· SERMONS ON ·

HEAVEN AND HELL

from sad + maria

25·12·19.

· SERMONS ON ·

HEAVEN AND HELL

HENDRICKSON
PUBLISHERS

Sermons on Heaven and Hell

ISBN 978-1-61970-756-6

Originally published by Hendrickon Publishers in *Sermons on the Last Days*.

Printed in the United States of America

Cover photo of Charles Haddon (C. H.) Spurgeon by Herbert Rose Barraud is used by permission of the University of Minnesota Libraries, Special Collections and Rare Books.

Contents

*In memory of Patricia Klein (1949–2014), our colleague
and friend, who spent her life caring for words
and who edited this series. She is truly missed.*

Preface

Charles Haddon Spurgeon
1834–1892

Ask most people today who Charles Haddon Spurgeon was, and you might be surprised at the answers. Most know he was a preacher, others remember that he was Baptist, and others go so far as to remember that he lived in England during the nineteenth century. All of this is true, yet Charles Haddon Spurgeon was so much more.

Born into a family of Congregationalists in 1834, Spurgeon's father and grandfather were both Independent preachers. These designations seem benign today, but in the mid-nineteenth century, they describe a family committed to a Nonconformist path—meaning they did not conform to the established Church of England. Spurgeon grew up in a rural village, a village virtually cut off from the Industrial Revolution rolling over most of England.

Spurgeon became a Christian at a Primitive Methodist meeting in 1850 at age sixteen. He soon became a Baptist (to the sorrow of his mother) and almost immediately began to preach. Considered a preaching prodigy—"a boy wonder of the fens"—Spurgeon attracted huge audiences and garnered a reputation that reached throughout the countryside and into London. As a result of his great success, Spurgeon was invited to preach at the New Park Street Chapel in London in 1854, when he was just nineteen. When he first preached at the church, they were unable to fill even two hundred seats. Within the year, Spurgeon filled the twelve-hundred-seat church to overflowing. He soon began preaching in larger and larger venues, outgrowing each, until finally in 1861 the Metropolitan Tabernacle was completed, which seated six thousand persons. This would be Spurgeon's home base for the rest of his career, until his death in 1892 at age fifty-seven.

Spurgeon married Susannah Thompson in 1856 and soon they had twin sons, Charles and Thomas, who would later follow him in his work. Spurgeon opened Pastors' College, a training school for preachers, which trained over nine hundred preachers during his lifetime. He also opened orphanages for underprivileged boys and girls, providing education to each of the orphans. And with Susannah, he developed a program to publish and distribute Christian literature. He is said to have preached to over ten million people in his forty years of ministry. His sermons sold over twenty-five thousand copies each week and were translated into twenty languages. He was utterly committed to spreading the gospel through preaching and through the written word.

During Spurgeon's lifetime, the Industrial Revolution transformed England from a rural, agricultural society to an urban, industrial society, with all the attendant difficulties and horrors of a society in major transition. The people displaced by these sweeping changes—factory workers and shopkeepers—became Spurgeon's congregation. From a small village himself and transplanted to a large and inhospitable city, he was a common man and understood innately the spiritual needs of the common people. He was a communicator who made the gospel so relevant, who spoke so brilliantly to people's deepest needs, that listeners welcomed his message.

Keep in mind that Spurgeon preached in the days before microphones or speakers; in other words, he preached without benefit of amplifier systems. Once he preached to a crowd of over twenty-three thousand people without mechanical amplification of any sort. He himself was the electrifying presence on the platform: he did not stand and simply read a stilted sermon. Spurgeon used an outline, developing his themes extemporaneously, and speaking "in common language to common people." His sermons were filled with stories and poetry, drama and emotion. He was larger than life, always in motion, striding back and forth across the stage. He gestured broadly, acted out stories, used humor, and painted word pictures. For Spurgeon, preaching was about communicating the truth of God, and he would use any gift at his disposal to accomplish this.

Spurgeon's preaching was anchored in his spiritual life, a life rich in prayer and the study of Scripture. He was not tempted by fashion, be it theological, social, or political. Scripture was the cornerstone of Spurgeon's life and his preaching. He was an expositional preacher mostly, exploring a passage of Scripture for its meaning both within the text as well as in the lives of each member of his congregation. To Spurgeon, Scripture was alive and specifically relevant to people's lives, whatever their social status, economic situation, or time in which they lived.

One has a sense that Spurgeon embraced God's revelation completely: God's revelation through Jesus Christ, through Scripture, and through his own prayer and study. For him, revelation was not a finished act: God still reveals himself, if one made oneself available. Some recognize Spurgeon for the mystic he was, one who was willing and eager to explore the mysteries of God, able to live with those bits of truth that do not conform to a particular system of theology, perfectly comfortable with saying, "This I know, and this I don't know—yet will I trust."

Each of the sermons in this collection was preached at a different time in Spurgeon's career and each has distinct characteristics. These sermons are not a series, as they were not created or intended to be sequential, nor have they been homogenized or edited to sound as though they are all of a kind. Instead, they reflect the preacher himself, allowing the voice of this remarkable man to ring clearly as he guides the reader into a particular account, a particular event—to experience, with Spurgeon, God's particular revelation.

As you read, *listen*. These words were meant to be heard, not merely read. Listen carefully and you will hear the cadences of this remarkable preaching, the echoes of God's timeless truth traveling across the years. And above all, enjoy Spurgeon's enthusiasm, his fire, his devotion, his zeal to recognize and respond to God's timeless invitation to engage the Creator himself.

The First Appearance of the Risen Lord to the Eleven

❦

Delivered on Lord's Day morning, April 10, 1887, at the Metropolitan Tabernacle, Newington. No. 1958.

And as they thus spake, Jesus himself stood in the midst of them, and saith unto them, "Peace be unto you." But they were terrified and affrighted, and supposed that they had seen a spirit. And he said unto them, "Why are ye troubled? and why do thoughts arise in your hearts? Behold my hands and my feet, that it is I myself: handle me, and see, for a spirit hath not flesh and bones, as ye see me have." And when he had thus spoken, he showed them his hands and his feet. And while they yet believed not for joy, and wondered, he said unto them, "Have ye here any meat?" And they gave him a piece of a broiled fish, and of an honeycomb. And he took it, and did eat before them. And he said unto them, "These are the words which I spake unto you while I was yet with you, that all things must be fulfilled, which were written in the law of Moses, and in the prophets, and in the psalms, concerning me."
—LUKE 24:36–44

This, beloved friends, is one of the most memorable of our Lord's many visits to his disciples after he had risen from the dead. Each one of these appearances had its own peculiarity. I cannot at this time give you even an outline of the special colorings which distinguished each of the many manifestations of our risen Lord. The instance now before us may be considered to be the fullest and most deliberate of all the manifestations, abounding beyond every other in "infallible proofs." Remember that it occurred on the same day in which our Lord had risen from the dead, and it was the close of a long day of gracious appearings. It was the summing up of a series of interviews, all of which were proofs of the Lord's resurrection. There was the empty tomb and the grave clothes left therein: the place where the Lord lay was accessible to all who chose to inspect it—for the great stone which had been sealed and guarded was rolled away. This in itself was most impressive evidence. Moreover, the holy women had been there and had seen a vision of angels, who said that Jesus was alive. Magdalene had enjoyed a special interview. Peter and John had been into the empty tomb and had seen for themselves. The report was current that "the Lord was risen indeed, and had appeared unto Simon." It was a special thing that he should appear unto Simon for the disciples painfully knew how Simon had denied his Master, and his appearance unto Simon seemed to have struck them as peculiarly characteristic: it was so like the manner of our Lord.

They met together in their bewilderment: the eleven of them gathered, as I suppose, to a social meal, for Mark tells us that the Lord appeared unto them "as they sat at meat." It must have been very late in the day, but they were loath to part, and so kept together till midnight. While they were sitting at meat, two brethren came in who, even after the sun had set, had hastened back from Emmaus. These newcomers related how one who seemed a stranger had joined himself to them as they were walking from Jerusalem, had talked with them in such a way that their hearts had been made to burn, and had made himself known unto them in the breaking of bread at the journey's end. They declared that it was the Lord who had thus appeared unto them, and, though they had intended to spend the night at Emmaus, they had hurried back to tell the marvelous news to the eleven. Hence the witness accumulated with great rapidity; it became more and more clear that Jesus had really risen from the dead. But as yet the doubters were not convinced, for Mark says: "After that he appeared in another form unto two of them, as they walked, and went into the country. And they went and told it unto the residue: neither believed they them."

Everything was working up to one point: the most unbelieving of them were being driven into a corner. They must doubt the truthfulness of Magdalene and the other saintly women; they must question the veracity of Simon; they must reject the two newly arrived brethren, and charge them with telling idle tales, or else they must believe that Jesus was still alive, though they had seen him die upon the cross. At that moment the chief confirmation of all presented itself; "for Jesus himself stood in the midst of them." The doors were shut; but, despite every obstacle, their Lord was present in the center of the assembly. In the presence of one whose loving smile warmed their hearts, their unbelief was destined to thaw and disappear. Jesus revealed himself in all the warmth of his vitality and love, and made them understand that it was none other than his very self, and that the Scriptures had told them it should be so. They were slow of heart to believe all that the prophets had spoken concerning him, but he brought them to it by his familiar communion with them. Oh, that in a like way he would put an end to all our doubts and fears!

Brethren, though you and I were not at that interview, yet we may derive much profit from it while we look at it in detail, anxiously desiring that we may in spirit see and look upon and handle the Word of life manifested in the flesh. Oh, to learn all that Jesus would teach us, as we now in spirit take our places at that midnight meeting of the chosen ones!

In this wonderful manifestation of our Lord to his apostles, I notice three things worthy of our careful observation this morning. This incident teaches us *the certainty of the resurrection of our Lord;* second, it shows us a little of *the character of our risen Master;* and, third, it gives us certain hints as to *the nature of our own resurrection,* when it shall be granted us. Oh, that we may be counted worthy to attain to the resurrection from among the dead!

1. First, then, let us see here *the certainty of our Lord's resurrection.*

We have often asserted, and we affirm it yet again, that no fact in history is better attested than the resurrection of Jesus Christ from the dead. The common mass of facts accepted by all men as historical are not one tenth as certainly assured to us as this fact is. It must not be denied by any who are willing to pay the slightest respect to the testimony of their fellowmen, that Jesus, who died upon the cross and was buried in the tomb of Joseph of Arimathea, did literally rise again from the dead.

Observe that when this person appeared in the room, the first token that it was Jesus was his speech: *they were to have the evidence of hearing:* he used the same speech. No sooner did he appear than he spoke. He was never dumb, and it was natural that the great teacher and friend should at once salute his followers, from whom he had been so painfully parted. His first accents must have called to their minds those cheering notes with which he had closed his last address. They must have recognized that charming voice. I suppose its tone and rhythm to have been rich with a music most sweet and heavenly. A perfect voice would naturally be given to a perfect man. The very sound of it would, through their ears, have charmed conviction into their minds with a glow of joy, had they not been frozen up in unbelief. "Never man spoke like this man": they might have known him by his speech alone. There were tones of voice as well as forms of language which were peculiar to Jesus of Nazareth.

What our Lord said was just like him; it was all of a piece with his former discourse. Among the last sounds which lingered in their ears was that word— "Peace I leave with you, my peace I give unto you: not as the world giveth, give I unto you"; and now it must surely be the same person who introduces himself with the cheering salutation, "Peace be unto you." About the Lord there were the air and style of one who had peace himself and loved to communicate it to others. The tone in which he spoke peace tended to create it. He was a peacemaker, and a peace giver, and by this sign they were driven to discern their leader.

Do you not think that they were almost persuaded to believe that it was Jesus when he proceeded to chide them in a manner more tender than any other chiding could have been? How gentle the accents when he said, "Why are ye troubled? And why do thoughts arise in your hearts?" Our Lord's chidings were comforts in disguise. His upbraidings were consolations in an unusual shape. Did not his upbraiding on this occasion bring to their minds his question upon the sea of Galilee when he said to them, "Why are ye fearful, O ye of little faith?" Did they not also remember when he came to them walking on the water, and they were afraid that he was a spirit, and cried out for fear; and he said to them, "It is I; be not afraid"? Surely they remembered enough of these things to have made sure that it was their Lord, had not their spirits been sunken in sorrow. Our Lord had never been unwisely silent as to their faults. He had never passed over their errors with that false and indulgent affection which gratifies its own ease by tolerating sin; but he had pointed out their faults with the fidelity of true love; and now that he thus admonished them, they ought to have perceived that it was none other than he.

When Jesus came at last to talk to them about Moses and the prophets and the psalms, he was upon a favorite topic. Then the eleven might have nudged each other and whispered, "It is the Lord." Jesus had, in his later hours, been continually pointing out the Scriptures which were being fulfilled in himself, and at this interview he repeated his former teaching. This is assuredly none other than he who always spoke his Father's mind and will and constantly did honor to the Holy Ghost by whom the sacred books were inspired. Thus in his tones and topics our Lord gave clear indications that it was himself who had suddenly appeared in that little assembly.

I want you to notice that this evidence was all the better, because they themselves evidently remained the same men as they had been. "They were terrified and affrighted, and supposed that they had seen a spirit"; and thus they did exactly what they had done long before when he came to them walking on the waters. In the interval between his death and his appearing, no change has come over them. Nothing has happened to them to elevate them as yet out of their littleness of mind. The Holy Spirit was not yet given, and therefore all that they had heard at the Last Supper, and seen in Gethsemane, and at the cross had not yet exercised its full influence upon them: they were still childish and unbelieving. The same men, then, are looking at the same person, and they are in their ordinary condition; this argues strongly for the correctness of their identification of their well-beloved Lord. They are not carried away by enthusiasm, nor wafted aloft by fanaticism, they are not even as yet upborne by the Holy Spirit into an unusual state of mind, but they are as slow of heart and as fearful as ever they were.

If *they* are convinced that Jesus has risen from the dead, depend upon it, it must be so. If they go forth to tell the tidings of his resurrection, and to yield up their lives for it, you may be sure that their witness is true, for they are not the sort of men to be deceived. In our day there has been a buzz about certain miracles of faith, but the statements usually come from persons whose impartiality is questionable—credulous persons who saw what they evidently wished to see. I know several good people who would not willfully deceive, who nevertheless upon some points are exceedingly unreliable, because their enthusiasm is prepared to be imposed upon. Any hawker of wonders would expect them to be buyers, they have a taste for the marvelous. As witnesses, the evidence of such people has no value in it as compared with that of these eleven men, who evidently were the reverse of credulous or excitable. In the apostles' case the facts were tested to the utmost, and the truth was not admitted till it was forced upon them. I am not excusing the unbelief of the disciples, but I claim that their witness has all the more weight in it, because it was the result of such cool investigation. These apostles were in special manner to be witnesses of the resurrection, and it makes assurance doubly sure to us when we see them arrive at their conclusion with such deliberate steps. These were men like ourselves, only perhaps a little less likely to be deceived: they needed to be convinced by overwhelming witness, and they were so: ever afterward they declared boldly that their crucified Lord had indeed risen from the dead.

Thus far in the narrative they had received the evidence of their ears, and that is by no means weak evidence, but now *they are to have the evidence of sight;* for the Savior says to them, "Behold my hands and my feet, that it is I myself"; "and when he had thus spoken, he showed them his hands and his feet." John says also "his side," which *he* specially noted because he had seen the piercing of that side, and the outflow of blood and water. They were to see and identify that blessed body which had suffered death. The nail prints were visible, both in his hands which were open before them, and also in his feet which their condescending Lord deigned to expose to their deliberate gaze. There was the mark of the gash in his side; and this the Lord Jesus graciously bared to them, as afterward he did more fully to Thomas, when he said, "Reach

hither thy hand, and thrust it into my side." These were the marks of the
Lord Jesus, by which his identity could be verified. Beyond this there was the
general contour of his countenance, and the fashion of the whole man by
which they could discern him. His body, though it was now in a sense glorified,
was so far veiled as to its new condition that it retained its former likeness: they
might perceive that the Lord was no longer subject to the pains and infirmities
of our ordinary mortality—else his wounds had not been healed so soon; but
yet there remained sure marks by which they knew that it was Jesus, and no
other. He looked like a lamb that had been slain: the signs of the Son of man
were in his hands and feet and side. Their sight of the Lord was not a hasty
glimpse, but a steady inspection, for John in his first epistle writes, "Which we
have seen and looked upon." This implies a lengthened looking, and such the
Lord Jesus invited his friends to take. They could not have been mistaken when
they were afforded such a view of those marks by which his identity was established. The same Christ that died had risen from the dead, the same Jesus that
had hung upon the cross now stood in the midst of those who knew him best.
It was the same body, and they identified it, although a great change had doubtless come over it since it was taken down from the tree.

Furthermore, that they might be quite sure, *the Lord invited them to receive
the evidence of touch or feeling.* He called them to a form of examination, from
which, I doubt not, many of them shrank; he said, "Handle me. Handle me,
and see; for a spirit hath not flesh and bones, as ye see me have." Writers have
remarked upon the use of the word "bones," instead of blood, in this case; but
I do not think that any inference can be safely drawn therefrom. It would have
been barely possible for the disciples to have discovered by handling that the
Lord had blood, but they could by handling perceive that he had bones; hence
the expression is natural enough, without our imputing to it a meaning which
it may never have been intended to convey. The Savior had a reason, no doubt,
other than some have imagined, for the use of the terms "a spirit hath not
flesh *and bones* as ye see me have." The Savior had not assumed a phantom
body: there was bone in it as well as flesh; it was to the full as substantial as
ever. He had not put on an appearance, as angels do when they visit the sons
of men. No, his body was solid substance, which could be handled. "Handle
me, and see that it is I myself." He bade them see that it was flesh and bone,
such as no spirit has. There were the substantial elements of a human frame
in that body of Christ which stood in the midst of the eleven. Jesus cried,
"Handle me, and see."

Thus our Lord was establishing to the apostles, not only his identity, but
also his substantial corporeal existence: he would make them see that he was

a man of flesh and bones, and not a ghost, airy and unsubstantial. This should correct a certain form of teaching upon the resurrection which is all too common. I was present some years ago at the funeral of a man of God for whom I had much respect. In the chapel a certain excellent doctor of divinity gave us an address before the interment, in which he informed us as to the condition of his departed friend. He said that he was not in the coffin: indeed, there was nothing of him there. This I was sorry to hear, for if so I was ignorantly mourning over a body which had no relation to my friend. The preacher went on to describe the way in which the man of God had ascended to heaven at the moment of death, his spirit fashioning for itself a body as it passed through the air. I believed in my friend's being in heaven, but not in his being there in a body. I knew that my friend's body was in the coffin, and I believed that it would be laid in the tomb, and I expected that it would rise again from the grave at the coming of the Lord. I did not believe that my friend would weave for himself a filmy frame, making a second body, nor do I believe it now, though I heard it so affirmed.

I believe in the resurrection of the dead. I look to see the very body which was buried raised again. It is true that as the seed develops into the flower, so the buried body is merely the germ out of which will come the spiritual body; yet still it will not be a second body, but the same body, as to identity. I shall enter into no dispute about the atoms of the body, nor deny that the particles of our flesh, in the process of their decay, may be taken up by plants and absorbed into the bodies of animals, and all that; I do not care one jot about identity of atoms; there may not be a solitary ounce of the same matter, but yet identity can be preserved; and it must be preserved if I read my Bible aright. My body today is the same as that which I inhabited twenty years ago, and yet all its particles are different: even so the body put into the grave and the body that rises from it are not two bodies, but one body. The saints are not at the coming of their Lord to remain disembodied spirits, nor to wear freshly created bodies, but their entire manhood is to be restored, and to enjoy endless bliss. Well said the patriarch of old, "in my flesh shall I see God." "He which raised up the Lord Jesus shall raise up us also by Jesus."

I cannot see how the doctrine of Christ goes beyond the doctrine of Plato and others if it be not a doctrine which respects this body. The immortality of the soul was accepted and known as a truth before the faith of Christ was preached, for it is dimly discoverable by the light of nature; but the resurrection of the body is a revelation peculiar to the Christian dispensation, at which the wise men of the world very naturally mocked, but which it ill becomes Christian men to spirit away. The body which is buried shall rise again. It is true it is sown a natural body and shall be raised a spiritual body, but it will be truly a body, and the same *it* which was sown shall be raised. It is true it is sown in weakness and raised in power, but the same *it* is thus raised. It is true that it is sown in weakness to be raised in power, and sown a corruptible body, to be raised in incorruption, but in each case it is the same body, though so gloriously changed. It will be of a material substance also; for our Savior's body was material, since he said, "Handle me, and see that it is I myself; for a spirit hath not flesh and bones, as ye see me have."

Still further to confirm the faith of the disciples, and to show them that their Lord had a real body, and not the mere form of one, *he gave them evidence which appealed to their common sense*. He said, "'Have ye any meat?' And they gave him a piece of a broiled fish, and of an honeycomb. And he took it, and did eat before them." This was an exceedingly convincing proof of his unquestionable resurrection. In very deed and fact, and not in vision and phantom, the man who had died upon the cross stood among them.

Let us just think of this and rejoice. This resurrection of our Lord Jesus is a matter of certainty; for, if you spirit this away, you have done away with the gospel altogether. If he is not risen from the dead, then is our preaching vain, and your faith is also vain; you are yet in your sins. Justification receives its seal in the resurrection of Jesus Christ from the dead; not in his appearing as a phantom, but in his very self being loosed from death, and raised to a glorious life. This is God's mark of the acceptance of the work of the great substitute, and of the justification of all for whom his atoning work was performed.

Note well that this is also our grand hope concerning those that are asleep. You have buried them forever if Christ was not raised from the dead. They have passed out of your sight, and they shall never again have fellowship with you, unless Jesus rose again from the dead; for the apostle makes the resurrection of all who are in Christ to hinge upon the resurrection of Christ. I do not feel it necessary, when I talk with the bereaved, to comfort them at all concerning those that are asleep in Christ, as to their souls: we know that they are forever with the Lord, and are supremely blessed, and, therefore, we need no further comfort. The only matter upon which we need consolation is that poor body, which once we loved so well, but which now we must leave in the cold clay. The resurrection comes in as a final undoing of all that death has done. "They shall come again from the land of the enemy." Jesus says, "Thy dead men shall live, together with my dead body shall they arise." If we question the resurrection of Christ, then is the whole of our faith questioned, and those who have fallen asleep in Christ have perished, and we are left just where others were before Christ brought this divine truth to light. Only as we are sure of the resurrection of Jesus can we cry, "O death, where is thy sting? O grave, where is thy victory?"

2. Second, will you follow me while I very briefly set forth *our Lord's character when risen from the dead?*

What is he now that he has quit death, and all that belongs to it? What is he now that he shall hunger no more, neither thirst any more? He is much the same as he used to be; indeed he is altogether what he was, for he is "the same yesterday, today, and forever."

Notice, first, that in this appearance of Christ we are taught that *he is still anxious to create peace in the hearts of his people.* No sooner did he make himself visible than he said, "Peace be unto you." Beloved, your risen Lord wants you to be happy. When he was here on earth, he said, "Let not your hearts be troubled": he says just the same to you today. He takes no delight in the distresses of his people. He would have his joy to be in them, that their joy may be full. He bids you rejoice in him evermore. He whispers to you this morning, as you sit in the pew, "Peace be unto you." He has not lost his tender care over the least of the flock; he would have each one led by the still waters and made to lie down in green pastures.

Note again, that *he has not lost his habit of chiding unbelief, and encouraging faith*; for as soon as he has risen, and speaks with his disciples, he asks them, "Why are ye troubled? And why do thoughts arise in your hearts?" He loves you to believe in him, and be at rest. Find if you can, beloved, one occasion in which Jesus inculcated doubt, or bade men dwell in uncertainty. The apostles of unbelief are everywhere today, and they imagine that they are doing God service by spreading what they call "honest doubt." This is death to all joy! Poison to all peace! The Savior did not so. He would have them take extraordinary measures to get rid of their doubt. "Handle me," he says. It was going a long way to say that, but he would sooner be handled than his people should doubt! Ordinarily it might not be meet for them to touch him. Had he not said to the women, "Touch me not"? But what may not be allowable ordinarily becomes proper when necessity demands it. The removal of their doubt as to our Lord's resurrection needed that they should handle him, and therefore he bids them do so. O beloved, you that are troubled and vexed with thoughts, and therefore get no comfort out of your religion because of your mistrust, your Lord would have you come very near to him, and put his gospel to any test which will satisfy you. He cannot bear you to doubt. He appeals tenderly, saying, "O thou of little faith, wherefore didst thou doubt?" He would at this moment still encourage you to taste and see that the Lord is good. He would have you believe in the substantial reality of his religion and handle him and see: trust him largely and simply, as a child trusts its mother and knows no fear.

Notice, next, that when the Savior had risen from the dead, and a measure of his glory was upon him, *he was still most condescendingly familiar with his people.* He showed them his hands and his feet, and he said, "Handle me, and see." When he was on earth, before his passion, he was most free with his disciples: no affectation of dignity kept him apart from them. He was their Master and Lord, and yet he washed their feet. He was the Son of the Highest, but he was among them as one that served. He said, "Suffer little children to come unto me." He is the same today.

> *His sacred name a common word*
> *On earth he loves to hear;*
> *There is no majesty in him*
> *Which love may not come near.*

Though he reigns in the highest heavens, his delights are still with the sons of men. Still he will permit us to sit at his feet, or even to lean our head upon his bosom. Jesus will hear us tell out our griefs; he will regard our cry when we are not pleading about a sword in our bones, but only concerning a thorn in our flesh. Jesus is still the brother born for adversity; he still manifests himself to us as he does not unto the world. Is not this clear, and also very pleasant to see, as we study this interview?

The next thing is that *the risen Lord was still wonderfully patient,* even as he had always been. He bore with their folly and infirmity; for "while they yet believed not for joy, and wondered," he did not chide them. He discerned between one unbelief and another, and he judged that the unbelief which grew out of wonder was not so blamable as that former unbelief which denied credible evidence. Instead of rebuke he gives confirmation. He says, "Have ye here any meat?" and he takes a piece of broiled fish, and of a honeycomb, and eats it. Not that he needed food. His body could receive food, but it did not require it. Eating was his own sweet way of showing them that if he could he would solve all their questions. He would do anything in his great patience that they might be cured of their mistrust. Just so today, beloved, Jesus does not chide you, but he invites you to believe him: he invites you, therefore, to sup with him and eat bread at his table. "He will not always chide, neither will he keep his anger forever"; but in his great mercy he will use another tone, and encourage you to trust him. Can you hold back? Oh, do not so.

Observe that our Savior, though he was risen from the dead, and there-fore in a measure in his glory, *entered into the fullest fellowship with his own*. Peter tells us that they did eat and drink with him. I do not notice in this narrative that he drank with them, but he certainly ate of such food as they had, and this was a clear token of his fellowship with them. In all ages eating and drink-ing with one another has been the most expressive token of communion, and so the Savior seems to say to us today, "I have eaten with you, my people, since I have quitted the grave. I have eaten with you through the eleven who repre-sented you. I have eaten, and I will still eat with you, till we sit down together at the marriage supper of the Lamb. If any man open unto me, I will come in to him, and will sup with him, and he with me." Yes, the Lord Jesus is won-derfully near to us still, and he waits to grant us the highest forms of fellow-ship which can be known on this side the gate of pearl. In this let our spirits quietly rejoice.

Let me call your attention to the fact that when Jesus had risen from the dead *he was just as tender of Scripture as he was before his decease*. I have dwelt for two Sunday mornings upon the wonderful way in which our Lord always magnified the Scriptures; and here, as if to crown all, he told them that "'all things must be fulfilled which were written in the law of Moses, and in the prophets, and in the psalms concerning' himself; and he opened their under-standing that they might understand the Scriptures, and said unto them, 'Thus it is written, and thus it behooved Christ to suffer, and to rise from the dead.'" Find Jesus where you may, he is the antagonist of those who would lessen the authority of holy Scripture. "It is written" is his weapon against Satan, his argument against wicked men. The learned at this hour scoff at the Book, and accuse of bibliolatry those of us who reverence the divine Word; but in this they derive no assistance from the teaching or example of Jesus. Not a word derogatory of Scripture ever fell from the lips of Jesus Christ; but evermore he manifested the most reverent regard for every jot and tittle of the inspired vol-ume. Since our Savior, not only before his death, but after it, took care thus to commend the Scriptures to us, let us avoid with all our hearts all teaching in which holy Scripture is put into the background. Still the Bible, and the Bible alone, should be and shall be the religion of Protestants, and we will not budge an inch from that standpoint, God helping us.

Once again, our Savior, after he had risen from the dead, *showed that he was anxious for the salvation of men;* for it was at this interview that he breathed upon the apostles, and bade them receive the Holy Ghost, to fit them to go forth and preach the gospel to every creature. The missionary spirit is the spirit of Christ—not only the spirit of him that died to save, but the spirit of him who has finished his work, and has gone into his rest. Let us cultivate that spirit, if we would be like the Jesus who has risen from the dead.

3. I can stay no longer, because I would draw your attention, in the third place, to the light which is thrown by this incident upon *the nature of our own resurrection.*

First, I gather from this text that our nature, *our whole humanity, will be perfected at the day of the appearing of our Lord and Savior Jesus Christ,* when the dead shall be raised incorruptible, and we that may then be alive shall be changed. Jesus has redeemed not only our souls, but our bodies. "Know ye not that your bodies are the temples of the Holy Ghost?" When the Lord shall deliver his captive people out of the land of the enemy, he will not leave a bone of one of them in the adversary's power. The dominion of death shall be utterly broken. Our entire nature shall be redeemed unto the living God in the day of the resurrection. After death, until that day, we shall be disembodied spirits; but in the adoption, to wit, the redemption, of the body, we shall attain our full inheritance. We are looking forward to a complete restoration. At this time the body is dead because of sin, and hence it suffers pain, and tends to decay; but the spirit is life because of righteousness: in the resurrection, however, the body shall be quickened also, and the resurrection shall be to the body what regeneration has been to the soul. Thus shall our humanity be completely delivered from the consequences of the fall. Perfect manhood is that which Jesus restores from sin and the grave; and this shall be ours in the day of his appearing.

I gather next that in the resurrection *our nature will be full of peace.* Jesus Christ would not have said, "Peace be unto you," if there had not been a deep peace within himself. He was calm and undisturbed. There was much peace about his whole life; but after the resurrection his peace becomes very conspicuous. There is no striving with scribes and Pharisees, there is no battling with anybody after our Lord is risen. A French author has written of our Lord's forty days on earth after the resurrection under the title of "The Life of Jesus Christ in Glory." Though rather misleading at first, the title is not so inaccurate as it appears; for his work was done, and his warfare was accomplished, and our Lord's life here was the beginning of his glory. Such shall be our life, we shall be flooded with eternal peace, and shall never again be tossed about with trouble and sorrow and distress and persecution. An infinite serenity shall keep our body, soul, and spirit throughout eternity.

When we rise again *our nature will find its home amid the communion of saints.* When the Lord Jesus Christ had risen again his first resort was the room where his disciples were gathered. His first evening was spent among the objects of his love. Even so, wherever we are we shall seek and find communion with the saints. I joyfully expect to meet many of you in heaven, and to know you, and commune with you. I should not like to float about in the future state without a personality in the midst of a company of undefined and unknown beings. That would be no heaven to me. No, brethren, we shall soon perceive who our comrades are, and we shall rejoice in them, and in our Lord. There could be no communion among unknown entities. You cannot have fellowship with people whom you do not recognize; and therefore it seems to me most clear that we shall in the future state have fellowship through recognition, and our heavenly bodies shall help the recognition and share in the fellowship. As the risen Christ wends his way to the upper room of the eleven, so will you by force of holy gravitation find your way to the place where all the servants of God shall gather at the last. Then shall we be truly at home, and go no more out forever.

Furthermore, I see that in that day *our bodies will admirably serve our spirits.* For look at our Lord's body. Now that he is risen from the dead he desires to convince his disciples, and his body becomes at once the means of his argument, the evidence of his statement. His flesh and bones were text and sermon for him. "Handle me," says he, "and see." Ah brethren! Whatever we may have to do in eternity, we shall not be hindered by our bodies as we now are. Flesh and blood hamper us, but "flesh and bones" shall help us. I want to speak sometimes, and my head aches, or my throat is choked, or my legs refuse to bear me up: but it is not so in the resurrection from the dead. A thousand infirmities in this earthly life compass us about; but our risen body shall be helpful to our regenerated nature. It is only a natural body now, fit for our soul; but hereafter it shall be a spiritual body, adapted to all the desires and wishes of the heaven-born spirit; and no longer shall we have to cry out, "The spirit indeed is willing, but the flesh is weak." We shall find in the risen body a power such as the spirit shall wish to employ for the noblest purposes. Will not this be well?

In that day, beloved, when we shall rise again from the dead, *we shall remember the past.* Do you not notice how the risen Savior says, "These are the words which I spoke unto you, while I was yet with you." He had not forgotten his former state. I think Dr. Watts is right when he says that we shall "with transporting joys recount the labors of our feet." It is rather a small subject, and probably we shall far more delight to dwell on the labors of our Redeemer's hands and feet; but still we shall remember all the way whereby the Lord our God led us, and we shall talk to one another concerning it. In heaven we shall remember our happy Sabbaths here below, when our hearts burned within us while Jesus himself drew near. Since Jesus speaks after he has risen of the things that he said while he was with his disciples, we perceive that the river of death is not like the fabled Lethe, which caused all who drank thereof to forget their past. We shall arise with a multitude of hallowed memories enriching our minds. Death will not be oblivion to us, for it was not so to Jesus. Rather shall we meditate on mercies experienced, and by discoursing thereon we shall make known to principalities and powers the manifold wisdom of God.

Observe that our Lord, after he had risen from the dead, *was still full of the spirit of service*, and therefore he called others out to go and preach the gospel, and he gave them the Spirit of God to help them. When you and I are risen from the dead, we shall rise full of the spirit of service. What engagements we may have throughout eternity we are not told, because we have enough to do to fulfill our engagements now; but assuredly we shall be honored with errands of mercy and tasks of love fitted for our heavenly being; and I doubt not it shall be one of our greatest delights while seeing the Lord's face to serve him with all our perfected powers. He will use us in the grand economy of future manifestations of his divine glory. Possibly we may be to other dispensations what the angels have been to this. Be that as it may, we shall find a part of our bliss and joy in constantly serving him who has raised us from the dead.

There I leave the subject, wishing that I could have handled it much better. Think it over when you are quiet at home, and add this thought to it, that you have a share in all that is contained in resurrection. May the Holy Ghost give you a personal grip of this vital truth! You yourself shall rise from the dead; therefore, be not afraid to die.

If any of my hearers have no share in our Lord's resurrection, I am truly sorry for them. O my friend, what you are losing! If you have no share in the living Lord, may God have mercy upon you! If you have no share in Christ's rising from the dead, then you will not be raised up in the likeness of his glorified body. If you do not attain to that resurrection from among the dead, then you must abide in death, with no prospect but that of a certain fearful looking for of judgment, and of fiery indignation. Oh, look to Jesus, the Savior! Only as you look to him can there be a happy future for you. God help you to do so at once, for his dear name's sake! Amen.

Great Difference

Delivered on Lord's Day morning, May 19, 1878, at the Metropolitan Tabernacle, Newington. No. 1415.

Where is the God of judgment? —MALACHI 2:17

Then shall ye return, and discern between the righteous and the wicked,
between him that serveth God and him that serveth him not. —MALACHI 3:18

You were not here, I am thankful to say, last Sabbath evening, for it was your duty and privilege to stay away to give others an opportunity of hearing; but my subject then was our heavenly Father, who makes his sun to rise upon the evil and upon the good, and sends rain upon the just and upon the unjust. Then I set forth the universal benevolence of God and the way in which he stays the operations of justice to give space for forbearance and longsuffering. Now this fact, this gracious fact, which ought to lead man to repentance, has through the perversity of human nature been used for quite another purpose. Men have said, "He blesses the evil as well as the good. The sun shines on all alike; the rain indiscriminately enriches the field of the churl and the pasture of the generous heart; where is the God of judgment? Is there such a God? Is it not one and the same whether we fear him or disregard him?" Side by side with this has run another circumstance perhaps even more readily misunderstood. God is in this life preparing his people for a better world and part of that process is effected by trial and affliction, so that it frequently happens that the godly are in adversity while the wicked are in prosperity. Having no such designs toward them as toward his people, the Lord permits the wicked to enjoy themselves while they may; so that oftentimes they are as bullocks fattened in rich pastures, but they forget that they are fattened for the slaughter; while the righteous are brought very low, are often in poverty, frequently in sickness, and not seldom in despondency of spirit, but all to prepare them for the glory land. From the trials of the godly, which are all sent in wisdom and in love, shortsighted man has inferred that God has no regard to human character and even treats those worst who serve him best. In Malachi's days the blaspheming crew even said that God takes sides with the wicked, and they wearied God by saying, "Everyone that doeth evil is good in the sight of the

Lord, and he delighteth in them." Then again they uttered the old rude but plainspoken question, "Where is the God of judgment?"

Truly brethren, in looking with these poor eyes upon the affairs around us, they do appear to be a great tangle and snarl, a mixed medley of strange accidents. We see the true princes of the earth walking in the dust and beggars riding upon horses. We mourn as we see servants of God and heirs of heaven lying, like Lazarus, sick at the gate of the ungodly miser, while the vicious libertine is rioting in luxury and drinking full bowls of pleasure. Until we perceive the clue, providence is a labyrinth into whose center we can never penetrate. But there is a clue which opens all its secrets. There is a God of judgment, not sitting in heaven in blind indifference, but looking down upon the sons of men and working out purposes of righteousness at all times.

At this time I purpose to speak upon the fact that God does put a difference between the righteous and the wicked, and makes no mistake between Egypt and Israel. The Lord knows them that are his, and in his dealings, which we cannot always understand, he nevertheless has not confounded his people with the world, nor does the rod of the wicked rest upon the lot of the righteous. He has a right hand of acceptance for them that fear him, he has a left hand of punishment for those that fear him not. This distinction is not so apparent yet as it shall be, but we shall now trace the gradual widening of the division between the two classes, and show that still there is a God of judgment, and that by and by even the blindest eye shall be able to discern between the righteous and the wicked, between him that serves God and him that serves him not.

1. First, then, *there are signs of separation* between the righteous and the wicked.

The first sign is seen in the evident difference of *character.* "They that feared the Lord" are spoken of. That is to say, there are still some on the face of the earth who believe that there is a God, who believe in the revelation which he has given, who accept the atonement which he has provided, and who delight to be obedient to the will which he has declared. How came they to fear the Lord? The answer is, it is a gift of his grace and a work of his Spirit wherever it is found. It makes a distinction very deep, and very vital, and consequently very lasting, for it shall continue throughout eternity. Let us bless God that in the worst times he still has a remnant according to the election of grace, and when blasphemers grow bold in sin and say, "Where is the God of judgment?," there are at least a few hidden ones who nevertheless look up and behold the Lord exalted above the rage of his foes. There will always be a band who bow the knee and worship the most High, because their hearts stand in awe of him. God is beginning to separate his chosen from the world, when he gives them an inward sense of his presence, and a consequent holy fear and sacred awe of him. The dividing work begins here, in the bent and current of the heart.

This difference in real character soon shows itself in a remarkable change of *thought* and meditation. According to the passage before us, those who are said to "fear the Lord" are also described as those who "thought upon his name." Their thoughts are not always toward the transient things of this world, but they are much engaged with the eternal God and his truth: they are not always groveling after the creature, but soaring toward the Creator. The Hebrew word has the idea of "counting": they reckon the Lord as the chief consideration when they count up their arguments for action. Others do not take him into the reckoning, they act as if there were no God at all: but the righteous make much of him, and account him to be the greatest factor in all their calculations; they fall back upon God in trouble, and joy most of all in him when they are glad. They reckon not without the Lord of hosts; they say, "The best of all is, God is with us." And concerning any action, if it be contrary to his mind, they reject it; if it be according to his will they think upon him, and they delight to carry it out. This makes a great difference in their course of life, and also in their happiness. Dear hearers, I trust there are many among you who can truly say that your meditation of God has been very sweet, you have been glad in the Lord. This, then, is working out a distinction between you and the wicked who forget God. You fear the Lord, and you take delight in meditating upon him in secret, but this the worldling cannot understand.

This makes a distinction between you and the careless, which does not long exist without operating in a further direction: you grow weary of their frivolous conversation, and they cannot endure your serious observations, and so two parties are formed, as of old there were two lines, the sons of God and the children of Cain. You will soon see Ishmael and Isaac, Esau and Jacob living over again if you watch the thoughtless worldling and the pious Christian, and mark how much they differ. Hence there grows out of this difference of thought and feeling a separation as to society. "Then they that feared the Lord spoke often one to another," which shows that they often met, and that they delighted in one another's company. Each man felt himself feeble in the midst of the ungodly, and therefore he sought out a brother that he might be strengthened by association. Each man felt himself to be like a sheep in the midst of wolves, but knowing the nature of sheep to be gregarious, each one sought to his fellow, that they might make up a flock, hoping that, as a flock, they might gather round the good Shepherd. Yes, and in the ungodliest times there are not only gracious people here and there, but these chosen souls by some means or other make mutual discoveries, and come together and so form the visible church of the living God.

In Rome in the days of the Caesars, when to be a Christian meant to be condemned to die without mercy, if believers could not meet in their houses they would meet in the abodes of the dead, in the catacombs: but they must meet. It is the nature of God's children that they do not like going to heaven alone, but prefer to go up to the temple in bands and companies, and the more the merrier, as the proverb has it, for they delight to go with the multitude that keep holy day, and they rejoice to fly in flocks like doves to their windows. There is a divine sweetness in Christian communion, and every true saint delights in it. The essence of our religion is love, and he that loves not the brethren loves not God, and lacks an essential point of the Christian character. By the exercise of holy brotherhood, the Lord continues to call out his own people, and thus to create a manifest separation. Likeness of character and thought produce a mutual attractiveness, and so a corporate body is formed, and the solitary secret ones become manifest in the mass. The chosen stones are quarried and are built into the similitude of a palace; what if I say that they come together bone to his bone to fashion the spiritual body of the Lord Jesus Christ?

This distinct association leads on to a peculiar *occupation*: for "they that feared the Lord *spoke* often one to another." They heard others speak against the Lord, and they resolved to speak too. Of others the Lord complained, "'Your words have been stout against me,' saith the Lord," and these men felt that it would be a shame if *they* were silent. They did not cast their pearls before swine, yet they wore their pearls where those who were not swine, but saints, could see them. In society where truth would be appreciated, they were not backward to declare it: they "spoke often one to another." It was a time of noise and tumult, it was a time of speaking very bitterly against the Lord: therefore when they met together they spoke for the Lord, and each one opened his mouth, that the Lord might not lack for witnesses. I take it that the expression means that they renewed and *repeated their testimony*. They "spoke often one to another." They said, "Ah, we can answer what the ungodly are saying, our experience testifies that they speak not aright. It is not a vain thing to serve God. How do you find it, brother?" Then the brother would say, "I find it exceedingly comforting and cheering to my soul. They have said, 'What profit is it that we have kept his ordinances?' but I have found it exceedingly profitable, for in keeping his commandments there is great reward." Then a third would say, "It has enriched our souls to walk according to the mind of God, and in the blessed ordinances of his house our souls have been fed and exceedingly nourished." A fourth would add, "The ungodly say it is in vain that we have walked mournfully before the Lord of hosts: do you find it so, brother?" The reply would be, "No, my mournful days have often been most profitable, like the days of shower and cloud, which have most to do with the harvest." "Besides," said another, "we do not walk mournfully before the Lord as a rule, for we rejoice before him, yes, in his name we do exceedingly rejoice." Thus, you see, by their testimony the one to the other they supported each other's minds against the popular infidelities of the time; they set their thoughtful experience against the vicious falsehoods of unbelieving men, and so they both honored God and benefited each other.

When they "spoke often one to another," I have no doubt *they expressed their affection* one for the other. They said, "Let us not marvel if the world hate us: did not our Master say, 'It hated me before it hated you'?" Did he not tell us to beware of man; did he not remind us that our worst enemies should be those of our own household. "Yes, brethren," they would say one to another, "let us love one another, for love is of God." The elders would speak like John the divine and say, "Little children, love one another," and the younger ones would respond by acts and words of loving respect to the older saints. Their mutual expressions of love would increase love. As when we lay live coals together they burn the better, so loving intercommunications increase the heat of affection till it glows like coals of juniper, which have a most vehement flame.

No doubt, for we know by what we see, this speaking one to another *assisted each other's faith.* One might be weak, but they were not all weak at once; one and another would be strong just then. We all have our ups and downs, but the mercy is that when one is sinking another is rising. It will frequently happen that if the sun does not shine on my side of the hedge it is shining on yours, and you can tell me that the sun is not snuffed out, but that it will shine on me too by and by. Commerce makes nations rich, and Christian intercourse makes believers grow in grace. Speaking often one to another with the view of helping the weak hands and confirming the feeble knees is a means of great blessing to the souls of Christians. When they met, one would tell what he knew which his brother might not know, and a third would say, "I can confirm that statement and add something more," and so the first speaker would learn as well as teach. Then a fourth brother would say, "But there is yet another truth which stands in relation to that which you have stated, do not overlook it." Thus by communion in experience, and each one expressing what the Lord had written upon his heart, the whole would be edified in righteousness.

Now, beloved, it is in proportion as the children of God speak often one to another in this way that the church is brought out into a visible condition. A silent church might grope through the world unobserved, but a speaking church, speaking often within itself, is of necessity soon heard beyond the doors of the house in which it dwells. Soon does the sound of gospel music steal over hill and dale. "Their sound hath gone forth throughout all the earth, and their words unto the end of the world." The speaking together of assembled saints at Pentecost led to the gift of tongues, and then they spoke so that every man in his own language heard the wonderful works of the Lord. An increase of private communion among the saints would lead to a fuller public communication to the outside, and the world would receive a blessing.

Thus I have shown you that the Lord thus gradually begins to separate a people to himself. The fear of the Lord in the heart, and the thought of God in the mind lead to association in persons of similar mold: hence arises the church. Then the interchange of expression between the godly makes them zealous, and this leads to public testimony, and the people of God are revealed. You will say that this does not prove that God is dealing differently with them from other men. "Where is the God of judgment?" is the question; and how is it to be answered? My reply is, but in all this the Lord is putting a difference. To work his fear in the heart is an act of sovereign grace, but to enable the soul to find deep enjoyment in meditating upon divine things is a reward as well as a gift of grace, and a reward more valuable than if he gave the God-fearing man wealth and fame.

Christian society is also no small token of the divine favor, and is another reward of the God-fearing. I do not know how you find it, but I can truly assert that my choicest delights are with the people of God. What a deal some of us owe to Christian fellowship! People whom we should never have known and never have thought of speaking to are now our choicest friends, and have been and are incalculably helpful to us. Christian love has enlarged our family circle wonderfully. We have come to be intertwisted the one with the other, and the separate threads have ceased to be such, for they have become a three-fold cord which cannot be broken, and this is no small gift of divine grace. Moreover, the communications which have arisen out of this society, in which we have edified one another, have they not been very precious to us? Can you not say you had rather dwell for a day in the courts of the Lord than reign in the tents of wickedness for ages? Is it not so that when we are able to rejoice together, and tell out our experience, we find a pleasure which makes the wilderness and the solitary place to be glad?

Best of all, it is in the midst of these communications, where holy society yields us gracious fellowship, that God himself is found. This is the grand distinction in God's relation to the universe at this present time, that he is with his people, and they know it; while he is far from the wicked. The Lord hearkened and heard of old, and he hearkens and hears still; and the Lord answers out of his holy place the prayers of his children, and sends tokens of acceptance to those who praise and magnify his name. "The Lord of hosts is with us, the God of Jacob is our refuge." Oh come, let us exult before him, for he is not far away, nor has he hidden his face from us, but he dwells between the cherubim and shines forth among his saints in the person of his dear Son, and manifests himself to us as he does not to the world. Even now Israel in Egypt is not Egypt, for God is pitying the sighs and cries of his people. Israel in the Arabian desert is not Arabian, for, lo, the fiery cloudy pillar, like an uplifted standard, gathers around it a separated people. Lo, "The people shall dwell alone, and shall not be reckoned among the nations." Even now the faithful in going out from the world and being separate find the promise fulfilled: "I will dwell in them, and walk in them; and I will be their God, and they shall be my people." There is the first answer to the question, "Where is the God of judgment?" The separation is already beginning; there are signs of it now.

2. Second, *there are preparations for a final separation,* and these are at this moment proceeding.

What these preparations are we learn from the sixteenth verse: "The Lord hearkened and heard it, and a book of remembrance was written before him for them that feared the Lord, and that thought upon his name." There is a day coming in which he will separate the two sorts of men the one from the other, as a shepherd divides the sheep from the goats. The great net is now dragging the sea bottom: the day comes when the net shall be hauled in, and drawn to shore. What a medley it contains of good and bad fish, of creeping things, and weeds, and shells, and stones: this mass must be parted. Then will come the putting of the good into vessels and the casting of the bad away. When that is done it will be executed with great solemnity and care. There will be great discrimination used in the dividing of the righteous from the wicked, and as at a trial *everything proceeds upon evidence,* the separating work is being prepared for us every day, because the evidence is being collected and recorded. The evidence in favor of the righteous might be forgotten if it were not duly preserved, in order that in the day when the separation shall be consummated there may be no mistake, and nobody may be able to challenge the decision of the great Judge.

Recollect this, dear friends, that *evidence is being written down in a book—evidence of fidelity to God* in evil times. When others were thinking against God, and speaking against God, there were some who spoke on his behalf, because they feared him, and thought upon his name, and their singular conduct was reported upon and chronicled. God's gracious eye never overlooks one single act of decision for him in the midst of blasphemy and rebuke. If the timid girl in the midst of a Christless family still patiently endures reproach, and holds on to her Master's truth, though she cannot speak eloquently, behold it is written in the book. Though her tears may often be her strongest expressions, they are in the book also, and shall not be forgotten. When the workman in the shop speaks a word against filthy language, a word for the sacredness of the Sabbath, a word for his Lord, it is all written in the book of remembrance. A commission is instituted for the collection of evidence as to those that fear the Lord, and think upon his name. Are you, dear friends, furnishing evidence, do you think, evidence which will prove that you are truly godly? Do you clearly stand out from among your fellows, and are you manifestly separate, so that even Satan himself at the last great day will not be able to challenge the evidence that will be given, that you did indeed fear the Lord when others reviled him?

This evidence is being taken by the Lord himself. There is much consolation in this, because others might be prejudiced, and give an unfavorable view of what we do, but when the Lord himself bears witness the truth will be manifested. "The Lord hearkened and heard." It is a very strong expression; he not only "hearkened" as one trying to hear, but he did actually hear all that was said. What a witness God will be in favor of his saints! If we really fear him and think upon his name, he will set our holy fear and our godly thought and our gracious talk in evidence on our behalf. He reads our motives, and these are a deep and vital part of character. Others might err, but he cannot: what he hears is accurately heard and correctly understood. Evidence is being collected, then, by a witness who is truth itself.

This evidence is before God's eye at all times. If you notice, "the book of remembrance was written *before him*," as if while every item was being put down, the book lay open before his gaze. From him the record is no more concealed than the act itself: past deeds of virtue are present to his eye. Every recorded act of grace is especially noticed by the Lord, every separate word of faithfulness and act of true God-fearing life is noted, weighed, estimated, valued, and safely preserved in memory to justify the verdict of the last grand dividing day. Do think of it, then, beloved, all that divine grace is working in you of humble faithfulness to God is being recorded. No annual report will proclaim it, it will never be printed in the magazine, nor advertised through the newspapers so as to bring you renown; but a book of remembrance is written before the Lord himself. There it lies before him whose single approval is more than fame. There, read a page, "Such a one thought upon my name; So-and-So spoke to his brother concerning me, and helped to the mutual edification of the body and to the bearing of powerful testimony for the truth against the assaults of error."

This evidence, moreover, dear friends, *is of a spiritual kind;* and this is one reason why it is taken down by God and by no one else, for it is evidence concerning the state of the heart in reference to God, and who is to form that estimate, but the Lord who searches the heart. Who is to know the thoughts of the mind, save God alone? There is an ear that hears thought: though it is not indicated by a sound so loud as the tick of a clock, nor so audible as the chirping of a little bird, yet every thought is vocal to the mind of the most High, and it is written down in the remembrance book. Certain great actions which every man applauds may never go into that book, because they were done from motives of ostentation; but the thought which nobody could have known and which must otherwise have remained in oblivion, is recorded of the Lord, and shall be published at the last assize. Perhaps it ran thus, "What can I do for Jesus? How can I help his poor people? How can I cheer such-and-such a languishing spirit? How can I defeat error? How can I win a wandering soul for my Master?" Such thoughts as these are reckoned worthy of record, and they are supplying evidence which in his gracious love the Lord is collecting, that the sentence of his great tribunal may be justified to all.

That evidence concerns apparently little things, for it mentions that "they spoke one to another." Of course people will gossip when they get together: what is there in talk? Oh, but what sort of gossip was it? That is the question. For a holy theme turns gossip into heavenly fellowship. It is written, they "thought upon his name." Surely it is not much to think. Ah brethren, thinking and speaking are two very powerful forces in the world, and out of them the greatest actions are hatched. Thoughts and words are the seeds of far-reaching deeds, and God takes care of these embryos and germs: men do not even know of them, and if they did know would not esteem them, but they are put down in the book of remembrance which lies always open before the most High.

Now, all this is going on every day and every night as certainly as time's sands drop through the hourglass. Letter after letter, and stroke by stroke, the

story is being written in the book of remembrance, and though men see it not
the evidence is being gathered up to be used in that dread solemnity, in which,
amid the pomp of angels, the great Infallible shall separate the blessed of his
Father from those who are accursed. Thus every day the God of judgment is
working toward the time when even the most careless shall discern between
the righteous and the wicked.

3. This brings us to the third point that *in that separation great
principles will be manifested.* I shall only have time to mention them
rapidly.

First, the principle of *election* will be displayed. God will have a people
who are more his than other men can be. "'They shall be mine,' saith the
Lord of hosts, 'in that day.'" "All souls are mine," says God, and his witness is
true, but he rejects some souls because of sin, and says, "Ye are not my people." As for his chosen, they are his portion, his peculiar treasure, his regalia,
his crown jewels, and they shall be his forever. Then will special love and
peculiar choice be manifest, for in the day of the separation it shall be seen
that the Lord knows them that are his, and while he counts others to be as
mere stones of the field, he has set his heart upon the saints who are the gems
of his crown.

But then will come as the next principle the fact of *essential value*: namely,
that the Lord's people are not only his, but they are his *jewels*. There is something in them which grace has put there, which makes them to be more precious than other men. "The righteous is more excellent than his neighbor":
God's grace makes his children to be purer, holier, heavenlier than the rest of
mankind; and they are rightly divided from the impure and worthless mass.
They will at the last by evidence be proved to have been jewels among men,
and nobody shall be able to question their worth. They shall be confessed by
all men to have been precious stones and pebbles, gold and dross.

Then will come up the next principle of *open acknowledgment*. They were
the Lord's, and they shall be owned as such. "'They shall be mine,' saith the
Lord of hosts, 'in that day.'" He himself will declare the fact, for it is written,
"He is not ashamed to call them brethren," and in that day the Lord Jesus will
say, "Here am I, and the children that thou hast given me." Oh, what a joy it
will be to be thus openly confessed by Jesus himself! Now, we are unknown if
we be God's people, for the world knows us not because it knew not our Master himself; for we are dead and our life is hid with Christ in God; but when
he who is our life shall appear then shall we also appear with him in glory.
"Then shall thy righteousness shine forth as the sun in the kingdom of their

Father." Then shall be carried out the principle that there is nothing hid which shall not be known; and those who were secretly servants of the Lord shall have evidence of that fact read aloud before assembled worlds, and God, the Judge of all, shall not be ashamed to declare, "They are mine; they are my peculiar treasure."

But even in their case the principle of *mercy* will be conspicuous. I want you to notice very specially. "When I make up my jewels they shall be mine, and I will spare them." Sparing applies to those who under another mode of judgment would not escape. Had it been a question of merit as under law, they would have been doomed as well as others, but the Lord says, "I will spare them." O God, even though you have made your chosen to be your treasure, yet you do spare them, for the evidence does not prove them meritorious, but shows that they were saved in Christ Jesus, and therefore taught to fear you. When the apostle had received great kindness from a friend whom he had valued, he offered a prayer for him, which you may be sure would be a very earnest and comprehensive one, but it was this: "The Lord have mercy upon him in that day." That is all we can expect, and, blessed be God, it is all we need. The matter of justice is settled by our great substitute, and to us mercy comes freely. The brightest saint that ever reflected the image of Christ on earth will have to be saved by mercy from first to last. "I will spare them," says he, for he might have dealt otherwise with them had he taken them on grounds of law, and judged them apart from the mercy which flows through the atoning sacrifice. True, they were jewels, and they were the Lord's own treasure, but if he had laid up their sins in evidence instead of their marks of grace, if that book of remembrance which is written before him had contained an account of their shortcomings and their transgressions as the basis of judgment, it would have gone otherwise with them, but now he calls to remembrance their godly fear, their sacred thoughts, and their holy conversation, and therefore he spares them.

They will be dealt with on the principle of *relationship* also. "I will spare them as a man spareth his own that serveth him." You spare your son when you know he is doing his best to serve you. He has made a blunder, and if he had been a mere hired servant, you might have been angry, but you say, "Ah, I know my boy was doing all he could, and he will do better soon, and therefore I cannot be severe. I see that he is imperfect, but I see equally well that he loves me, and acts like a loving son." The word here used signifies pity or compassion, "Like as a father pitieth his children, so the Lord pitieth them that fear him." He will even at the last look upon us with a love which has pity mingled with it, for we shall need it in that day. He will "remember that we are dust," and will accept us, though cognizant of all the faults there were, and of all the infirmities that there had been: he will accept us still, because we are his own sons in Christ Jesus, and by grace desire to serve him. We do not serve him to become sons, but because we are sons. It is a sweet name for a child of God: a son-servant, one who is a servant to his father, and therefore, because he is his son, serves not for wage, nor of compulsion, but out of love. Such service is mentioned as evidence of sonship, and not as a claim; and we shall be saved through grace, our holy service of sonship being the proof of that grace.

Beloved, on these principles will God make the final division. He will say, "You are mine: I chose you. You are my saints, and there is a gracious excellence in you. I acknowledge you as mine, and I am not ashamed to do so, for you bear my nature. I chose you in mercy, and in consequence of my having chosen you, I have made you to be my son-servants, and so I accept your holy conversation as the token of your sincere love to me, and I receive you into my glory to be mine forever and ever.

4. And now, last, comes the sure truth that *the separation itself will be clear to all.*

Then shall you mourn, you sorcerers and adulterers, you that oppress the hireling and turn aside the stranger from his right, you false swearers and enemies of God. You now can go on your way and say, "God cares nothing about righteous or wicked, he deals with all alike, or even smites his children worst of all"; but you shall look another way by and by. Compelled to turn your heads in another direction from that of this poor fleeting world, you shall see something that will astound you; for though you wish it not, even you and much more the godly shall then "discern between the righteous and the wicked, between him that serveth God and him that serveth him not."

The division will be sharp and decisive. Wherever you read in the Bible you find only two classes; you never read of three; but you find the righteous and the wicked, him that fears God and him that fears him not. A certain order of persons puzzle us in making division here below, because we do not know to which party they belong; but when the book of remembrance is finished and shall be opened, there will be no sort of difficulty in knowing them; the two classes shall roll apart like the two portions of the Red Sea when Moses lifted up his rod, and there shall be a space between. On which side, my dear hearer, you that are halting between two opinions—on which side will you be? There will be no borderland, no space for noncommittal and neutrality; you will then be among the fearers of God or among those that fear not his name. Who may abide the day of his coming? That coming may be very speedy, for none of us knows the day nor the hour when the Son of man shall appear.

The separation will be sharp and decisive, there will be no undecided ones left. And *it will obliterate a host of pretensions,* for the day comes that shall burn as an oven, and all the proud shall be as stubble. The Pharisee who thought he took his place among those that were the jewels of creation will find that the coming of the Lord will burn up his phylacteries and his broad hems, and utterly consume all his boasting as to fasting thrice in the week and taking mint and anise and cumin, for these things were never written in the book, nor worth recording there. What was put there was fearing the Lord, and thinking upon his name, and speaking one to another; but ceremonials and niceties of observance are not thought worth a stroke of the recording pen. There is nothing in the book to act as evidence for the proud, but everything to condemn him; and therefore the day shall burn him up and utterly consume him and his hopes.

That division will be *universal,* for all they that do wickedly shall be as stubble, not one of them escaping. Though they hid their wickedness and bore a good name, though they concealed their sin even from those who watched them, they entered the church and gained honors in it, as Judas did in the college of the apostles; yet that day shall discover all that do wickedly. Talk how they may, and speak as they please, their outward conduct will be the index of their inner alienation from God, and in the hour of their judgment the fire shall consume them from off the earth.

Then shall both classes perceive that the distinction *involves two very different fates.* Once the righteous were in the fire, and according to the third chapter and the third verse, the Lord sat as a refiner and purified them in a furnace like silver, but now the tables are turned, and the proud, and they that do wickedly, are in a more terrible fire. The day shall burn as an oven! The righteous were profited by their fire, for they were good metal, and to part with the dross was no loss, but the wicked are such base metal that they shall utterly fail in the testing fire. The tables will be turned again, for the righteous were under the feet of the wicked—they ridiculed and mocked them, and called them "cants and hypocrites"; but then the ungodly shall be laid low, and the righteous shall tread them as ashes under their feet. The cause of evil will be a worn-out thing, it will be burned up, and there will be nothing left of it upon the earth but memories of its former power and of the fire by which it perished. That day comes, and let the mighty ones among the sons of men who rebel against God know it: they shall no more be able to resist the terror of his presence than the stubble is able to stand against the blazing fire. When they pine forever in the place where their worm dies not and their fire is not quenched, they will know the God of judgment, and see how utterly he consumed them out of the land.

Look at the lot of the righteous. When Christ the Sun of righteousness shall arise upon the earth and gild it with his own light, there shall be a new heaven and a new earth, and the righteous shall go forth and leap for joy, like cattle which formerly had been penned in the stall. No works of the ungodly shall be left. As far as this world is concerned, they shall be utterly and altogether gone. There shall then be no tavern songs or alehouse ribaldry; there shall be no village profligate around whom shall gather the youth of the hamlet to be led away by his libidinous and blasphemous words; there shall then be no shameless reviler who shall provide a hall where blasphemers may congregate to try which can utter the blackest profanities against the Lord of hosts. There shall be no shrine of virgin, or of saint or idol or image or crucifix. Superstition shall be swept away. There shall be no congregations where pretended preachers of the gospel shall deal out new philosophies and suggest newly invented skepticisms, or which at least they hoped men would accept as new, though they were the old errors of the past picked from off the dunghill upon which they had been thrown by disgusted ages. Sin shall all be gone and not a trace of it shall be left, but here shall dwell righteousness and peace; the meek shall inherit the earth, and the saints shall stand each one in his lot, for the Lord himself shall reign among his ancients gloriously. From every hill and every vale shall come up the one song of glory unto the most High and every heart that beats shall magnify his name, who at last has answered the question, "Where is the God of judgment?" Then, cast into the nethermost hell, in the place appointed for the devil and his angels, the ungodly shall never ask again, "Where is the God of judgment?," and saints triumphant in their Lord, with whom they shall reign forever in eternity, shall also perceive that he "discerneth between the righteous and the wicked, between him that serveth God and him that serveth him not." Beloved hearer, where? oh, where will you be? Where shall I be—"in that day"?

The Plumb Line

＊

Published on Thursday, October 6, 1904; delivered on Lord's Day evening, August 27, 1876, at the Metropolitan Tabernacle, Newington. No. 2904.

Thus he showed me: and, behold, the LORD stood upon a wall made by a plumb line, with a plumb line in his hand. And the LORD said unto me, "Amos, what seest thou?" And I said, "A plumb line." Then said the LORD, "Behold, I will set a plumb line in the midst of my people Israel: I will not again pass by them anymore." —AMOS 7:7–8

God usually speaks by men according to their natural capacity. Amos was a herdsman. He was not a man of noble and priestly rank, like Ezekiel, nor a man of gigantic intellect and mighty eloquence, like Isaiah. He was a simple herdsman, and therefore God did not cause him to see the visions of Isaiah, or dazzle his mind with the wondrous revelations that were given to Ezekiel. God's rule is, "Every man in his own order," and if we depart from that, we get out of place ourselves, and we are apt to try to make others do that which they are not fit to do, and then blame them when they fail to accomplish what they should never have attempted. God always uses his servants in the best possible way, and as they ought to be used; so, when the herdsman Amos had a vision, he simply saw a piece of string with a plumb of lead at the bottom of it—a plumb line—a thing which he could easily understand. There was a mystery about the vision, but the vision itself was not mysterious. It was a very simple emblem indeed, exactly suited to the mind of Amos, just as the visions of Ezekiel and Isaiah were adapted to the more poetic minds of men of another class.

You and I, dear brethren, may be very thankful if God should use us as he did Amos; and, if he does, we must not be aping the Isaiahs and Ezekiels. If we see a plumb line, let us preach about a plumb line; and if God should ever enable us to understand the visions of Zechariah or Ezekiel, then let us preach about them. Let every preacher or teacher testify according to the measure of light and grace that God has given him; then we shall do well. Amos can see a plumb line, and he sees it well; and when he has seen it, he tells what he has seen, and leaves God to set his seal upon his testimony.

Now, on this occasion, we have nothing before us but this plumb line, but there is a great deal to be learned from it. The first thing is this, *the plumb line is used in construction*; second, *the plumb line is used for testing what is built*; and, third, it appears from the text that *the plumb line is used in the work of destruction*, for the casting down of that which is found not to be straight.

1. First, *the plumb line is used in construction.*

We are told, in the text, that "the Lord stood upon a wall made by a plumb line," that is to say, a wall which had been constructed with the help of a plumb line; and, therefore, he tested it with that which was supposed to have been used in its construction, which was a fair and proper thing to do. If the wall only professed to be run up without a plumb line, then it might be hard to try it with the plumb line; but as it was a wall which professed to have been constructed according to the rules of the builder's art, it was fair and reasonable that it should be tested by the plumb line.

First, then, dear friends, a plumb line is used in building when it is done as it ought to be; and I remind you that *God always uses it in his building.* Everything that God builds is built plumb and straight and square and fair. You see that rule at work in nature; there is nothing out of proportion there. Those who understand these things, and look deeply into them, will tell you that the very form and size of the earth have a connection with the blooming of a flower or the hanging of a dewdrop upon a blade of grass; and that, if the sun were larger or smaller than it is, or if the material of which the earth is formed were more dense, or different in any degree from what it is, then everything, the most magnificent and the most minute, would be thrown out of gear.

Someone of old used to say that God is the great arithmetician, the great master of geometry; and so he is. He never makes any mistakes in his calculations; there is not anything in the world that he has made in a careless manner. The mixing of the component parts of the air we breathe is managed with consummate skill; and if you could resolve a drop of water into its original elements, you would be struck by the wisdom with which God has adapted the proportions of each particle so as to make a liquid which man can drink. Everything is done by order and rule, as in the changes of the various seasons, the movements of the heavenly bodies, and the arrangements of divine providence. God always has the plumb line in his hand. He never begins to build, as a careless workman would, that which might turn out to be right or might turn out to be wrong; but he makes sure work of all that he does.

In spiritual matters, it is very manifest that, whenever God is dealing with souls, he always uses the plumb line. In beginning with us, he finds that the very foundation of our nature is out of the perpendicular; and, therefore, he does not attempt to build upon it, but commences his operations by digging it out. The first work of divine grace in the soul is to pull down all that nature has built up. God says, "I cannot use these stones in my building. This man has been behaving himself admirably in some respects, and he thinks that he is building up a temple to my honor and glory with his own natural virtues, his own good works, and other things of a like character. But all this must be dug out." The man has taken a great deal of pains in putting it together, but it must all come out, and there must be a great hole left; the man must feel himself emptied, and abased, and humbled in the sight of God; for, if God is to be everything to the man, then he himself must be nothing; and if Christ is to be his Savior, he must be a complete Savior, from beginning to end. So the foundation of human merit must be cleared right out and flung away, for God could not build squarely upon it. With such a foundation as that, the plumb line would never mark a perpendicular wall.

After all human merit has been flung out, the Lord begins his gracious work by laying the foundation stone of a simple faith in Jesus Christ, and that faith, though simple, is very real. When a man professes to convert his fellowman, he only gives him a fictitious faith which is of no value to him; but when God saves a sinner, he gives him real faith. There may be little knowledge of the truth, but the little that the man knows is truth; and faith, though it be but as a grain of mustard seed, if it be of the right sort, is better than that faith which is as big as a mountain, yet all of the wrong sort, which will not stand in the time of testing. But the faith which the Holy Spirit gives is the faith of God's elect, the real faith which will endure even the tests which God applies to it.

Side by side with that faith, God puts true repentance. When a man attempts to convert his fellowman, he gives him a sham repentance, or perhaps he tells him that there is no need of any repentance at all. Certain preachers have been telling us, lately, that it is a very easy matter to obtain salvation, and that there is no need of repentance; or if repentance is needed, it is merely a change of mind. That is not the doctrine that our fathers used to preach, nor the doctrine that we have believed. That faith, which is not accompanied by repentance, will have to be repented of; so, whenever God builds, he builds repentance fair and square with faith. These two things go together; the man just as much regrets and grieves over the past as he sees that past obliterated by the precious blood of Jesus. He just as much hates all his sin as he believes that his sin has been all put away.

The Lord never builds anything falsely in any man or teaches him to reckon that to be true which is not true; but he builds with facts, with substantial verities, with true grace, and with a real and lasting work in the soul.

When the Lord builds in a man, he builds with the plumb line in the sense of always building up that which is toward holiness. Have any of you fallen into sin, rest assured that God did not build you in that way. Have sinful desires and lustings after evil been excited within you by any doctrine to which you have listened? Then you may be sure that it was not of God. "By their fruits shall ye know them" is an infallible test of doctrines as well as of disciples; and if any of you have embraced any form of doctrine which hinders you from being watchful, prayerful, careful, and anxious to avoid sin, you have embraced error and not truth, for all God's building tends toward holiness, toward carefulness, toward a gracious walk to the praise and glory of God. When the Lord builds a man up, he makes him conscientious, makes him jealous of himself, makes him detect the very shadow of sin, so that, before the sin itself comes upon him, he holds up his all-covering shield of faith, that he may be preserved from its deadly assaults. You may always know God's building because it is pure building, clean building; but if anybody builds you up in such a style that you can talk of sin as a trifle, and think that you may indulge in it, at least in a measure, with impunity, that is certainly not God's building.

And, blessed be his name, when our souls are really given up into the Lord's hands, he will continue to build in us until he has built us up to perfection. There will come a day when sin, which now makes its nest in this mortal body of ours, shall find this body dissolving and crumbling back to the earth of which it was made; and then our emancipated spirits, delivered from the last taint and trace of sin—free from even the tendency to evil—shall soar away to be with Christ, which is far better, and to wait for the trumpet of the resurrection, when the body itself shall also be delivered from corruption, for the grave is a refining pot; and, at the coming of Christ, our body shall be pure and white, like the garments of a bride arrayed to meet her bridegroom, and the soul, reunited with the body, shall have triumphed over every sin. This is the way that God builds. He does not build us up so that we can go to heaven with our sin still working in us. He does not build us up to be temples for him to dwell in, and let the devil also dwell in us. Antinomian building is not according to the fashion of God's building; but God builds up surely, solidly, truthfully, sincerely, and until we have reached that state of perfection which makes us fit for heaven.

Now, beloved, as God thus uses the plumb line in his building, I gather that *we also should use the plumb line in our building*. First, with regard to the uplifting of our own soul, I would urge upon myself first, and then upon you next, the constant use of the plumb line. It is very easy to seek after speed, but to neglect to ensure certainty. There is such a thing as being in a dreadful hurry to do what had better never be done, or else be done in a very different style. We see some people who become Christians in about two minutes; and I am devoutly thankful when that is really the case. We see some others become full-grown Christians in about two days, and instructors of others in the course of a week; and, very speedily, they attain to such vast dimensions that there is no ordinary church that is big enough to hold them. That is very quick work; that is the way that mushrooms grow, but it is not the way that oaks grow. I urge you all to remember that, often, the proverb, "the more haste, the less speed," is true in spiritual things as well as in temporal. My dear brother, if you only grow an inch in the course of ten laborious years, yet that growth is real, it is better than appearing to grow six feet in an hour, when that would only be disease puffing you up and blowing you out. Often and often, the soul needs to use the plumb line to see whether that which is built so very quickly is really built perpendicularly, or whether it does not lean this way or that. As the work goes on, we should frequently stop and say to ourselves, "Now, is this right? Is this real? Is this true?" Many a time, if we did that, we should have to fall upon our knees, and cry, "O Lord, deliver me from exalting myself above measure and counting myself to be rich and increased with goods, when, all the while, I am wretched and miserable and poor and blind and naked."

I would like you young men who are here to use the plumb line when you begin your spiritual life-building. I mean this: your father and mother are members of a certain church, but do not you, therefore, go and join that church without a thorough investigation of the principles on which it is founded. Use the plumb line to see whether it is all straight and square. Try all the doctrines that are taught and do not embrace that which is popular, but that which is biblical. Then try with the plumb line the ordinances of the church; do not submit to them simply because other people do so, but use the plumb line of Scripture to test them all. You know that, as a body, we are not afraid that you will ever read your Bible too much. We, as Baptists, have no objection to your bringing everything that is taught to the test of the Bible, for we know that we should be the gainers if you were to do that; but, instead of using the plumb line of the Bible, many people have a newly invented test— the Book of Common Prayer or Minutes of the Conference or something else equally valueless. Now, whatever respect I have for books of that sort, I prize my Bible infinitely above them all, and above all the volumes of decretals of popes and councils and conferences put together. I should not like to feel that I had been building and building and building and building, and yet that there had been a radical error in the whole structure, for I had commenced with a mistake, and I had been building myself up, not in the most holy faith of the apostles, but in the most mischievous error of my own notions. Do, I pray you, apply the Bible plumb line continually to all your beliefs and views and practices.

But, even before you do that, use the gospel plumb line to see whether you really were ever born again, for our Lord Jesus said to Nicodemus, "Except a man be born again, he cannot see the kingdom of God." Do test yourselves as to whether you have really believed in Jesus Christ, for "without faith it is impossible to please God"; and if you have believed in him, take care that, while you think you are getting more faith, more love, more patience, more of every grace, you keep the plumb line going; otherwise, you may get a great deal into the structure that you will have to take out again, and you will get the building out of the perpendicular, and the whole of it may come down with a crash.

And this plumb line is also to be used upon all work that is done on behalf of other people. There is much teaching which has been given with a pure motive, but which, nevertheless, cannot endure this test. There are some little sects, still existing upon the face of the earth, that were formed with much labor by their originators; but they are evidently not gold or silver or precious stones, for they are passing away with the lapse of time. I would like, as a minister of the gospel, to do for God that which will endure the supreme test of the day of judgment. I should not like to build up a great church here, and then, when I was dead and gone, for it to be scattered to the four winds, and to learn in heaven that I had been mistaken except as to the matter of my own salvation; and that, consequently, while some good was done, there was ill done as well. No; we must constantly use the plumb line, so that what we build may be perpendicular, and may stand the test of the ages, and the test of God's great judgment seat. Look to it, sirs, you who are diligent, that you are diligent in spreading truth and not error. See to it, you who count up your many converts, that they are real converts, and not the mere fruit of excitement. See to it, you who plod on from day to day so industriously seeking to save souls, that they are really saved and truly brought to Christ; for, if not, your work will be in vain. Churches that are built in a hurry will come down in a hurry; wood, hay, and stubble, that look all right in the building, will look terrible in the burning, when the day of the trial by fire shall come.

So that is our first point, that the plumb line is to be used in the construction of the building.

2. **Second,** *the plumb line is to be used for testing the building when it is built.*

Do not let us judge either ourselves or one another simply by the eye. I have frequently thought that a building was out of the perpendicular when it was not; and I have sometimes thought it perpendicular when it really was not so. The human eye is readily deceived, but the plumb line is not; it drops straight down, and at once shows whether the wall is upright or not. *We must continually use upon ourselves the plumb line of God's Word.* Here is a wall that needs to be tested—the wall of self-righteousness. This man thinks he is all right. He never did anything very wrong. Moreover, he is religious in his way. He says that he has kept the law from his youth up. That is a fine piece of wall, is it not?—with some very handsome stones inlaid therein with fair colors. You are very proud of it, my dear friend; but if I put the Bible plumb line to your life, you will be astonished to find how much out of the perpendicular it is. The plumb line is according to this standard, "If any man will be saved by his own works, he must keep the law of the Lord perfectly; for he who is guilty of the breach of any one of God's commandments, has broken the whole law: 'therefore by the deeds of the law there shall no flesh be justified in his sight.'" That condemns your wall, does it not?—because you have not at all times kept the whole law in the fullness of the meaning which Christ gave to it. If you are to be saved by works, there must not be a single flaw in the whole wall of your life. If there is, it is not in the perpendicular.

Here is another wall, built by a man who says that he is doing his best, and trusting to Christ to make up for his deficiencies. Well, my dear friend, your wall is sadly out of the perpendicular, because there is a text which says, "Christ is all"; and I know that the Lord Jesus Christ will never be willing to be put side by side with such a poor creature as you are, to be jointly used with yourself to your soul's salvation. Remember that in the gospel plan it is not Christ and Co.; it must be all Christ, or no Christ at all. So, if you are depending partly upon self, and partly upon him, my plumb line shows that your wall is out of the perpendicular, and that it will have to come down.

Another man is depending upon rites and ceremonies. Now, there are some very strong texts in Scripture concerning that matter. Here is one: "To obey is better than sacrifice, and to hearken than the fat of rams." Will you come before God bringing the blood of beasts or costly offerings? Has he not told you that, to come before him with a broken and a contrite heart, and, especially, to come unto him through the merit of the one great sacrifice offered by his Son, is the only acceptable way of approaching him? The most gorgeous ceremonies in the whole world cannot save a single soul. That wall is out of the perpendicular and must come down.

Here is another man, who says, "I am, as often as I can be, a hearer of the Word." I am glad that you are; but if you are only a hearer, and not a doer of the Word, your wall is out of the perpendicular; for, if it is good to hear what is right, it is better still to do it; and your condemnation will be all the more terrible if you have known what you ought to do, and yet have not done it. There are many of you who come here and who have been coming for a long time who, I hope, will be led to do much more than simply come to hear; for I trust that you will be led by the Holy Spirit to lay hold on eternal life. If not, your wall will not endure the test of the Bible plumb line, which plainly shows that you are quite out of the perpendicular.

There are many other bowing walls besides those I have mentioned, but I cannot stop to try them now. I would, however, most earnestly urge you all to remember that, if you do not test yourself by the plumb line of God's Word, *if you are God's servant, you will be tried and tested.* Have you never known what it is to be laid aside, on a bed of sickness, and to have everything about you tried? In times of acute pain, I have had every morsel of what I thought to be gold and silver put into the fire, piece by piece, by the Master himself, until he has put it all in. Thank God, some of it has been proved to be gold, and has come out all the brighter for the testing; but, oh, how much of it has proved to be alloy or even worthless dross! You can have a great deal of patience when you have not any pain; and you can have a great deal of joy in the Lord when you have got joy in your worldly prosperity; and you can have any quantity of it when you have no troubles to test its reality. But the real faith is that which will endure the trial by fire. The real patience is that which will bear intense agony without a murmur of complaint. The Lord will test and try you, my brother, sooner or later, if you are his. He will be sure to use the plumb line, so you had better use it yourself. It may save you much anxiety in the future if you stop now to question yourself and to inquire whether these things be real and true to you or not.

And remember, once more, that *God will use the plumb line, at the last great day, to test everything.* How many of us could hear, without a tremor, the intimation that God had summoned us to appear before his bar? O my brethren and sisters, if the great scales of divine justice were swinging from this ceiling now, and the Judge of all said to you, "Step in, and let me see what is your weight," is there one of us who could solemnly and sincerely rise and say, "Lord, I am ready for the weighing"? Yes; I trust that many could say, each one for himself or herself, "There is not anything good in me, but my hope is fixed on Christ alone; and though I am not what I ought to be, nor what I want to be, nor what I shall be, yet 'by the grace of God I am what I am.' My profession of being a Christian is not a lie; it is not a pretense; it is not a piece of religious masquerade; it is true, great God; it is true." My brother, my sister, if you can say that, you may step into the scales without any fear, for the contrite and believing heart can endure being weighed. But into the scales you will have to go whether you are ready or not. Your building will all have to be tested and tried. Some of you have built fine mansions and towers and palaces; but the plumb line will be applied to them all, and it is God himself who will use the plumb line in every case. No counterfeit will be allowed to pass the pearly gates, nor anything that defiles or works abomination or makes a lie. At the last great day, none shall pass from beneath the eye of the Judge of all without due examination. He will not suffer even one of the guilty to escape, nor condemn any one of those who have been absolved for Christ's sake. It will be a right and just judgment that will be given in that day; but judgment there will be.

3. My last point is this, *the plumb line is used in the work of destruction.*

When a city wall was to be battered down, the general would sometimes say, "This wall is to be taken down to this point," and then the plumb line was hung down to mark how far they were to go with the work of destruction. They thus marked out that part which might be spared and that which must be destroyed.

Now, in the work of destruction, God always uses the plumb line, and *he goes about that work very slowly.* He shows that he does not like it. When the Lord is going to save a sinner, he has wings to his feet; but when he is going to destroy a sinner, he goes with leaden footsteps, waiting, and warning many times, and while he waits and warns, sighing, and crying, "How shall I give thee up?" He even goes so far as to use an oath, saying, "As I live, saith the Lord God, I have no pleasure in the death of the wicked; but that the wicked turn from his way and live." God never brings men to judgment, as the infamous Judge Jeffreys did, in a great haste. He would hurry them off to the gallows with indecent speed; but, at the last great day, there will be a solemn and stately pomp about the whole dread assize, the sounding of the trumpet, the bursting of the graves, the setting up of the great white throne, the opening of the books, and the majestic appearance of him from whose face heaven and earth will flee away. And when the judgment begins, it will not be without due order, nor will it be without keen perception of all differences. There will hang the infallible plumb line. That which is perpendicular will be declared to be perpendicular, and that which bows will be shown tottering to its fall; for, before the Judge's eye, and before the eyes of the assembled universe, shall hang a plumb line, with these words above it: "He which is filthy, let him be filthy still; . . . and he that is holy, let him be holy still."

The whole judgment shall be according to the plumb line. *Not a soul, in that great day, will be sent to hell who does not deserve to go there.* If there be any man who can plead that it would be unjust to condemn him—if he can truthfully prove that he has been obedient up to the measure of his light, if he can prove that justice is on his side—God will not do an unjust turn to him, or to any other man. Those awful gates, which grind upon their iron hinges, never yet opened to receive a soul damned unjustly. It would be impossible, in the very nature of things, for such a thing to happen. If any man could truly say, "This is unjust," he would have taken away the sting of hell, for this is the essence and the soul of helldecretal—"I am wrong and can never get right. I am wrong and do not want to get right. I am so wrong that I love the wrong and make evil to be my good, and good to be my evil. I hate God, for it is impossible, while I am in such a state as this, that I can be otherwise than unhappy; and this is the greatest hell that can happen to a man, not to love God, and not to love right." That is the flame of hell, the worm that gnaws forever—that being out of gear with God—that being out of harmony with the most High forever. I imagine that there needs to be no fiercer hell than that. So, the final judgment will be according to the plumb line, so that no one will be condemned unjustly.

You talk to me about the fate of the heathen who have never heard the gospel, and I reply, "I know very little about them; but I know that God is just, so I leave them in his hands, knowing that the Judge of all the earth will do right." There will not be one pang, to a soul in hell, more than that soul deserves, not a single spasm of despair, or a sinking in hopelessness, that is imposed by the arbitrary will of God. It will be a terrible reaping for them, when they reap sheaves of fire; but they will only reap what they have sown. There will be an awful pouring out of divine vengeance upon the vessels of wrath fitted to destruction; but no one will be able to say that the judgment is unjust. The lost will themselves feel that they only have to eat as they baked and to drink as they brewed. It will all be just to them; and this is what will make the teeth of the serpent of hell, and the flame of its fire—that it is all just—that if I were myself judge, I must condemn myself to what I have to suffer. Think of that, and escape from the wrath to come.

And as that plumb line hangs there, in that great day of account, *there will be differences made between some lost men and other lost men.* All hell is not the same hell, any more than all flesh is the same flesh. That man knew his Lord's will and did it not; lay on the lashes to the full that the law allows. That other man did not obey his Lord's will, but, then, he did not know it, so he shall be beaten with few stripes. Few will be too many for anyone to bear; so do not run the risk of them. But, oh, the many stripes, what will they be. There are the lost that perished in Sodom and Gomorrah—those filthy beings whose sins we dare not think upon. There they are, and there is the hell they suffer. There hangs the plumb line; and, by his unerring justice, God awards their doom. But what will he award to you and you and you, who have heard the gospel simply and plainly preached, and yet have rejected Christ? You will have to go lower down in hell than the inhabitants of Sodom and Gomorrah, for God's plumb line tells us that sin against light is the worst of sin, and that the willful rejection of the atoning blood flowing from the loving Savior's wounds is the climax of all iniquity. That is how the plumb line will work.

And when you come up, you rich man, who have spent your money in sin, and when you come up, you poor man, who work so hard, there shall be a difference between the one of you and the other, between the seducer, whom the world allows to enter into her drawing room, and the poor girl whom he led astray; for, though both are guilty, God will make a difference, not as men make it here, but quite the other way. The man of talent and of rank and of position who frittered away his whole existence in the life of a butterfly, there will be a difference between his sentence and that of the obscure, uneducated individual who did sin, but not as he did who had the greater gifts. To put one talent in a napkin brings its due punishment; but to bury or misuse ten talents shall bring a tenfold doom; for there will hang that plumb line, and by the rules of infinite justice everything shall be determined.

"This is dreadful talk," some of you may be saying. It is; it is; and it is a dreadful business altogether for the lost, that being driven from God's presence when you die, hearing him say, "Depart, ye cursed, into everlasting fire, prepared for the devil and his angels." You do not like to hear about this, and I do not like to preach about it; only I must do so, lest you come unto that place of torment because I failed to warn you. Then might you say, in your despair, "O cursed preacher! O unfaithful minister! You tried to tickle our ears with pleasant things, but you left out all allusions to the wrath to come. You toned down the truth, you softened it, and now we are ruined forever through your wicked desire to please our foolish ears. O sirs, you will never be able truthfully to say that, for I do pray you to escape from that awful future. Run no risk of it. I think every one of you would like to have his house insured against fire, and to know that, as far as proper title deeds go, whatever you have is held on a good tenure. Then, I implore you, make sure work for eternity by laying hold on Christ Jesus. Yield yourself up to him, that he may make you right where you are wrong, put you in gear with God, and set you running parallel with the will of the most High; that he, indeed, may build you up on the perpendicular, on the solid foundation of his eternal merits by faith, through the power of the ever-blessed Spirit, that you may be so built that, when God himself holds the plumb line, it may hang straight down, and he will be able to say, "It is all right." Happy will you be if you hear his verdict, "Well done, good and faithful servant; thou hast been faithful in a few things, I will make thee ruler over many things. Enter thou into the joy of thy Lord."

May God grant this mercy to every one of you, for Jesus Christ's sake! Amen.

Preparation for Heaven

~ᴧᴖᴄ~

Published on Thursday, November 16, 1916; delivered at the Metropolitan Tabernacle, Newington. No. 3538.

Now he that hath wrought us for the selfsame thing is God, who also hath given unto us the earnest of the Spirit. —2 CORINTHIANS 5:5

How very confidently Paul contemplates the prospect of death! He betrays no trembling apprehensions. With the calmness and serenity, not merely of resignation and submission, but of assurance and courage, he appears joyous and gladsome, and even charmed with the hope of having his body dissolved, and being girded about with the new body which God has prepared for his saints. He that can talk of the grave and of the hereafter with such intelligence, thoughtfulness, faith, and strong desire as Paul did is a man to be envied. Princes might well part with their crown for such a sure and certain hope of immortality. Could emperors exchange their treasures, their honors, and their dominions, to stand side by side with the humble tentmaker in his poverty, they would be great gainers. Were they but able to say with him, "We are always confident, and willing rather to be absent from the body, and to be present with the Lord," they might well barter earthly rank for such a requital.

This side heaven, what can be more heavenly than to be thoroughly prepared to pass through the river of death? On the other hand, what a dreary and dreadful state of mind must they be in who, with nothing before them but to die, have no hope and see no outlet—the pall and the shroud their last adorning; the grave and the sod their destination. Without hope of rising again in a better future or realizing a better heritage than that which should know us no more before long; no prospects of seeing God face to face with rejoicing—well may men dislike any reference to death. So they shrink from the thought of it; far less can they tolerate its being talked of in common conversation. No marvel that they recoil from the shade of mortality when they are so ill prepared to face the reality of the soul's departure. But, dear friends, since it is so desirable to be ready to depart, it cannot be inexpedient sometimes to talk about it; and on my part the more so, because there is a proneness in all our minds to start aside from that grave topic which, as God shall help us, shall be our subject this evening—preparation for the great hereafter. "For," says the apostle, "God hath wrought us for this selfsame thing"; he has prepared us for the dropping of the present body, and the putting on of the next, and he has "given us the earnest of his Spirit."

Our three departments of meditation will be—*the work of preparation itself*; *the Author of it*; and *the seal which he sets to it,* the possession of which may resolve all scruples as to whether we are prepared or not.

1. *The work of preparation* stands first.

Is it not almost universally admitted that some preparation is absolutely essential? Whenever the death of a friend or comrade is announced, you will hear the worst instructed say, "I hope, poor man, he was prepared." It may be but a passing reflection or a common saying. Yet everybody will give expression to it, "I hope he was ready." Whether the words be well understood or not, I do not know; but the currency given to them proves a unanimous conviction that some preparation is necessary for the next world. And, in truth, this doctrine is in accordance with the most elementary facts of our holy religion. Men by nature need something to be done for them before they can enter heaven and something to be done in them, something to be done with them, for by nature they are enemies to God. Dispute it as you will, God knows best. He declares that we are enemies to him and alienated in our hearts. We need, therefore, that some ambassador should come to us with terms of peace and reconcile us to God. We are debtors as well as enemies to our Creator—debtors to his law. We owe him what we cannot pay, and what he cannot pardon. He must exact obedience, and we cannot render it. He must, as God, demand perfection of us, and we, as men, cannot bring him that perfection.

Some mediator, then, must come in to pay the debt for us, for we cannot pay it, neither can we be exempted from it. There must be a substitute who shall stand between us and God, one who shall undertake all our liabilities and discharge them, and so set us free, that the mercy of God may be extended to us. In addition to this, we are all criminals. Having violated the law of God, we are condemned already. We are not, as some vainly pretend, introduced to this world on probation; but our probation is over; we have forfeited all hope; we have broken the law and the sentence is gone out against us, and we stand by nature as condemned criminals, tenants of this world during the reprieve of God's mercy, in fear of a certain and terrible execution, unless someone come in between us and that punishment; unless some gracious hand bring us a free pardon; unless some voice divine plead and prevail for us that we may be acquitted. If this be not done for us, it is impossible that we should entertain any well-grounded hope of entering heaven.

Say, then, brethren and sisters, has this been done for you? I know that many of you can answer, "Blessed be God, I have been reconciled to him through the death of his Son; God is no enemy of mine, nor I of his; there is no distance now between me and God; I am brought near to him and made to feel that he is near to me and that I am dear to him." Full many here present can add, "My debts to God are paid; I have looked to Christ, my substitute; I have seen him enter into suretyship engagements for me, and I am persuaded that he has discharged all my liabilities; I am clean before God's bar; faith tells me I am clean." And, brethren, you know that you are no longer condemned. You have looked to him who bore your condemnation, and you have drunk in the spirit of that verse, "There is, therefore, now no condemnation to them that are in Christ Jesus, who walk not after the flesh, but after the Spirit." Surely this is a preparation for heaven. How could we enter there if our debts were not discharged? How could we obtain the divine favor eternally if we were still condemned criminals? How could we dwell forever in the presence of God if we were still his enemies? Come, let us rejoice in this: that he has worked us for this selfsame thing having championed our cause from the cradle to the grave.

Preparation for heaven consists still further in *something that must be worked in us,* for observe, brethren, that if the Lord were to blot out all our sins, we should still be quite incapable of entering heaven unless there was a change wrought in our natures. According to this Book, we are dead by nature in trespasses and sins—not some of us, but all of us; the best as well as the worst; we are all dead in trespasses and sins. Shall dead men sit at the feasts of the eternal God? Shall there be corpses at the celestial banquets? Shall the pure air of the New Jerusalem be defiled with the putrefaction of iniquity? It must not, it cannot be. We must be quickened; we must be taken from the corruption of our old nature into the incorruption of the new nature, receiving the incorruptible seed which lives and abides forever. Only the living children can inherit the promises of the living God, for he is not the God of the dead, but of the living; we must be made living creatures by the new-creating power of grace or else we cannot be made meet for glory.

By nature we are all worldly. Our thoughts go after earthly things. We "mind earthly things," as the apostle says. We seek after the world's joys; the world's maxims govern us; the world's fears alarm us; the world's hopes and ambitions excite us. We are of the earth earthy, for we bear the image of the first Adam. But, brethren, we cannot go to heaven as worldly men; for there would be nothing there to gratify us. The gold of heaven is not for barter to use, nor for covetousness to hoard. The rivers of heaven are not for commerce, neither are they to be defiled by men. The joys and glories of heaven are all spiritual, all celestial.

> *Pure are the joys above the skies*
> *And all the region peace.*

Such peace is of a heavenly kind and for heavenly minds. Carnal spirits, greedy, envious spirits—what would they do in heaven? If they were in the place called heaven, they could not be in the state called heaven, and heaven is more a state than a place. Though it is probably both, yet it is mainly the former, a state of happiness, a state of holiness, a state of spirituality, which it would not be possible for the worldly to reach. The incongruity of such a thing is palpable. Therefore, you see, brethren, the Holy Spirit must come and give us new affections. We must have a fresh object set before us. In fact, instead of minding the things that are seen, we must come to love and to aspire to the things that are not seen. Our affections, instead of going downward to things of earth, must be allured by things that are above, where Christ sits at the right hand of God.

In addition to our spiritual death and worldliness, we are all unholy by nature. Not one of us is pure in the sight of God. We are all defiled and all defiling, but in heaven they are "without fault before the throne of God." No sin is tolerated there; no sin of thought or word or deed. Angels and glorified spirits delight to do God's will without hesitation, without demur, without omission; and we, like them, must be holy, or we cannot enter into their sacred fellowship.

> *Those holy gates forever bar*
> *Pollution, sin, and shame.*
> *None shall obtain admission there*
> *But followers of the Lamb.*

But what a change must come over the carnal man to make him holy! Through what washings he must pass! What can wash him white, indeed, but that far-famed blood of the Son of God? Through purification he must pass! What, indeed, can purify him at all but the refining energy of God the Holy Ghost? He alone can make us what God would have us to be, renewed in his image in holiness and righteousness.

That a great change must be wrought in us, even ungodly men will confess, since the idea of the heaven of the Scriptures has always been repulsive, never agreeable, to unconverted men and women. When Muhammad would charm the world into the belief that he was the prophet of God, the heaven he pictured was not at all the heaven of holiness and spirituality. His was a heaven of unbridled sensualism, where all the passions were to be enjoyed without let or hindrance for endless years. Such the heaven that sinful men would like; therefore, such the heaven that Muhammad painted for them and promised to them.

Men in general, be they courtly, or be they coarse in their habits, when they read of heaven in the Scriptures with any understanding of what they read, curl their lips and ask contemptuously, "Who wants to be everlastingly psalm singing? Who could wish to be always sitting down with these saints talking about the mighty acts of the Lord and the glorious majesty of his kingdom?" Such people cannot go to heaven, it is clear; they have not character or capacity to enter into its enjoyment. I think Whitefield was right. Could a wicked man be admitted into heaven, he would be wretched there; being unholy, he must be unhappy. From sheer distaste for the society of heaven, he might fly to hell for shelter. With the tumult of evil passions in his breast, he could not brook the triumph of righteousness in the city of the blessed. There is no heaven for him who has not been prepared for it by a work of grace in his soul. So necessary is this preparation—a preparation for us, and a preparation in us.

And if we ever have such a preparation, beyond all question we must have it on this side of our death. It can only be obtained in this world. The moment one breathes his last, it is all fixed and settled. As the tree falls, so it must lie. While the nature is soft and supple, it is susceptible of impression, stamp what seal you may upon it; once let it grow cold and hard, fixed and frigid, you can do so no more, it is proof against any change. While the iron is flowing into the mold, you can fashion it into what implement you please; let it grow cold, in vain you strive to alter its form. With pen of liquid ink in your hand, you write what you will on the paper, but the ink dries, the impress remains, and where is the treachery that shall tamper with it? Such is this life of yours. It is over, all over with you for eternity, beyond alteration or emendation, when the breath has gone from the body. Your everlasting state is fixed then.

> *There are no acts of pardon passed*
> *In the cold grave to which we haste;*

But darkness, death, and long despair
Reign in eternal silence there.

We have no intimation in the Word of God that any soul dying in unbelief will afterward be converted to the faith. Nor have we the slightest reason to believe that our prayers in this world can at all affect those who have departed this life. The masses of priests are fictions, without the shadow of divine authority. Purgatory, or "pick-purse," as old Latimer used to call it, is an invention for making fat larders for priests and monks, but the Scriptures of truth give it no countenance. The Word of God says, "He that is holy, let him be holy still; he that is filthy, let him be filthy still." Such as you are when death comes to you, such will judgment find you, and such will the eternal reward or the eternal punishment leave you, world without end. Preparation is needed, and the preparation must be found before we die.

Moreover, we ought to know—for *it is possible for a man to know whether he is thoroughly prepared.* Some have said not, but they have usually been persons very little acquainted with the matter. The writings of those grand old divines of the Puritan period abundantly prove how thoroughly they enjoyed the assurance of faith. They did not hesitate to express themselves in such language as the apostle used: "We *know* that if this earthly house of our tabernacle be dissolved, we have a house not made with hands, eternal in the heavens." They were apt to speak as Job does when he says, "I know that my Redeemer liveth." And indeed, many of the children of God among us at this present time are favored with a confident, unstaggering confidence that, let their last hour come when it may, or let the Lord himself descend from heaven with a shout, there will be nothing but joy and peace for them—no cause of trembling, nothing that can give them dismay. Why, some of us live from year to year in constant assurance of our preparation for the bliss that awaits and the rest that remains for God's people.

Beloved, God has not so left us in such a dubious case that we always need to be inquiring, "Am I his, or am I not?" He has given us good substantial grounds to go upon to make sure work of it. He tells us that "he that believeth and is baptized shall be saved"; if we have been obedient to these two commands, we shall be saved, for our God keeps his word. He tells us that such believers, patiently continuing in well doing, inherit eternal life. If we are kept by his grace, walking in his fear, we may rest assured that we shall come to the ultimate end of such a life, namely, the glory which abides for the faithful. We need not harbor endless questionings. What miserable work it is to stand in any doubt on this matter. Let us not be satisfied till we are sure and confident that heaven will be ours.

Alas, how many put off all thoughts of being prepared to die! They are prepared for almost anything except the one thing for which it is most needful to be ready. If the summons should come to some of you at this moment, how dread it would be! Were we to see an angel hovering in the air, and should we have intelligence by a message from the clouds that someone of us must, on a sudden, leave his body behind him and appear before God, what cowering down, what trembling, what muttering of forgotten prayers there would be with some of you! You are not ready. You never will be ready, I fear. The carelessness in which you have lived so long has become habitual. One would think you had resolved to die in your sins.

Have you never heard the story of Archaeus, the Grecian despot, who was going to a feast, and on the way a messenger brought him a letter, and seriously importuned him to read it? It contained tidings of a conspiracy that had been formed against him, that he should be killed at the feast. He took the letter and put it into his pocket. In vain the messenger urged that it was concerning serious matters. "Serious matters tomorrow," said Archaeus, "feasting tonight." That night the dagger reached his heart while he had about him the warning which, had he heeded it, would have averted the peril. Alas, too many men say, "Serious things tomorrow"! They have no misgiving that, when their sport is over, they will have alike the leisure and the leanings for these weighty matters. Were it not wiser, sirs, to let these grave affairs come first? Might ye not, then, find some better sport of nobler character than all the froth and frivolity to which fashion leads on? A holy merriment and a sacred feasting that well become immortal spirits. How vain and groveling the mirth which reduces men to children, pleased with a rattle, tickled with a straw; then brings them down to driveling fools and degrades them often till they become worse than brutes. I wish I could imprint a solemn thought on the mind of some careless individuals. You care not that time is short, that life is precarious, that opportunities cross your path at lightning speed, that hope flatters those on whom the fangs of death are fixed; that there is no vestibule in which to fit your frame of mind, that the shock will always come sudden at last. What sentence more trite; what sentiment more prevalent; yet what solemnity more neglected than this: "Prepare to meet your God"! Propound it, profess it, preach it as we may, the most of men are unprepared. They know the inevitable plight, they see the necessity of preparation, but they postpone and procrastinate instead of preparing. God grant you may not trifle, any of you, until your trembling souls are launched into that sphere unknown, but not unfeared, and read your doom in hell.

2. Now, *as to the Author of this preparation for death*, the text says, "he that hath wrought us for the selfsame thing is God."

It is God alone, then, who makes men fit for heaven. He works them to the selfsame purpose. Who made Adam fit for paradise but God? And who must make us fit for the better paradise above but God? That we cannot do it ourselves is evident. According to the Scriptures, we are dead in trespasses and sins. Can the dead start from the grave of their own accord? Do you think to see coffins opened and gravestones uplifted by the natural energy of corpses? Such things were never dreamed of. The dead shall surely rise, but they shall rise because God raises them. They cannot vitalize their inert frames, neither can the dead in sin quicken themselves and make themselves fit for the presence of God. Conversion, which prepares us for heaven, is a new creation. That word "creation" puts all the counsel, the conceit, and the contrivance of man into the background. If anyone says that he can make a new heart, let him first go and make a fly. Not until he has created such a winged insect let him presume to tell us that he can make a man a new creature in Christ Jesus. And yet to make a fly would not demonstrate that a fly could make itself, and it would offer but a feeble pretext for that wonderful creation which is supposed in a man's making himself a new heart. The original creation was the work of God, and the new creation must likewise be of God. To take away a heart of stone and give a heart of flesh is a miracle. Man cannot do it; if he attempts it, it shall be to his own shame and confusion. The Lord must make us anew. Have not we, who know something of the Lord's working in us, this selfsame thing, been made to feel that it is all of his grace? What first made us think about eternal things? Did we, the stray sheep, come back to the fold of our own accord? No; far from it.

> *Jesus sought me when a stranger,*
> *Wandering from the fold of God.*

And ever since, we have been living men in Christ Jesus. To whom must we ascribe our preservation and our progress? Must we not attribute every victory over sin, and every advance in the spiritual life, to the operation of God and nothing at all to ourselves?

A poor simpleton once said, "'Twas God and I did the work." "Well, but Charlie, what part did you take in it?" "Sure, then," said he, "I did all I could to stop the Lord, and he beat me." I suppose, did we tell the simple truth, we should say much the same. In the matter of our salvation we do all we can to oppose it—our old nature does—and he overcomes our evil propensities. From first to last, Jesus Christ has to be the Author and the Finisher of our salvation, or it never would have been begun, and it never would have been completed. Think, beloved, of what fitness for heaven is. To be fit for heaven a man must be perfect. Go, you who think you can prepare yourselves, be perfect for a day. The vanity of your own mind, the provocation of this treacherous world, and the subtle temptation of the devil, would make short work of your empty pretensions. You would be blown about like chaff. Creature perfection, indeed! Was ever anything so absurd? Men have boasted of attaining it, but their very boastings have proved that they possessed it not. He that gets nearest to perfection is the very man who sighs and cries over the abiding infirmities of his flesh. No, if perfection is to be reached—and it must be, or we shall not be fit for heaven—by the operation of God it must be wrought. Man's work is never perfect; it is always marred on the wheel. His best machinery may still be improved upon; his finest productions of art might still be excelled. God alone is perfect, and he alone is the perfecter. Blessed be God, we can heartily subscribe to this truth: "He that hath wrought us for the selfsame thing is God."

But what shall I say to those of you, my friends, who have no acquaintance with God? You certainly cannot be fitted for heaven. Your cause is not committed to him. He is doing nothing for you. He has not begun the good work in you. You live in this world as if there were no God. The thought, the stupendous thought, of his "being" does not affect you. You would not act any differently if there were twenty Gods or if there were no God. You utterly ignore his claims on your allegiance and your responsibility to his law. Virtually in thought and deed you are without God in the world. Poor forlorn creature, you have forgotten your Creator. Poor wandering soul, you have fallen out of gear with the universe; you have become alienated from the great Father who is in heaven. I tremble at the thought. To be on the wide sea without rudder or compass; to be lost in the wilderness, where there is no way! Cheerless as your condition is, remember this: though you see not God, God sees you. God sees you now; he hears you now. If you breathe but a desire toward him, that desire shall be accepted and fulfilled. He will yet begin to work in you that gracious preparation which shall make you meet to be a partaker of the inheritance of the saints in light.

3. And now, third: *let the seal of this preparation* be briefly but attentively considered.

The apostle says, "He that hath wrought us for the selfsame thing is God, who also hath given unto us the earnest of the Spirit." Masters frequently pay during the week a part of the wages which will be due on Saturday night. God gives his Holy Spirit, as it were, to be a part of the reward which he intends to give to his people, when, like hirelings, they have fulfilled their day. Our country friends just before harvest go out into the fields, and they pick half a dozen ears that are ripe, braid the ends, and hang them up over the mantel as a kind of earnest of the harvest. So God gives us his Holy Spirit to be in our hearts as an earnest of heaven; and as the ears of wheat are of the same quality and character as the harvest, so the gift of the Holy Spirit is the antepast of heaven. When you have him, you have a plain indication to your soul of what heaven will be. You have a part of heaven—"a young heaven," as Dr. Watts somewhere calls it, within you.

Ask yourself, then, dear hearer, this question, "Have I received the earnest of the Spirit?" If so, you have the preparation for heaven; if not, you are still a stranger to divine things, and you have no reason to believe that the heaven of the saints will be your heritage. Come, now, have you received the Holy Spirit? Do you reply, "How may I know?" Wherever the Holy Spirit is, he works certain graces in the soul—repentance, to wit. Have you ever repented of sin? I mean, do you hate it? Do you shun it? Do you grieve to think you should once have loved it? Is your mind altogether changed with regard to sin, so that what once seemed pleasure now is pain, and all the sweetness of sin is poison to your taste? Where the Holy Spirit is, repentance is followed by the whole train of graces, all in a measure, not any in perfection, for there is always room to grow in grace and in the knowledge of Jesus Christ. Such is patience, which submits to the Lord's will; such, too, the gracious disposition of forgiveness, which enables us to bear injuries and to forgive those that vex us; such, likewise, that holy courage which is not ashamed to own our Lord, or to defend his cause. In fact, where the Holy Ghost is bestowed, all the graces of the Spirit will be communicated in some degree. Though they will all need to grow, yet there will be the seeds of them all. Where the Holy Spirit is, there will be the joy.

No delight can be more animating or more elevating than that which springs from the indwelling of God in the soul. Think of God coming to abide in this poor bosom! Why, were a cross of diamonds or pearls glittering on your breast, some might envy you the possession of such a treasure; but to have God within your breast is infinitely better. God dwells in us, and we in him. Oh! sacred mystery! Oh! birth of joy unspeakable! Oh! well of bliss divine that makes earth like heaven! Have you ever had this joy—the joy of knowing that you are pardoned; the joy of being sure that you are a child of God; the joy of being certain that all things work together for your good; the joy of expecting that before long, and the sooner the better, you shall be forever beyond gunshot of fear and care and pain and want? Where the Spirit of God is, there is more or less of this joy, which is the earnest of heaven.

This gift, moreover, will be conspicuously evidenced by a living faith in the Lord Jesus Christ. The Holy Ghost is not in you if you rely on anything but Jesus; but if, as a poor guilty sinner, you have come to him, partaken of his gracious pardon, kissed his blessed feet, and are now depending upon him alone, you have received the Holy Ghost, and you have got the antepast of heaven.

Brethren and sisters, it is intensely desirable that we should seek more to be consciously filled with the Holy Spirit. We get easily contented with a little spiritual blessedness. Let us grow more covetous of the best gifts. Let us crave to be endued with the Holy Spirit and to be baptized in the Holy Ghost and in fire. The more we get of him, the more assurance we shall have of heaven for our peace, the more foretastes of heaven for our happiness, and the more preparation for heaven in lively hope.

Thus have I shown you the need of preparation, the Author of preparation, and the great seal which proves the verity of that preparation. If your honest conscience allows your humble claim to have received this sacred token of salvation, how happy you would be! Do not be afraid to be happy. Some Christians seem to court the gloom of despondency as if they dared not bask in the sunshine of heaven. I have sometimes heard people say that they have not enjoyed themselves. No, dear friends; pity, I think, if any of us ever should. It would be a poor kind of enjoyment if we merely enjoyed ourselves. But oh! it is delightful when you can enjoy your God, and when you can enjoy the mercies that are in him and the promises that are in him and the blessings which through him come to you. When you gather round the table of the Lord's love, do not be afraid to partake of the feast. There is nothing put there to be looked at. There is no confectionery spread out for show. If you dare conclude that you are living in Christ, and living on Christ, do not be afraid to sing as you go home—

> *Now I can read my title clear*
> *To mansions in the skies;*
> *I bid farewell to every fear,*
> *And wipe my weeping eyes.*

It will be a blessing to your family for you to be happy. You may find that something has gone wrong while you have been away. Go home as happy as you can be, and you will be better able to bear the cares and vexations that must and will befall you. Keep your spirit well worked up to the fear of the

Lord and the enjoyment of his presence. Then, if some little cross matter should come to disquiet you, you can say, "Who am I that I should be vexed and chafed, or lose my temper, or be cast down about such a matter as this? This is not my sphere of well-being; this is not my heaven; this is not my God."

> *If thou shouldst take them all away,*
> *Yet should I not repine;*
> *Before they were possess'd by me*
> *They were entirely thine.*

> *Nor would I speak a murmuring word,*
> *Though the whole world were gone,*
> *But seek enduring happiness*
> *In thee, and thee alone.*

But oh! suppose you feel persuaded and honestly admit that you are not prepared to die, not made meet for heaven. Do not utterly despair, but be grateful that you live where the gospel is preached. "Faith cometh by hearing, and hearing by the Word of God." Be much in hearing the Word, and be much in earnest prayer that the hearing may be blessed to your soul. Above all, give diligence to that divine command which bids you trust in Jesus Christ, whom he has sent. Eternal life lies in the nutshell of that one sentence, "Believe in the Lord Jesus Christ, and thou shalt be saved." All that is asked of you—and even that grace gives you—is simply to trust in him who, as Son of God, died for the sins of men. God give you that faith, and then may you meet death with joy or look forward to the coming of the Lord with peace, whichever may be your lot. Amen.

The Strait Gate

Published on Thursday, April 19, 1917; delivered at the Metropolitan Tabernacle, Newington. No. 3560.

Strive to enter in at the strait gate; for many, I say unto you, will seek to enter in, and shall not be able. —LUKE 13:24

The precepts of our Lord Jesus Christ are dictated by the soundest wisdom. He has given us divine prescriptions for the health of our souls, and his commandments, though clothed with sovereign authority, are spoken in such infinite kindness that we may regard them as the advice of a true and faithful friend. This is not a legal but a gospel exhortation: "Strive to enter in at the strait gate." He himself is the only gate, or the door, by which we can find admission, and the way to enter in through Jesus Christ is not by working, but by believing. Then, as to the strife we are urged to carry on, it is an earnest endeavor to steer clear of all the rocks and shoals and quicksands of popular fallacies and deceitful traditions, and to sail in the deep waters, with his covenant for our chart, and his Word for our compass, in simple obedience to his statutes, trusting to him as our pilot, whose voice we always hear, though his face we cannot see. The storm signal may well rouse your fears; the cry of peril had need excite your caution. The mere mention sounds like a menace. "Many shall seek to enter in, and shall not be able." Listen to that warning, lest you be among the "many" that founder—perhaps you shall be among the few that escape. Hearken to what Jesus tells you shall come to pass with the multitude, that it may never come to pass with you as individuals.

1. Mark now, first, *a gate which it is most desirable to enter.*

Surely "many" would not seek to enter if they were not convinced of the desirableness of passing through it. The very fact that so many, although they fail, will at least seek to enter, proves that there is a desire, a reason, and a motive why men should aim to enter.

This gate—that is, Christ—it is most desirable for us to pass through, *because it is the gate of the city of refuge.* Cities of refuge were appointed for manslayers, that when they were pursued by the avenger of blood, they might pass the gate and be secure within the sanctuary or city. The gospel of Jesus

Christ is intended as a refuge for those who have broken the law of God, whom vengeance is pursuing, who will certainly be overtaken, to their eternal destruction, unless they fly to Christ and find shelter in him. Outside of Christ the sword of fire pursues us swift and sharp. From God's wrath there is but one escape, and that is by a simple faith in Christ. Believe in him, and the sword is sheathed, and the energy and the love of God will become your everlasting portion; but refuse to believe in Jesus, and your innumerable sins, written in his book, shall be laid at your door in that day when the pillars of heaven shall reel, and the stars shall fall like withered fig leaves from the tree.

Oh! who would not wish to escape from the wrath to come! Mr. Whitefield, when preaching, would often hold up his hands and cry, "Oh! the wrath to come! the wrath to come! the wrath to come!" There is more weight and meaning in these words than tongue can tell or heart conceive. The wrath to come! the wrath to come! When past that gate, like Noah after he had passed into the ark, you are safe from the overwhelming deluge; you are sheltered from the devouring conflagration which shall consume the earth; you are rescued from the death and the doom that await the countless multitudes of the impenitent. Who would not wish to enter where there is salvation, the only place where salvation can be found?

It is desirable to enter this gate *because it is the gate of a home.* There is sweet music in that word "home." Jesus is the home of his people's hearts. We are at rest when we get to Christ. We have all we want when we have Jesus. Happiness is the portion of the Christian in this life while he lives upon his Savior. I have seen outside the night refuges crowds of persons waiting an hour beforehand, till the doors were opened. Poor souls! Shivering in the cold, but in expectation of being warmed and comforted in a little time for a little while, when they should be admitted. What think you, O homeless men and women—were there a permanent home for you, a home from which you never could be banished, a home into which you could be introduced as dear children, would it not be worth your while to wait long at the door, and to knock again and again right vehemently, could you but ultimately gain admission? Jesus is a home for the homeless, a rest for the weary, a comfort for the comfortless.

Is your heart broken? Jesus can comfort you. Have you been banished from your family, or one by one have the dear ones been taken to their last resting place? Do you feel solitary, friendless, cheerless, accounting "the black flowing river" to be preferred before this troubled stream of life, and that pitiless society of men and women, eager all for gain and gaiety, caring nothing of your griefs or your groans? Oh, come to Jesus! Trust in him, and he will light up a star in the black midnight sky; he will kindle a fire in your hearts that shall make them glow with joy and comfort, even now. It were worthwhile to be a Christian, irrespective of the hereafter. Such present comfort as a belief in Jesus imparts is an inestimable compensation. This is the gate of refuge, and it is the gate of a home.

Moreover, it *leads to a blessed feast*. We read just now of the supper that was spread. Jesus does not feed our bodies, but he does what is better, he feeds our minds. A hungry stomach is terrible, but a hungry heart is far more dreadful, for a loaf of bread will fill the one, but what can satisfy the other? Oh! when the heart gets craving and pining and yearning after something it cannot get, it is like the sea that cannot rest; it is like the grave that never can be filled; it is like the horse leech, whose daughters cry, "Give, give, give." Happy the man who believes in Jesus, for he becomes at once a contented man. Not only does he find rest in Christ, but joy and gladness, peace and abiding satisfaction are the portion of his lot. I tell you what I do know—and I would not lie, even for the Lord himself—I tell you that there is a mirth to be found in faith in Christ which cannot be matched. Speak you of their buoyant spirits who make merry in the dance or of the festive glee of those that are filled with wine? It is but the crackling of a handful of thorns under a pot—how soon it is gone! But the joy of the man who meditates on the love of Christ which embraces him, on the blood of Christ which cleanses him, on the arm of Christ which upholds him, on the hand of Christ which leads him, on the crown of Christ which is to be his portion—the joy of such a man is constant, deep, overflowing, beyond the power of expression.

The meanest Christian in all the world, bedridden, living on parish allowance, full of pains and ready to die, when his heart is stayed upon Christ, would not change places with the youngest, brightest, richest, noblest spirit to be found outside the church of God. No, kings and emperors, boast no more of your beggarly crowns; their glitter will soon fade; your purple robes will soon be moth-eaten; your silver shall soon be cankered; of your palace, not a stone shall be left upon its fellow. Bitter shall be the dregs of your wine cups, and all your music shall end in discord. I tell you that the poorest of all the company of the faithful in Christ Jesus excel you, and "would not change their blest estate for all that earth calls good or great." So abundantly worthwhile is it to come to Christ for the happiness, as well as the repose, which we find in him.

Well likewise, dear friends, may men desire to pass through the strait gate, knowing it is *the gate which leads to paradise*. There was one gate of paradise through which our father—Adam—and our mother—Eve—went weeping as they left the garden all behind them, to wander into the desert world. Can you picture them to yourselves, with the cherubim behind them and the flaming sword bidding them begone, for paradise was no place for rebels? Men have wandered up and down the world since then to find the gate of paradise, that they might enter yet again. They have scaled the peaks of Sinai, but they have not found it there. They have traversed the tracks of the wilderness, weary and footsore, jaded and faint, but they have found no gate to paradise anywhere in all their expeditions. The scholar has searched for it in the ancient books; the astronomer has hunted for it among the stars; sages, as they were called, have sought to find it by studying their arts; and fools have tried to find it among their viols and their bowls.

But there is only one gate. See, there it is. It is in the form of a cross, and he that will find the gate of heaven finds the cross and the man that did hang thereon. Happy he who can come up to it and pass through it, reposing all his confidence in the atonement once made by the Man of suffering on Calvary's tree. On earth he is saved, and in the article of death he shall pass through that gate of pearl unchallenged, walk the streets of gold unabashed, and bow before the excellent glory without a fear. He is free of heaven. The cross is a mark of a citizen of the skies. Having truly believed in Jesus, everlasting felicity is his beyond all doubt. Who, then, would not pass through the strait gate?

And who would not wish to pass through it when he considers what will be the lot of those outside the gate? How we tremble at the thought of that outer darkness, where shall be weeping and wailing and gnashing of teeth! There are many inquiries nowadays about eternal punishment. O men and brethren, do not rashly or carelessly challenge the bitter experience of such condemnation! Speculate as you will about the doctrine, but I pray you do not trifle with the reality. To be lost forever, let that mean what it may, will be more than you can bear though your ribs were iron and your bones were brass. Tempt not the avenging angel. Beware that you forget not God, lest he tear you in pieces, and there be none to deliver. By the living God, I pray you fear and tremble, lest you be found out of Christ in the day of his appearing. Rest not, be not patient, much less merry, till you are saved. To be in danger of hellfire is a peril that no heart can adequately realize, no language fitly paint. Oh! I beseech you, halt not, give yourself no rest, till you have got beyond that danger! Flee for your lives, for the fiery shower will soon descend! Escape! God, in his mercy, quicken your pace that you may escape full soon, lest the hour of mercy cease and the day of judgment come! Surely these are reasons enough for wanting to pass in at the strait gate.

2. Observe still further what our Lord tells us. *There is a crowd of people who will seek to enter and will not be able.*

Who are these? If you look closely at *the crowd who this day seek to pass,* I think you will see a considerable difference between seeking and striving. You are not merely advised to seek; you are urgently bidden to strive. Striving is a more vehement exercise than seeking. Are you among those who coolly seek admission because, indeed, they suppose it is the proper thing? Many there be who come up to the gate of mercy and seek to enter, not striving, not particularly anxious, certainly far enough from being agitated. And when they look at the gate they object to the lintel because it is too low, nor will they deign to stoop. There is no believing in Jesus with a proud heart. He that trusts Christ must feel himself to be guilty and acknowledge it. He never will savingly believe till he has been thoroughly convinced of sin. But many say, "I will never stoop to that. Unless I have something to do in the work, and share some of the merit, I cannot enter." No, sirs, some of you are quite unable to believe in Christ because you believe in yourselves. As long as a man thinks himself a fine fellow, how can he think well of Jesus? You eclipse the sun; you hold up your own little hands before the sunlight; how can you expect to see? You are too good to go to heaven or, at least, too good in your own apprehension. O man! I pray God prick that bubble, that blown-up bladder, and let out the gas, that you may discern what you really are, for you are nothing, after all, but a poor worm, contemptible, notwithstanding your conceit and pride, in spite of your poverty, an arrogant worm, that dares to lift up its head when it has nothing to glory in. Oh! bow yourself in lowly self-abhorrence, else you may seek to enter, but shall not be able!

Some are unable to enter *because the pride of life will not let them.* They come to this gate in their carriage and pair, and expect to drive in, but they cannot get admission. There is no different way of salvation for a peer of the realm than for a pauper in the workhouse. The greatest prince that ever lived must trust Jesus just as the meanest peasant does. I recollect a minister once telling me that he attended the bedside of a very proud woman, of considerable wealth, and she said to him, "Do you think, sir, that when I am in heaven, such a person as Betty-My-Maid will be in the same place as I am? I never could endure her company here. She is a good servant in her way, but I am sure I could not put up with her in heaven." "No, madam," said he, "I do not suppose you will ever be where Betty will be." He knew Betty to be one of the humblest and most consistent of Christian women anywhere, and he might have told her proud mistress that in the sight of God meekness is preferable to majesty. The Lord Jesus, in the day of his coming, will wipe out all such distinctions as may very properly exist on earth, though they cannot be recognized beyond the skies. O rich man, glory not in your riches! All your wealth, if you could take it with you, would not buy a single paving stone in the streets of heaven. This poor stuff—do not trust in it. Oh! lay it aside as a crown of glorying and pass humbly through the gate with Lazarus!

Some are unable to enter *because they carry contraband goods with them.* When you land in France, there stands the gendarme, who wants to see what you are carrying in that basket. If you attempt to push by, you will soon find yourself in custody. He must know what is there; contraband goods cannot be taken in. So at the gate of mercy which is Christ, no man can be saved if he desire to keep his sins. He must give up every false way. "Oh!" says the drunkard, "I'd like to get to heaven, but I must smuggle in this bottle somehow." "I would like to be a Christian," says another; "I do not mind taking Dr. Watts's hymns with me, but I should like sometimes to sing a Bacchanalian song, or a lightsome serenade." "Well," cries another, "I enjoy myself on Sunday with God's people, but you must not deny me the amusements of the world during the week; I cannot give them up." Well, then, you cannot enter, for Jesus Christ never saves us in our sins; he saves us from our sins. "Doctor," says the fool, "make me well, but I'd like to keep my fever." "No," says the doctor, "how can you be well while you keep the fever?" How can a man be saved from his sins while he clings to his sins? What is salvation but to be delivered from sin? Sin lovers may seek to be saved, but they shall not be able; while they hug their sins, they cannot have Christ. Some of you are in this grievous predicament. You have been attending this house of prayer a good long time. I do not know what hinders you, but this I do know, there is a worm somewhere eating out the heart of that fair-looking apple. Some private sin that you pamper is destroying your souls. Oh! that you had grace to give it up, and to come in by the strait gate, trusting in Jesus Christ!

Not a few are unable to enter in because *they want to postpone the matter until tomorrow.* Today, at any rate, you are engaged with other plans and projects. "A little longer let me revel in some of the sensual enjoyments of life, and afterward I will come in." Procrastinators are among the most hopeless of people. He that has "tomorrow" quivering on his lips is never likely to have grace reigning in his heart.

Others, and these are in the worst plight of all, *think that they are in,* and that they have entered. They mistake the outside of the gate for the inside. A strange mistake to fall into, but many do thus delude themselves. They rub their backs against the posts, and then they tell us they are as near heaven as anybody else. They have never passed the threshold; they have never found shelter in Christ, albeit they may have felt wonderfully excited at a revival meeting, and sung as loudly and lustily as any of the congregation: "I do believe, I will believe." There is a considerable show of reformation about them. Although they have not got a new garment, they have mended up the old one. They are not new creatures, but still they are better behaved creatures than they were before. And they are "all right." Be not deceived, my dear friends; do beware of mistaking a work of nature for the operation of God's grace. Do not be taken in by the devil's counterfeits. They are well made; they look like genuine; when they are brand new they shine and glitter like fine gold, but they will not stand the test; every one of them will have a nail driven through them one day; they will never pass current with God. If you have a religion, let it be real and true, not feigned and hypocritical. Of all cheats, the man who cheats himself is certainly the least wise, and, as I think, he is the least honest. Do not play the knave with your own soul. Suspect yourself too much rather than too little. Better journey to heaven in terror of hell than dream of the happy land while drifting in the other direction. "Ah! that deceit should steal such gentle shapes!" Be on your guard, every one of you. Let not any man deceive himself.

Thus it is that a crowd—I had almost said a countless crowd—of people nowadays seek to enter in, but for manifold reasons they are not able to do so. And yet there is a more appalling aspect to the same fact. "Many, I say unto you, *will* seek to enter in, and shall not be able." *The dying are not able.* Panic-stricken, the dying man sends for the minister whom he never went to hear when his health was good and hours hung heavy on his hands. The charm of Sundays lay in their dissipation; an excursion up the river or a cheap trip to Brighton and back; anything—everything sooner than hear the gospel. He never read his Bible; he never prayed. Now the doctor shakes his head and the nurse suggests that they "fetch a clergyman." Poor soul! She means right; but what, think you, can he do? What can we ministers do for you? What can any man do for his fellow creature? "None of us can by any means redeem his brother, nor give to God a ransom for him." He begins to seek, when, alas! he cannot think, poor fellow, for he is in *articulo mortis*, with the throes of his last struggle. His head swims, pains grow at his vitals, a glassy film is over his eyes, rambling words fall from his lips. Could he think, he has got something else to think about than the dread future that awaits him. Look at his weeping wife. See those dear children, brought in to get a last kiss from their father. Were his mind more vigorous, it were not likely to be taken up with spiritual thoughts; there is too much in the solemn farewell to occupy the moments left in preparation for the future. "Pray for me, sir," he says, with fainting, failing breath. Yes, he is seeking to enter in. In ninety-nine cases out of a hundred, I fear the answer is, he shall not be able. Little hope have I for deathbed repentances. Never trust to them, I beseech you. Such a vestibule as a deathbed you may never have. To die in the street may be your lot. Should you have a deathbed, you will have something else to think about besides religion. Oh! how often have I heard Christian men say, when they have been dying, "Ah sir, if I had a God to seek now, what a misery it would be! What a blessing it is that, with all the cares that now come upon me, I have a sure and certain hope in Christ, for I found him years ago." O dear hearers, do not be among those who postpone and procrastinate, till, in a dying hour, after a fashion you seek to enter and find you shall not be able.

Some years ago I was awakened about three o'clock in the morning by a sharp ring of the doorbell. I was urged without delay to visit a house not very far off London Bridge. I went, and up two pairs of stairs I was shown into a room, the occupants of which were a nurse and a dying man. There was nobody else. "O sir," said she, "Mr. So-and-So, about half an hour ago, begged me to send for you." "What does he want?" I asked. "He is dying, sir," she replied. I said, "I see that. What sort of a man was he?" "He came home last night, sir, from Brighton. He had been out all day. I looked for a Bible, sir, but there is not one in the house; I hope you have got one with you." "Oh!" I said, "a Bible would be of no use to him now; if he could understand me, I could tell him the way of salvation in the very words of Holy Scripture." I spoke to him, but he gave me no answer. I spoke again; still there was no reply. All sense had fled. I stood a few minutes gazing at his face, till I perceived he was dead; his soul had departed. That man in his lifetime had been inclined to jeer at me. In strong language he had often denounced me as a hypocrite. Yet he was no sooner smitten with the darts of death than he sought my presence and my counsel, feeling no doubt in his heart that I was a servant of God, though he did not care to own it with his lips. There I stood, unable to help him. Promptly as I had responded to his call, what could I do but look at his corpse and go home again? He had, when too late, sighed for the ministry of reconciliation, sought to enter in, but he was not able. There was no space left in him then for repentance; he had wasted the opportunity. Therefore, I pray and beseech you, my dear hearers, by the near approach of death—it may be much nearer than you think—give earnest heed to these things. I look round on this building and note the pews and sittings from which hearers, whose faces were once familiar to us, have gone—some to glory, some I know not where. God knows. Oh! let not the next removal, if it be yours, vacate the seat of a scoffer or of a neglecter or of one who, having been touched in his conscience, silenced the secret monitor and would not turn. As the Lord lives, you must turn or burn; you must either repent or be ruined forever. May God give you wisdom to choose the better part!

It appears from Scripture that *even after death there will be some who will seek to enter and shall not be able.* I do not attempt to explain what I cannot understand, but I find the Master represents those on the left hand asking a question, "When saw we thee hungry, and fed thee not?" as if they had some glimmering hope that the sentence upon them might be reversed. And I read in another place of those who will come and knock at the door, and say, "Lord, Lord, open to us." But the Master of the house, having already risen up and shut to the door, will answer, "Verily, I say unto you, I know you not." Is there, then, such a thing as prayer in hell? When the soul has passed out of the body without hope, will it seek for hope hereafter? Perhaps so. Did not the rich man pray to Abraham to send Lazarus? It is but natural to expect that, as they doubted God's promises on earth, they may doubt God's threatenings in hell, and may hope, perhaps, that there will be a way of escape. They will seek, they will seek, but they shall not be able, not able to enter heaven. They said they were not able on earth; they shall find they are not able in hell. *Non possumus* is the sinner's cry. "We are not able to leave our sins; we are not able to believe; we are not able to be serious; we are not able to be prayerful"; and then, how it will be thrown back into their teeth! Not able to enter heaven; not able to escape from torment; not able to live; not able to die; not able, because the gate of heaven admits no sinner who has not been washed in the Redeemer's blood. Back with you, sir! You would not come to the fountain, you would not wash. Back with you.

You are not able; not able, because heaven is a prepared place for a prepared people, and you never thought of preparation. Away with you, sir! How can you enter when you are not prepared? Heaven is a place for which a fitness is needed. Men cannot enjoy that which would be contrary to their natures. Away with you, sirs! You could not enjoy heaven if you were admitted, for you are not changed in heart. Away with you! What, do you linger? Do you cry? Do you pray? Do you weep? Do you entreat? Away with you! No, the angels shall sweep you away, for is it not written: You yourselves shall be thrust out—unceremoniously driven and scourged away from the gate of glory, because you would not come to the gate of grace. These are terrible things to utter.

I well might shrink from speaking thus, were it not that fidelity to your souls makes such demands that I must ring the warning. If you die without faith in Christ, behold there is *a gulf fixed* between you and heaven. I do not know what that means, but I know what idea it gives to me, and should give to you. Between heaven and hell there is no traffic. None ever passed from hell to heaven.

> *There are no acts of pardon passed*
> *In the cold grave to which we haste;*
> *But darkness, death, and long despair*
> *Reign in eternal silence there.*

They would fain pass the gulf—were it fire, they could be glad to pass it; were it full of torments, many and manifold as a Spanish Inquisition could invent, they would be glad to bear them; could they but hope to cross the gulf. But no, the voice is heard—an angel's voice: "He that is filthy, let him be filthy still; he that is unjust, let him be unjust still." The wax has cooled; you cannot alter the impression. The die is cast; you cannot remold it. The tree has fallen; there it lies.

I wish I could speak now in words that should burn their way right into your inmost hearts. Alas! I cannot. I must, however, just repeat the text again, and leave it with you. Many shall seek in that dread day to enter, but shall not be able. Oh! enter then, enter you! Enter now, while yet the gate stands open wide, and mercy bids you come! Make haste to enter while yet the avenging angel lingers, and the angel of mercy stands with outstretched arms and cries, "Whosoever will, let him come and take of the water of life freely." May God, the ever-blessed Spirit, without whom no warning can be effectual, and no invitation can be attractive, sweetly constrain you to trust Christ tonight.

Here is the gospel in a few words. Jesus suffered the wrath and torment we justly merited. He doubtless bore the penalty of your transgressions, if you penitently believe in his sacrifice. When you trust in him for pardon, 'tis proof your sins were laid on him for judgment. You are, therefore, a forgiven man, a pardoned woman; you are saved—saved forever. If you have a simple, childlike trust, you may go home, singing for joy of heart, knowing that you have already entered the strait gate, and before you lie grace on earth and glory in heaven. May God bless you richly, and may you adore him gratefully, for his dear name's sake. Amen.

A Last Lookout

Delivered at the Metropolitan Tabernacle, Newington. No. 989.

The time of my departure is at hand. —2 TIMOTHY 4:6

So near, so very near the change—his removal from this to another world; and so very conscious of it; yet Paul looked back with calm satisfaction; he looked forward with sweet assurance; and he looked round with deepest interest on the mission that had engaged his life. As you must have noticed while we were reading the chapter, in his case "the ruling passion was strong in death." Writing what he well knows is the last letter he shall ever write, its main topic is care for the church of God—anxiety for the promotion of the truth—zeal for the furtherance of the gospel. When he is dead and gone from the post of service, the scene of suffering, the field of enterprise, on whom shall his mantle fall? He desires that in Timothy he may find a worthy successor, strong in the faith, sincere of heart, and having dauntless courage withal, one who will wield the sword and hold the banner when his hand is palsied in death.

Men have usually shown us what lies at the bottom of their heart when they have come to die. Often their last expiring expressions have been indicative of their entire character. Certainly you have before you in the last sentences of Paul's pen a fair epitome of his entire life. He is trusting in the Savior; he is anxious to show his love for that Savior. The welfare of the Christian church and the advancement of the holy cause of the gospel are uppermost in his mind. May it be yours and mine to live wholly for Christ and to die also for him. May this ever be foremost in our thoughts: "How can I advance the kingdom of our Lord and Savior? By what means can I bless his church and people?" It is very beautiful to observe the way in which Paul describes his death in this verse. According to our translation, he speaks of it as an offering. "I am now ready," says he, "to be offered." If we accept this version, he may be supposed to mean that he felt as one standing like a bullock or a lamb, ready to be laid on an altar. He foresaw he would die a martyr's death. He knew he could not be crucified as his brother Peter had been, for a Roman citizen was, as a rule, exempt from that ignominious death. He expected to die in some other manner. Probably he guessed it would be by the sword, and so he describes himself as waiting for the sacrificial knife to be used, that he might be presented as a sacrifice.

So I say the words of our translation would lead us to think. But the original is far more instructive. He here likens himself, in the Greek, not to an offering, but to the drink offering. Every Jew would know what that meant. When there was a burnt sacrifice offered, the bullock or the victim then slain was the main part of the sacrifice. But sometimes there was a little, what if I say an unimportant, supplement added to that sacrifice—a little oil and a little wine were poured on to the altar or the bullock, and thus a drink offering was said to be added to the burnt offering. Now Paul does not venture to call himself an offering—Christ is his offering. Christ is, so to speak, the sacrifice on the altar. He likens himself only to that little wine and oil poured out as a supplement thereto, not necessary to its perfection, but tolerated in performing a vow, or allowed in connection with a freewill offering, as you will find if you refer at leisure to the fifteenth chapter of Numbers, from the fourth to the eighth verses. The drink offering was thus a kind of addendum, by which the person who gave it showed his thankfulness. So Paul is resolved to show his thankfulness to Christ, the great sacrifice, and he is willing that his blood should be poured as a drink offering on the altar where his Lord and Master was the great burnt offering. He rejoices when he can say, "I am ready to be presented as a drink offering unto God."

We have mainly to do with the second description which he gives of his death. What does he say when the hour that this grim monster must be grappled with is at hand? I do not find him sad. Those who delight in gloomy poetry have often represented death in terrible language. "It is hard," says one—

> To feel the hand of death arrest one's steps,
> Throw a chill blight on all one's budding hopes,
> And hurl one's soul untimely to the shades.

And another exclaims—

> O God, it is a fearful thing
> To see the human soul take wing,
> In any shape, in any mood!
> I've seen it rushing forth in blood,
> I've seen it on the breaking ocean,
> Strive with a swollen, convulsive motion.

Not so the apostle Paul. I do not even hear him speak of flying through the gate as our grand old poet has described death. He does not say, "The hour of my dissolution is at hand"—a very proper word if he had used it; but he is not looking so much at the process as at the result of his dying. He does not even say, "The hour of my death is at hand," but he adopts a beautiful expression, "the time of my departure"—words which are used sometimes to signify the departure of a vessel from the port; the pulling up of the anchor so that it looses its moorings, when about to put out to sea—so he feels himself like a ship lying at the harbor for a while—but he says, "The time for pulling up the anchor, the time for letting loose the cable, and cutting from the mooring is at hand; I shall soon be launched upon my voyage." And he knew right well where that voyage would end, in the fair havens of the port of Peace in the better country, whither his Lord had gone before him.

Now we will proceed very briefly to say a word about *departure*; and then a shorter word still about the time of our departure; and then a little more about *the time* of our departure *being at hand*—trying here, especially, to bring forward some lessons which may be of practical usefulness to each one of us.

1. First, then, dear brethren, let us think a little about *our departure*.

It is quite certain we shall not dwell here forever: we shall not live here below as long as the first man did, or as those antediluvian fathers, who tarried some eight or nine hundred years. The length of human life then led to greatness of sin. Monstrosities of evil were ripened through the long continuance of physical strength and the accumulating force of eager passions. All things considered, it is a mercy that life is abridged and not prolonged to a thousand years. Amid the sharp competition of man with man, and class with class, there is a bound to every scheme of personal aggrandizement, a limit to all the spoils of individual despotism, a restraint upon the hoardings of anyone's avarice. It is well, I say, that it should be so. The narrow span of life clips the wings of ambition and balks it of its prey. Death comes in to deprive the mighty of his power, to stay the rapacity of the invader, to scatter abroad the possessions of the rich. The most reprobate men must end their career after they have had their threescore years and ten or their fourscore years of wickedness.

And as for the good and godly, though we mourn their exit, especially when we think that they have been prematurely taken from us, we remember how the triumphs of genius have been for the most part achieved in youth, and how much the world has been enriched by the heads and hearts of those who have but sown the seeds of faith and left others to reap the fruits. If into less than the allotted term they have crowded the service of their generation, we may save our tears, for our regrets are needless. The summons will reach each one of us before long. We cannot stop here as long as the gray fathers of our race: we expect, and it is meet that we should prepare, to go. The world itself is to be consumed one day. "The elements shall melt with fervent heat." The land on which we stand we are apt to call *terra firma*, but beneath it is probably an ocean of fire, and it shall itself feel the force of the ocean. We must not marvel, the house being so frail, that the tenants are unsettled and migratory. Certainly, whether we doubt it or not, we shall have to go. There will be a departure for us.

Beloved believer in Christ Jesus, to you the soft term "departure" is not more soft than the truth it represents. To die is to depart out of this world unto the Father. What say you about your departure? What say you of that from which you go, and what think you of that land to which you go? Well, of the land from which we go, my brethren, we might say many hard things if we would, but I think we had better not. We shall speak more correctly if we say the hard things of ourselves. This land, my brethren, has been a land of mercy to us: there have been sorrows in it; but in bidding it farewell, we will do it justice and speak the truth concerning it. Our sorrows have usually sprung up in our own bosoms, and those that have come from the soil itself would have been very light if it had not been for the plague of our hearts, which made us vex and fret over them. Oh, the mercy you and I have enjoyed even in this life! It has been worthwhile to live for us who are believers. Even had we to die like a dog dies, it has been worthwhile to live for the joy and blessedness which God has made to pass before us. I dare not call that an evil country in which I have met my Savior and received the pardon of my sin. I dare not call that an ill life in which I have seen my Savior, though it be through a glass darkly. How shall I speak ill of that land where Zion is built, beautiful for situation, the joy of the whole earth, the place of our solemn assemblies, where we have worshiped God? No; cursed of old as the earth was to bring forth the thorn and the thistle, the existence of the church of God in that land seems to a great degree to have made reparation for the blight to such as know and love the Savior.

Oh, have we not gone up to the house of God in company with songs of ecstatic joy, and have we not when we have gathered round the table of the Lord—though nothing was upon it but the type and emblem—have we not felt it a joyous thing to be found in the assembly of the saints, and in the courts of the Lord's house even here? When we loose our cable and bid farewell to earth, it shall not be with bitterness in the retrospect. There is sin in it, and we are called to leave it; there has been trial in it, and we are called to be delivered from it; there has been sorrow in it, and we are glad that we shall go where we shall sorrow no more. There have been weakness and pain and suffering in it, and we are glad that we shall be raised in power; there has been death in it, and we are glad to bid farewell to shrouds and to knells; but for all that there has been such mercy in it, such loving-kindness of God in it, that the wilderness and the solitary place have been made glad, and the desert has rejoiced and blossomed as a rose. We will not bid farewell to the world, execrating it, or leaving behind us a cold shudder and a sad remembrance, but we will depart, bidding adieu to the scenes that remain and to the people of God that tarry therein yet a little longer, blessing him whose goodness and mercy have followed us all the days of our life, and who is now bringing us to dwell in the house of the Lord forever.

But, dear brethren, if I have had to speak in a somewhat apologetic manner of the land from which we depart, I shall need to use many apologies for my own poor talk about the land to which we are bound. Ah, where do you go, spirit loosened from your clay—do you know? Where do you go? The answer must be, partly, that we know not. None of us have seen the streets of gold of which we sang just now; those harpings of the harpers, harping with their harps, have never fallen on these ears; eye has not seen it, ear has not heard it: it is all unrevealed to the senses; flesh and blood cannot inherit it, and, therefore, flesh and blood cannot imagine it. Yet it is not unknown, for God has revealed it unto us by his Spirit. Spiritual men know what it is to feel the spirit, their own newborn spirit, living, glowing, burning, triumphing within them. They know, therefore, that if the body should drop off, they would not die. They feel there is a life within them superior to blood and bone and nerve and sinew. They feel the life of God within them, and none can dispute it. Their own experience has proven to them that there is an inner life.

Well, then, when that inner life is strong and vigorous, the spirit often reveals to it what the world of spirits will be. We know what holiness is, do we not, brethren? Are we not seeking it? That is heaven—perfect holiness is heaven. We know what peace means; Christ is our peace. Rest—he gives us rest: we find *that* when we take his yoke. Rest is heaven. And rest in Jesus tells us what heaven is. We know, even today, what communion with God is. If anyone should say, "I do not know it," I should reply to him thus: Suppose I said to you, "You know not what it is to eat and drink": the man would tell me that I belied him, for he knew, as he knew his own existence, what it was to eat and drink; and, as surely as I live, I have communion with God. I know it as certainly as you know that I have declared it to you. Well, friends, that is heaven. It has but to be developed from the germ to the produce, and there is heaven in its full development.

Communion with saints in like manner—know we not what that is? Have we not rejoiced in each other's joys, been made glad with the experience of our brethren? That, too, carried to perfection, will be heaven. Oh, to throw yourself into the bosom of the Savior and lie there taken up with his mind and his love, yielding all things to his supremacy, beholding your King in him! When you have been in that state you have had an antepast of heaven. Your view may have been but as one seeing a man's face in shadow yet you would know that man again even by the shadow; so know we what heaven is. We shall not be strangers in a strange land when we get there. Though, like the Queen of Sheba, we shall say, "The half has not been told me," yet we shall reflect on it thus: "I did surmise there would be something of this sort. I did know from what I felt of its buddings in my soul below that the full-blown flower would be somewhat of this kind." Where away, then, spirit that is departing to soar through tracks to yourself unknown? Your answer is, "I am away: away to the throne of him whose cross first gave me life and light and hope. I am away to the very bosom of my Savior, where I hope to rest and to have fellowship with the church of the Firstborn, whose names are written in heaven." This is your departure that you have in near prospect.

Suppose, dear friend, the thought of departing from this world to the glory world should ever startle you, let me remind you that you are not the first that ever went that way. Your vessel is in the pool, as it were, or in the dock; she is going out on her voyage; oh, but you will not go alone, nor have to track your course through paths unnavigated or unknown before! When the Portuguese captain first went by the Cape of Storms it was a venturous voyage, and he called it the Cape of Good Hope when he had rounded it. When Columbus first went in search of the New World, his was a brave spirit that dared cross the unnavigated Atlantic. But oh, there are tens of thousands that have gone where you go. The Atlantic that severs us from Canaan is white with the sails of the vessels that are on voyage there. Fear not, they have not been wrecked; we hear good news of their arrival; there is good hope for you. There are no icebergs on the road, no mists, no counter currents, and no sunken vessels or quicksands; you have but to cut your moorings, and with Christ on board you shall be at your desired haven at once.

Remember, too, your Savior went that way. Have you to depart? So Christ departed too. Some of my brethren are always so pleased—pleased as some children are with a new toy—at the idea that they shall never die; that Christ will come, it may be, before the time of their decease; for, "we shall not all sleep, but we shall all be, changed." Well, let him come, yes, let him come;

come quickly. But if I had my choice, were it permitted me to choose, I would prefer to pass through the portals of the grave. Those that are alive and remain unto the coming of the Lord will not prevent, go before, or steal a march on them which are asleep. But surely they will lack one point of conformity to their Lord, for he disdained not to sojourn awhile in the tomb, though it was impossible that he should be held of death. Let the seal of death, then, be set upon this face of mine, that my fate in the matter may be like his. Enoch and Elijah were exempt from this privilege—privilege, I call it—of conformity to his death. But it is safe to go by the beaten track and desirable to travel by the ordinary route to the heavenly city. Jesus died. Through the valley of shadows, the vale of death shades, there are the footprints of Emmanuel all the way along: go down into it and fear not. Do you consider, too, dear brethren and sisters, that we may well look forward to our departure and look forward to it comfortably too? Is it not expedient by reason of nature? Is it not desirable by reason of grace? Is it not necessary by reason of glory?

I say, is not our departure needful by reason of nature? Men are not, when they come to hoary age, what they were in the prime of their days. The staff is needed for the foot, and the glass is wanted for the eye; and after a certain number of years, even those on whom Time has gently laid his hand find the taste is gone. They might proclaim, like old Barzillai, that they know not what they eat or drink. The hearing fails, the daughters of music are silent, the whole tenement gets very crazy. Oh, it were a melancholy thing if we had to continue to live! Perhaps there is no more hideous picture than that which the satirist drew of men who lived on to six or seven hundred years of age—that strange satirical man, Swift. Be thankful that we do not linger on in imbecility. Kind nature says we may depart; she gives us notice, and makes it welcome by the decays that come upon us. Besides, grace desires it; for it were a poor experience of his kindness as our best and truest friend that did not make us long to see our Savior's face. It is no mere driveling sentiment, I hope, when we join to sing—

> Father, I long, I faint to see
> The place of thine abode;
> I'd leave thy earthly courts, and flee
> Up to thy seat, my God!

I must confess there was one verse in the hymn we sang just now which I could not quite chime in with. I am not eagerly wishing to go to heaven this night. I have a great deal more to do here; therefore I do not want to take a hasty leave of all below. To full many of us, I suppose, there are times of quiet contemplation and times of rapt devotion, when our thoughts surmount these lower skies, and look within the veil and then, oh, how we wish to be there! Yet there are other times; times of strenuous activity when we buckle on the armor and press to the front; and then we see such a battle to be waged, such a victory to be won, such a work to be worked, that we say: "Well, to abide in the flesh, to continue with you all for the joy and furtherance of your faith, seems more loyal to Christ, more needful for you, and more in accord with our present feelings." I think it is idle for us to be crying to go home; it is too much like the lazy workman that wants Saturday night to come when it is only Tuesday morning. Oh no; if God spare us to do a long life's work, so much the better. At the same time, as a spark flies upward to the sun, the central source of flame, so does the newborn spirit aspire toward heaven, toward Jesus, by whom it was kindled. And, I add, that glory demands it, and makes our departure needful. Is not Christ in heaven praying that we may be with him where he is? Are there not the saints in heaven, of whom it is said, they without us cannot be perfect? The circle of the skies cannot be completed until all the redeemed be there. The grand orchestra of glory misses some notes as yet. What if the bass be full, there are wanting still some trebles and tenors! There are some sopranos that will be requisite to swell the enchanting melodies and consummate the worship of the Eternal! What, therefore, nature prepares for, grace desires, and glory itself demands, we have no just cause to shudder at. Our departure need not make us afraid.

2. Having thus occupied so much time on this first point, I have little or no room to enlarge on the second. *The time of our departure,* **though unknown to us, is fixed by God, unalterably fixed; so rightly, wisely, lovingly settled, and prepared for, that no chance or haphazard can break the spell of destiny.**

The wisdom of divine love shall be proven by the carefulness of its provision. Perhaps you will say: "It is not easy to discern this; the natural order of things is so often disturbed by casualties of one kind or another." Let me remind you, then, that it is through faith, only through faith, we can understand these things; for it is as true now of the providence of God as it was of old of the creation of God that *"things* which are seen were not made of things which do appear." Because the *mode* of your departure is beyond your own knowledge, it does not follow that the time of your departure is not foreseen by God. "Ah but," say you, "it seems so shocking for anyone to die suddenly, unexpectedly, without warning, and so come to an untimely end!" I answer you thus. If you take counsel with death, your flesh will find no comfort; but if you trust in God, your faith will cease to parley with these feverish anxieties, and your spirit will enjoy a sweet calm.

Dire calamities befell Job when he was bereaved of his children and his servants, his herds and his flocks. Yet he took little heed of the different ways in which his troubles were brought about—whether by an onslaught of the Sabeans or by a raid of the Chaldeans, whether the fire fell from heaven or the wind came from the wilderness, it mattered little. Whatever strange facts broke on his ear, one thought penetrated his heart, and one expression broke from his lips. "The Lord gave, and the Lord hath taken away; blessed be the name of the Lord." So, too, beloved, when the time of your departure arrives—be it by disease or decay, be it by accident or assault, that your soul quits its present tenement—rest assured that "thy times are in his hand"; and know of a surety that "all his saints are in his hand" likewise.

Besides this, dear friends, since the time of our departure must come, were the manner of it at our own disposal, I think we should most of us say, "What I shall choose, I know not." Fevers and agues, the pangs and tortures of one malady and another, or the delirium incident to sickness, are not so much to be preferred to the shock of a disaster or the terror of a wreck at sea, because one is the prolonging of pain, and the other the dispatch of fate, that we need to covet, and desire weeks or months spent in the vestibule of the grave. Rather should we say, "Let the Lord do with me as seems him good." To live in constant communion with God is a sure relief from all these bitter frettings. Those who have walked with him have often been favored with such presentiments of their departure as no physician could give them. Survivors will tell you that though death seemed to come suddenly to the godly merchant, he had in the last acts of his life appeared to expect and prepare for it, and even to have taken an affecting farewell of his family while in the vigor of health, as though he were aware that he was setting out on his last journey, which a few hours afterward it proved to be. So, too, the minister of Christ has sometimes fallen, expiring in his pulpit with a *nunc dimittis*, "Now lettest thou thy servant depart in peace," on his lips—secretly, but surely, made ready to depart and to be with his Lord. There is a time to depart; and God's time to call me is my time to go.

3. Now, to our third point—*the time is at hand.* "The time of my departure is at hand."

In a certain sense, every Christian here may say this; for whatever interval may interpose between us and death, how very short it is! Have you not all a sense that time flows faster than it did? In our childish days, we thought a year was quite a period of time, a very epoch in our career; now as for weeks—one can hardly reckon them! We seem to be traveling by an express train, flying along at such a rate that we can hardly count the months. Why, the past year only seemed to come in at one door and go out at the other; it was over so soon. We shall soon be at the terminus of life, even if we live for several years; but in the case of some of us, God knows of whom, this year, perhaps this month, will be our last. I think tomorrow night we shall have to report at the church meeting the deaths of nine members of this church within the last eight or nine days. Since these have gone, some of us may expect to follow them. There are those who will evidently go; disease has set in upon them. Some of those disorders that in this land seem to be always fatal, tell these dear friends that the time of their departure is undoubtedly at hand. And then old age, which comes so gracefully and graciously to many of our matrons and our veterans, shows, past all dispute, "the time of your departure is at hand." The lease of your life is almost up. Not indeed that I would address myself to such special cases only. I speak to every brother and sister in Christ here. "The time of our departure is at hand." What then, dear friends?

Is not this a reason for surveying our condition again? If our vessel is just launching, let us see that she is seaworthy. It would be a sad thing for us to be near departing, and yet to be just as near discovering that we are lost. Remember, dear friends, it is possible for anyone to maintain a decent Christian profession for fifty years, and be a hypocrite after all; possible to occupy an office in the church of God, and that of the very highest, and yet to be a Judas; and one may not only serve Christ, but suffer for him too, and yet, like Demas, may not persevere to the end; for all that looks like grace is not grace. Where true grace is, there it will always be; but where the semblance of it is, it will oftentimes suddenly disappear. Search yourself, good brother; set your house in order, for you must die and not live. Have you the faith of God's elect? Are you built on Christ? Is your heart renewed? Are you verily an heir of heaven? I charge every man and woman within this place, since the time of his departure may be far nearer than he thinks, to take stock and reckon up and see whether he be Christ's or no.

But if the time of my departure be at hand, and I am satisfied that it is all right with me, is there not a call for me to do all I can for my household? Father, the time of your departure is at hand; is your wife unsaved? Will you pass another night without lovingly speaking to her of her soul? Are those dear boys unregenerate? Is that girl still thoughtless? The time of your departure is at hand. You can do little more for the lads and lasses; you can do little more for the wife and the brother. Oh! do what you can now. Sister, you are consumptive; you will soon be gone. You are the only Christian in the family. God sent you there to be a missionary. Do not have to say, when you are dying, "The last hope of my family is going out, for I have not cared for their souls." Masters, you that have servants about you, you must soon be taken away. Will you not do something for their souls? I know if there were a mother about to go to Australia, and she had to leave some of her children behind, she would fret if she thought, "I have not done all that needs to be done for those poor children. Who will care for them now their mother is gone?" Well, but to have neglected something necessary for their temporal comfort would be little in comparison with not having cared for their souls! Oh, let it not be so! Let it not be a thorn in your dying pillow that you did not fulfill the relations of life while you had the opportunity. "The time of my departure is at hand."

Then there is a third lesson. Let me try to finish all my work, not only as regards my duty to my family, but in respect to all the world so far as my influence or ability can reach. Rich men, be your own executors. Do what you can with your substance while it is your own. Men of talent, speak for Jesus before your tongue has ceased to articulate and becomes a piece of clay. George Whitefield may supply us with a fine model of this uniform consistency. He was so orderly and precise in his habits, and so scrupulous and holy in his life, that he used to say he would not like to go to bed if there were a pair of gloves out of place in the house, much less were his will not made or any part of his duty unfulfilled to the best of his knowledge. He wished to have all right, and to be fully prepared for whatever might happen, so that, if he never woke again from the slumbers of the night, nobody would have cause to reflect upon anything he had left undone, entailing needless trouble on his wife or his children. Such care bestowed on what some account to be trifles is a habit; worthy of our imitation. The main work of life may be sadly spoiled by negligence in little things. This is a striking test of character. "He that is faithful in that which is least is faithful also in much: and he that is unjust in the least is unjust also in much." Oh then! time is fleeting, dispatch is urgent; gather up your thoughts, quicken your hands, speed your pace, for God commands you to make haste. If you have anything to do, you must do it soon. The wheels of eternity are sounding behind you. Press on! If you are to run a race you must run it fast, for death will soon overtake you. You may almost feel the hot breath of the white horse of death upon your cheeks already. O God, help us to do something ere we go hence and be no more seen. It was grand of the apostle that in the same breath, when he said, "The time of my departure is at hand," he could also say, "I have fought a good fight, I have finished my course, I have kept the faith." So may we be able to say when the time of our departure has arrived.

If the time of our departure is at hand, let it cheer us amid our troubles. Sometimes, when our friends go to Liverpool to sail for Canada or any other distant region, on the night before they sail they get into a very poor lodging. I think I hear one of them grumbling, "What a hard bed! What a small room! What a bad lookout." "Oh," says the other, "never mind, brother; we are not going to live here; we are off tomorrow." Consider in like manner, you children of poverty, this is not your rest. Put up with it; you are away tomorrow. You sons of sorrow, you daughters of weakness, you children of sickness, let this cheer you:

> *The road may be rough,*
> *But it cannot be long*
> *And I'll smooth it with hope,*
> *And cheer it with song.*

Oftentimes when I have been traveling on the Continent, I have been obliged to put up at a hotel that was full, where the room was so inconvenient that it scarcely furnished any accommodation at all. But we have said, "Oh, never mind: we are off in the morning! What matters it for one night?" So, as we are soon to be gone and the time of our departure is at hand, let us not be ruffling our tempers about trifles, nor raise evil spirits around us by caviling and finding fault. Take things as you find them, for we shall soon be up and away.

And if the time of my departure is at hand, I should like to be on good terms with all my friends on earth. Were you going to stop here always, when a man treated you badly, apart from a Christian spirit, you might as well have it out with him; but as we are going to stop such a little while, we may well put up with it. It is not desirable to be too ready at taking an offense. What if my neighbor has an ugly temper, the Lord has to put up with him, and so I may. There are some people with whom I would rather dwell in heaven forever than abide with them half an hour on earth. Nevertheless, for the love of the brethren, and for the peace of the church, we may tolerate much during the short time we have to brook with peevish moods and perverse humors. Does Christ love them, and shall not we? He covers their offenses; why, then, should we disclose them or publish them abroad? If any of you have any grievances with one another, if there is any bickering or jealousy between you, I should like you to make it up tonight, because the time of your departure is at hand.

Suppose there is someone you spoke harshly to, you would not like to hear tomorrow that he was dead. You would not have minded what you said to him if he had lived, but now that the seal is set upon all your communications one with another, you could wish that the last impress had been more friendly. There has been a little difference between two brothers—a little coldness between two sisters. Oh, since one or other of you will soon be gone, make it up! Live in love, as Christ loved you and gave himself for you. If one of you were going to Australia tomorrow, never to come back again, and you had had a little tiff with your brother, why, I know before you started, you would say, "Come, brother, let us part good friends." So now, since you are so soon to depart, end all strife, and dwell together in blessed harmony till the departure actually occurs.

If the time of my departure is at hand, then let me guard against being elated by any temporal prosperity. Possessions, estates, creature comforts dwindle into insignificance before this outlook. Yes, you may have procured a comfortable house and a delightful garden, but it is not your rest: your tenure is about to expire. Yes, you may say, "God did prosper me last year, the bank account did swell, the premises were enlarged, and the business thrived beyond all expectation." Ah! hold them loose. Do not think that they are to be your heaven. Be very jealous lest you should get your good things here, for if you do you will not have them hereafter. Be not lifted up too much when you grasp the pain, of which you must so soon quit your hold. As I said of the discomfort of the hotel, we did not think much of it, because we were going away. So, if it happens to be very luxurious, do not be enamored of it, for you must go tomorrow. "These are the things," said one, when he looked at a rich man's treasures, "that make it hard to die." But it need not be so if you hold them as gifts of God's kindness, and not as gods to be worshiped with self-indulgence. You may take leave of them with composure, "knowing in yourselves that you have in heaven a better and an enduring substance."

Last, if the time of our departure is at hand, let us be prepared to bear our testimony. We are witnesses for Christ. Let us bear our testimony before we are taken up and mingle with the cloud of witnesses who have finished their course and rested from their labors. Do you say, "I hope to do that on my dying bed"? Brother, do it now: do it now, for you may never have opportunity to do it then. Mr. Whitefield was always desirous that he might bear a testimony for Christ in the hour of death; but he could not do so at that momentous crisis, for as you well know, he was suddenly taken ill after preaching and very soon expired. Was this to be grievously deplored? Ah no. Why, dear friends, he had borne so many testimonies for his Lord and Master while he was alive, there was no need to add anything in the last few moments before his death, or to supply the deficiencies of a life devoted to the proclamation of the gospel. Oh, let you and me bear our testimony now! Let us tell to others wherever we can what Christ has done for us. Let us help Christ's cause with all our might while it is called today. Let us work for Jesus while we can work for him. As to thinking we can undo the effect of our idleness by the spasmodic effort of our dying breath, that were a vain hope indeed compared with living for Jesus Christ. Your dying testimony, if you are able to bear it, will have the greater force if it is not a sickly regret, but a healthy confirmation of your whole career.

I only wish these words about departure were applicable to all here. "Precious in the sight of the Lord is the death of his saints." But, "'As I live,' says the Lord God, 'I have no pleasure in the death of the wicked, but that the wicked turn from his ways, and live.'" O unconverted man, the time for letting loose your cable draws nigh; it is even at the door. You must shortly set sail for a far country. Alas, then yours is not the voyage of a passenger, with a sweeter clime, a happier home, a brighter prospect in view. Your departure is the banishment of a convict, with a penal settlement looming in the distance; fear all rife and hope all blank, for the term of your banishment is interminable. I fear there are some of you who may depart before long full of gloom with a fearful looking for of judgment and of fiery indignation. I seem to see the angel of death hovering over my audience. He may, perhaps, select for his victim an unconverted soul. If so, behind that death angel attends there something far more grim. Hell follows death to souls that love not Christ. Oh, make haste, make haste! Seek Christ. Lay hold on eternal life; and may infinite mercy save you, for Jesus Christ's sake. Amen and amen.

A Precious Promise for a Pure People

-⭒⭒-

Published on Thursday, December 14, 1916, at the Metropolitan Tabernacle, Newington. No. 3542.

Thine eyes shall see the king in his beauty. —ISAIAH 33:17

No doubt these words originally had a timely and strictly literal meaning for the people of Jerusalem. When the city was besieged by Sennacherib, the inhabitants saw Hezekiah in garb of mourning. How had he rent his clothes in sorrow! But the day would come, according to prophecy, when Sennacherib must fall. Those who counted the resources and estimated the strength or the weakness of the city would be far away; and then there would be times of liberty. The people would be able to travel to the utmost ends of Palestine, so they would see the land that is very far off. Hezekiah himself would come out in his robes of excellency and majesty on a joyful occasion to praise the Lord, and thus would the people's eyes see the king in his beauty.

The passage, however, has been frequently used with quite another import, and that properly enough if it be thoroughly understood that it is by way of accommodation we take it, and that it is typically we trace it out. Have we not by faith seen our King in his robes of mourning? Have we not seen Jesus in the sorrowful weeds of affliction and humiliation while here below? Our faith has gazed upon him in the rent garments of his passion. We have beheld him in his agony and bloody sweat, in his crucifixion and his death. Well, now, another and a brighter view awaits us. Our eyes shall one day see the King in a more glorious array. We shall behold him as John saw him on Patmos. We shall behold the King in his beauty, and then we shall enter and enjoy the land which is at present very far off.

I think it meet and right to take such a word as this tonight when there are so many in our midst who are seeking and finding the Savior; because it is very certain that not long after their conversion they will have to encounter some of the difficulties of the way. Sometimes within a few hours of their starting on pilgrimage, they are met by some of the dragons, or they fall into some Slough of Despond, or they are surprised by some Hill Difficulty; therefore, they ought to be stimulated with encouragements; they need to be cheered and consoled by the prospect which lies before them. You will recol-

lect how Christian is represented by Bunyan in his famous allegory to be reading in his book as he went along concerning the blessed country, the celestial
land where their eyes should behold the King in his beauty, and this beguiled
the roughness of the road, and made the pilgrim hasten on with more alacrity
and less weariness.

Now I am going to turn over one of the elementary pages of this book. I
want to show the young convert a vision pleasing and profitable for all Christians, young or old, the glory that awaits him, the rest which is secured by the
promise of God to every pilgrim who continues in the blessed road and holds
on and holds out to the end. Your eyes, beloved, you who have lately been converted to God, if by divine grace your conversion prove genuine, your eyes
shall one day behold the King in his beauty. This may well inspire you with
courage and dispose you to endure with patience all the difficulties of the way.
When God brought his servant Abraham into the separated position of a
stranger in a strange land, it was not long before he said to him, "Lift up now
thine eyes, and look to the north, and to the south, and to the east, and to the
west, for all this land will I give to thee and to thy seed forever," as if to solace
and cheer him in the place of his sojourn by the picture and the promise that
greeted him. In like manner, you children of faithful Abraham, you who have
left all for Christ's sake, look upon your future heritage from the spot of your
present exile, and your hearts will exceedingly rejoice.

We shall notice, first, *the object to be seen*—the King in his beauty! Then,
second, *the nature of this vision*, for our eyes shall see the admirable spectacle;
and, third, we shall draw your attention to *those to whom this favor will be
granted*. The context will help us to discover of whom it is the Lord speaks
when he says, "Thine eyes shall see the king in his beauty." Not all eyes, but
your eyes shall see the King in his beauty. What is this vision which is here
promised to God's people? They are to see the King.

1. They are to see *the King in his beauty*.

The King—a sweet title which belongs to our Lord Jesus Christ as his
exclusive prerogative, crowned with the thorn crown once, but now wearing
the diadem of universal monarchy. Other kings there are, but theirs is only a
temporary title to temporal precedence among the sons of men. I had almost
said theirs was a mimic sovereignty. He is the real King—the King of kings—
the King that reigns forever and forever. He is King, for he is God. Jehovah
reigns. The Maker of the earth must be her King. He in whose hands are the
deep places of the earth, and the strength of the hills; he by whom all things
exist and all things consist; he must of necessity reign. The government shall

be upon his shoulders. His name shall be called Wonderful, Counselor, the mighty God. From the very fact that he is the Son of God, the express image of his Father's glory, he must be King. Because he condescended to veil himself in our flesh, he derives a second title to the kingdom—he is King now by his merits. "Wherefore God also has highly exalted him, and given him a name which is above every name, that at the name of Jesus every knee should bow, of things in heaven, and things in earth, and things under the earth." For the suffering of death, he was made for a little while lower than the angels; but now, seeing he has been obedient even unto death, even the death of the cross, he has obtained a more excellent name than the angels, and he is crowned with glory and honor.

He is Head over all things now. In him dwells all the fullness of the Godhead bodily. We rejoice to reflect upon him as King by nature, and then as King by due desert over a kingdom which he has inherited by right divine. He is King at this time by virtue of the conquests he has made, having spoiled the principalities and powers of darkness. In this world he fought the battle, and so bravely did he fight it out that he could say, "It is finished." He made an end of sin; he made reconciliation for iniquity; he trampled death and hell beneath his feet, and now he is King by force of arms. He entered into the strong man's house, wrestled with him, and vanquished him, for he is stronger than he; he has led captivity captive, and he has ascended upon high—King of kings and Lord of lords. He reigns supremely, moreover, in some of our hearts. We have yielded to the sway of his love. We rejoice to crown him. We never feel happier than when our hearts and tongues are singing—

> Bring forth the royal diadem
> And crown him Lord of all.

I trust there are many more among you who have not yet yielded that yet yield your hearts to his power. Fresh provinces shall be added to his empire; new cities of Mansoul will open their gates that the Prince Emmanuel may ride in, and may sit in triumph there. Oh! that it may be so, for a multitude that no man can number shall cheerfully, joyfully own his sway, and kiss the Son lest he be angry. But mark, the limit of his power is not according to the will of man, for where he does not reign by the joyful consent of his people and the mighty conquest of his love, he still exercises absolute dominion. Even the wicked are his servants. They shall be made in some way or other to subserve his glory, for he must reign till he has put all enemies under his feet. Why do the heathen rage, and the people imagine a vain thing? The King is anointed upon God's holy hill of Zion. King he is. He has a bit in the mouth of his most violent adversaries, and he turns them about according to his own will. What though with mingled cruelty and rage men attack the gospel of Christ, they strive in vain to thwart the divine decree. In ways mysterious and unknown to us, the Lord asserts his own supremacy. He reigns even where the rulers conspire, and the people rebel against him.

Beloved, the sovereignty of our Lord Jesus Christ, to which he is entitled by inheritance, is due to him for his merits and in the equitable claim of his conquests—this reign of Christ extends over all things. He is the universal Lord. In this world he is regent everywhere. By him all things exist and consist. When I think of him, it seems to me that the sea roars to his praise, and the trees of the wood rejoice in his presence. There is not a dewdrop that twinkles on the flower at sunrise but reflects his bounty; there is not an avalanche that falls from its alp with thundering crash but resounds with tokens of his power. The great Shepherd reigns. The Lord is King. As Joseph was made ruler over all the land of Egypt, even so, according unto the word of Jesus, all the people are ruled. He has all things put under his feet; for it was of him the prophet sang of old, "Thou hast made him a little"—(or as the margin has it, a little while)—"lower than the angels, and hast crowned him with glory and honor; thou hast put all things under his feet, all sheep and oxen, yea, and the beasts of the field; the fowl of the air, and the fish of the sea, and whatsoever passeth through the paths of the seas." Though we see not yet all things put under man, yet we see Jesus, who, for the suffering of death, was made, for a little while, lower than the angels, crowned with glory and honor. At this hour he rules on earth. Death and hell are under his scepter. Satan, and the spirits that have followed his leadership, bite their iron bonds while they confess the power of the Lord divine to be paramount. He can crush his enemies and break them with a rod of iron as a potter's vessel. His mighty power is felt and feared.

But oh! yonder, up in heaven, where the full beams of his glory are unveiled, he reigns in matchless splendor. The angels worshiped him when he was brought forth as the only begotten into the world. So spoke the oracle, "Let all the angels of God worship him." Seraphim and cherubim, are they not his messengers? He makes them like flames of fire. The redeemed by blood, what could they do? What is their joy, their occupation, their delight, but to sing forever, "Worthy is the Lamb that was slain to receive honor, and glory, and dominion, and power"? Oh! tell us not of emperors; there is but one imperial brow! Tell us not of monarchs, for the crown belongs to the blessed and only potentate. He alone is King. As such, we think of him and long for his appearing, when we shall hail him the King in his beauty. I love to see his courtiers. That is a happy hour in which I can talk with one who has my Master's ear. I love to see the skirts of his garment as I come in fellowship with him to his table. I love to tread his courts; I love to hear his voice, even though I cannot yet see the face of him that speaks with me. But to see the King—to see the King himself! Oh! joy unspeakable! It is worth worlds even to have a good hope of beholding a sight so resplendent with glory.

Note well the promise, "Thine eyes shall see the king in his *beauty*." Does not this suggest to us that the King has been seen, though not in his beauty? He was seen on earth as the prophet foretold, "despised and rejected of men, a man of sorrows, and acquainted with grief." And as seen then, we are told there is no beauty that we should desire him. There was a time when many were astonished at him. His visage was more marred than any man and his form more than the sons of men; that was in the day of his humiliation.

But we are yet to see the King in his beauty, and I know, beloved, that in part that vision does beam, even now, upon spirits before the throne. I would not exactly say that they have eyes, for they have left these organs of sense behind them. They have not received the fullness of this promise, yet in a measure they see the beauty of the King, that beauty which his Father has put upon him now that he has ascended up on high and returned to the Father, having obeyed all his precepts and fulfilled all his will. His father has already rewarded him. He sits enthroned on the right hand of the Majesty on high; he is adored and worshiped. It is no small sight for our disimprisoned spirits to behold him and adore. But remember the spirits in heaven, without us, cannot be made perfect, so says the apostle. They are waiting for the adoption—to wit, the redemption of the body—waiting for the trumpet of resurrection. It is then, I think, that this blessed hope will be fully verified, "Thine eyes shall see the king in his beauty." As Job puts it, "I know that my Redeemer liveth, and that he shall stand at the latter day upon the earth; and though, after my skin worms destroy this body, yet in my flesh shall I see God, whom I shall see for myself, and mine eyes shall behold, and not another." Our bodies shall be raised from the dead.

> These eyes shall see him in that day,
> The God that died for me;
> And all my rising bones shall say—
> Lord, who is like to thee?

From the dark chambers of the grave, we shall come forth with all the blood-bought company of the faithful. Then we shall see the King in his beauty. What beauty that will be! We steadfastly look for his appearing when he shall come the second time. This personal manifestation must be welcome to the saints. To see him then must be to see his beauty. Our senses, relieved of infirmity, will be endowed with full capacity, our graces being increased and our spirits lively and vigorous to appreciate his wonderful person. As God and Man we do now believe in him; but how little can our faith anticipate the vision! We acknowledge the mystery which is as yet unveiled. How little are we affected by the wonderful information which must astonish angels—that the infinite can be joined with the finite, that the Godhead can be in perfect union with the manhood, the bush of the manhood burning with the glow of the Godhead, yet not thereby consumed. 'Tis matchless that the Eternal should link himself with finite flesh; that he should hang upon his mother's breast, who bears up the columns of the universe. Strange conjunction! Till we wake up in his likeness, we shall never thoroughly understand it. Oh! how amazement will resolve itself into admiration as we gaze upon him who has a nature that we have been familiar with, the proper divinity which no man has seen or can see! What grandeur to behold! What rapture to experience when our eyes see the King in his beauty! The sight will overwhelm us.

But in other respects than that which is essential to his kingly dignity, the spectacle will be illustrious. In the hour of conquest he will take possession of a throne which no rival dare dispute. Judas will be there, but he will not think of betraying him. Pilate will be there, but he will not think of questioning him. The Jews will be there, but they will not cry, "Crucify him." The Romans will be there, but they will not think of hauling him away to execution. His enemies in that day shall lick the dust. They shall be like chaff before the whirlwind in the day of his coming. And what will be the splendor of his glory when he shall be proclaimed King of kings in his beauty, with all the insignia of his royal power!

He will have the beauty of state pageant too, for he will assume office as Judge of quick and dead. Then will the trumpet sound, and all the solemn pomp of the great assize will encircle him round about. The vivid lightning will flash through the universe, and the roar of his thunder shall awake the dead, while an irresistible summons shall compel them to appear before his dread tribunal. From his searching gaze no creature shall be hid, and every eye shall see him. They also that pierced him, and all the kindreds of the earth, shall weep and wail because of him. But to us that awful pomp will not be appalling, but a fit accessory on which his royal beauty is displayed. We shall admire the hand that holds the scepter, for we shall recognize it as the same hand that was once pierced for us. We shall admire the voice that condemns the wicked and bids them, "Depart!," for that voice shall pronounce our welcome, saying, "Come, you blessed." We shall admire the Shepherd's crook with which he shall separate the sheep and the goats, for it will apportion us to eternal bliss, though it shall dismiss the goats to their eternal doom. Thrice happy and most blessed shall we be in that day. Terror and trouble shall be the lot of the world; trust and triumph shall then be the portion of the saints. He shall be admired in all them that believed; and when that final judgment shall have fulfilled its destined purpose, he shall be in his beauty seen as the conqueror of all evil, the conqueror of sin, of death, and hell. The last enemy that shall be destroyed is death. How shall we see him in his beauty when death itself shall die!

I cannot attempt to describe that beauty. It is far too dazzling for me to picture. I have dreamed of it sometimes in sacred soliloquies. My faith has tried to realize the facts which are revealed unto us by his Spirit. Still the tongue cannot tell so much as the heart has conceived. There are unspeakable words which greet us in seasons of rapture which it is not lawful to utter. Whenever we are caught up to the third heaven in rapturous meditation, we have but small news to tell to men. But how inconceivable to us now is the glory of Christ as it shall be when all his people are present with him in heaven!

I have not touched upon the millennial age or the latter-day glory. Your thoughts can fill up the vacancy. But what will be the beauty of Christ in heaven in that day "when he shall make up his jewels"! What are the jewels of our King but his redeemed people? What will be the ornaments of his state but those for whom he shed his blood? And when they are all there, then we shall see the King in his beauty with all his jewels. Beauty! A shepherd's beauty lies much in his simple garb; a mother's beauty—very much of it is to be seen as she appears in the center of a happy and lovely family. So, beyond all doubt, the beauty of Christ will be most conspicuous when all his saints are with him. I was in company with some good people lately, who were discussing the question whether we should see the saints in heaven. I do not know whether they settled the question to their satisfaction, but I settled it very well to mine. I expect to see and know all the saints, to recognize them, and rejoice with them, and that without the slightest prejudice to my being wholly absorbed in the sight of my Lord. Let me explain to you how this can be. When I went the other day into a friend's drawing room, I observed that on all sides there were mirrors. The whole of the walls were covered with glass, and everywhere I looked I kept seeing my friend. It was not necessary that I should fix my eyes upon him, for all the mirrors reflected him. Thus, brethren, it seems to me that every saint in heaven will be a mirror of Christ, and that as we look upon all the loved ones, gazing round upon them all, we shall see Christ in every one of them; so we shall still be seeing the Master in the servants, seeing the head in all the members. It is I in them, and they in me. Is it not so? It will be all the Master. This is the sum total of heaven. "Thine eyes shall see the king in his beauty," and they shall see the beauty of the King in all his people. Nor does it appear that the manifestation shall be ever withdrawn, or that we shall ever leave off seeing the beauty of our King. There is the mercy. "Thine eyes shall see the king in his beauty," on and on, and on still, and on, forever on, discerning more and more of the beauty, the inexhaustible beauty and splendor of the Sun of righteousness world without end. The theme grows upon us. We must curb ourselves. We can but skim the surface as the swallow does the brook.

2. Now, as to *the nature of this vision,* we know it is in the future.

"Thine eyes *shall* see the king in his beauty." You poor sinners must be content with seeing the King in his majesty. Happy souls who come to see Jesus on the cross! Oh! it is joy for them to look unto him and be saved! Behold the Lamb of God—behold the Lamb slain from the foundation of the world. Poor sin-sick soul, are you looking to Jesus to be saved? If it be so in the present, then in the future you shall see him in his beauty. It will be a vision for all. Their natural sense shall discern the real Savior, "Thine eyes shall see the king in his beauty." It is not merely your spiritual perception, but your natural eyes. Does not Job express this conviction, "whom mine eyes shall see"? Oh yes! not as it now is with this flesh and blood, but still with this body! I call you a vile body sometimes, my poor flesh and blood, and so you are. Yet in your origin there was something good, and in your destiny there is something better, "Bone of thy bone, and flesh of thy flesh." Born of a woman as you were and fed on bread as you must be, and though the worms devour you, yet shall you rise again. Oh body! you are even now the temple of God. Know you not that your *bodies* are the members of Christ? Know you not that your body is the temple of the Holy Ghost? These eyes shall see him. They may be weeping eyes, aching eyes, weary eyes, and sleepy eyes, yes, or even blind eyes, or your failing eyes on which the curtain is being drawn about you—your eyes shall see the King. When heaven is in sight there will be no need for glasses to assist your vision. Your eyes all strengthened to bear the light, as the eagle's eye, when the sun shines in his strength—"Thine eyes shall see the King in his beauty."

It *will be a personal vision.* "Whom mine eyes shall see, and not another." It shall not be somebody else repeating another's testimony, "Yes, I see him." I like to hear what John saw, but I like better to have John's privilege; we shall be like John, and shall ourselves behold him. Can you realize it? You recollect in Bunyan's *Pilgrim's Progress* how Mercy laughed in her sleep, and Christiana asked her what made her laugh so. Mercy replied that she had seen a beautiful vision. Is it not enough to make us laugh in our sleep, to think that "thine eyes shall see the king in his beauty"? To think that this head shall wear a crown; that these hands shall grasp the palms; that these feet shall stand on the transfigured globe; that these ears shall hear the symphonies of eternity; and that this tongue shall help to swell the everlasting chorus. Oh! who would not rejoice? This is the wine which, as it goes down, makes the lips of him who drinks to speak. Oh! that we may all have a personal sight of the King in his beauty!

And *it will be a near sight,* because it will be clear and distinct. "Thine eyes shall see the king in his beauty." This does not imply a distant view of a remote object; a dim vision of the dazzling splendor; but you shall behold him in such close proximity that you can discern every feature of his person, every phase of his comeliness. You shall discern all the insignia of his offices, his conquests, his titles, his dominion, and his glory. Now you only see a picture of him reflected as in a glass darkly, then you shall see him face to face. Oh! that the curtain might be drawn up, the veil rent, the vision unfolded!

It will be a delightful sight. When he shall appear in his beauty, we cannot wear the vestments of our mourning and sorrow. As he is, so are we in this world. As he shall be revealed, so shall we be also in that world. "It doth not yet appear what we shall be, but we know that when he shall appear we shall be like him, for we shall see him as he is." Thus we shall be beautiful when we shall see him in his beauty. He shall say to us, "Thou art all fair, my love; there is not a spot in thee." Oh! the delight, the pure unclouded joy, reflective as the light of heaven. What an introduction to eternal felicity this will be when your eyes shall see the King in his beauty! There is no period, no finale, no end put to it.

This is no transient spectacle. His beauty never fades. Our festival can never terminate. Long as he appears in his beauty we shall see him, and be enamored of his loveliness. Is it not written, "Because I live, ye shall live also"? Without his people, without the complement of his saints with him, he would not be a full Christ at any time. "Know ye not that the church is the fullness of him who filleth all in all?" So all his disciples must be forever with him, and they must forever see his face and be partakers of his glory.

We find a remarkably full description of these people. Read the fifteenth verse [Isa. 33]. Their ordinary gait distinguishes them. *"He that walketh righteously."* "The pure in heart shall see God"; but if your deportment disgraces you, how deep will be your dishonor. Unholy creatures will never see a holy God. It is not possible. O sinners, what think you of this? You must be changed; you must be cleansed; you must be converted; the Holy Ghost must regenerate you; otherwise, you cannot walk uprightly or stand in the presence of the King in his beauty.

Next to this they are known by their tongues: *"and speaketh uprightly."* No liar shall enter into heaven. Those who talk lasciviously, those who swear profanely, the singers of idle songs, those who lend their lips to slander, backbite their neighbors, and circulate evil reports in malice—these and such as these can have no inheritance in the kingdom of God. Oh! may the Lord wash your tongues, rinse your mouths, and make them sweet and clean; else you will never sing the songs of heaven. "He that walketh righteously and speaketh uprightly" is so far approved.

But let him take heed to his commercial character; for it is further said, *"he that despiseth the gain of oppressions,"* or, as the margin has it, of deceit. A man that gets money by squeezing others, by oppressing the poor by hard bargains, shall not enjoy the beatific vision. If you buy and sell and get gain by lying, by false pretenses, by tricks of trade—yes, even by the customs that are commonly allowed, though they would look fraudulent if thoroughly exposed, you shall have no inheritance in the kingdom of God. How can you be gracious when you are not honest? He that is not able to hold the scales lightly, measure out an even yard, or make out a bill equitably, may well tremble at being poised in the balances of the sanctuary. When such as these are weighed, they will be found wanting. Thorough integrity must stand the test of disinterestedness.

"He that shaketh his hands from holding of bribes." Some men cannot help preferring coin to conscience. This is the way of bribery. Palm oil was largely used when Isaiah wrote. It is much in vogue still; perhaps not so much in this country as in others; but there are plenty of ways of receiving bribes besides selling one's vote at the polling booth. How many men are bribed by a smile or a crown—bribed to Sabbath breaking—bribed to the follies of the world— bribed to I know not what of error! But drop a shilling into a conscientious man's hand, and he shakes it from his hand; he does not like the touch of it; he is like Paul, who shook off the viper into the fire. So the man who is to see the King in his beauty shakes his hand from holding bribes.

Moreover, *"he stoppeth his ears from hearing of blood."* He does not like to hear of cruelty, of outrage, or wantonly causing pain. He stops his ears, he will not listen to any proposal either to gratify a resentment or to seek a personal advantage whereby his neighbor would be injured. In this wicked world it is often wise to stop one's ears. A deaf ear is a great blessing when there is base conversation in the neighborhood.

The good man who thus keeps guard over his hands and his feet, his tongue and his ears, is likewise known by his eyes. *"He shutteth his eyes from seeing evil."* He shuns the temptations to which a vain curiosity would expose him. Oh! if our mother Eve had shut her eyes when the serpent pointed out yon rosy apple on the tree! Oh! that she had shut her eyes to it! Oh! that she had said, "No, I will not even look at it." Looking leads to longing, and longing leads to sin. Do you say, "There can be no harm in looking, just to see for yourself; are we not told to prove all things?" "Just come here, young man," says the tempter; "you do not know what life is; one evening will suffice to show you a little gaiety, and let you see how the frolic is carried on. You need not share in it, you know. You may learn a thing or two you never dreamed of before. Surely a man is not to go through the world a baby. Just come for an hour or two and look on." "Ah no," says the man, whose eyes are to see the King in his beauty, "the tree of knowledge of good and evil never brought any man good yet, so please let me alone. I shut my eyes from the sight of it. I do not want to participate, even as a spectator. I do not care to look upon that which God will not look upon without abhorrence. I know that his love has put my sins behind his back; what, then, he puts behind his back shall I put before my face? That were ingratitude indeed!

Perhaps you say, "Well, if this is the character of such as shall see the King in his beauty, I shall never come up to the standard." "No, but you must, else you will never enjoy the beatific vision." "But I cannot convert myself after this fashion." I know you cannot, but there is One who can. Has not Jesus Christ come into the world to make us new creatures? It is his object and intent. "Behold, I make all things new." He changes a man, gives him new desires, new longings, and new hopes. And he can change you. Let me ask you, have you ever seen, by faith, the King? Have you ever looked to Jesus on the cross, and did you ever recognize that Jesus Christ, if he is to be your Savior, must be your King? You say you have believed in Jesus. Yes, but did you take him to be your King? Did you mean to obey him as well as to trust him? Did you intend to serve him as well as to lean upon him? Remember you cannot have a half of Christ. You cannot have him as your Redeemer, but not as your Ruler. You must take him as he is. He is a Savior, but he saves his people from their sins. Now, if you have ever seen Christ as your Savior, you have seen beauty in him; he is lovely in your eyes, for the loveliest sight in the world to a sinner is his Savior. "What is the latest news," said a certain squire to a companion, accustomed to hunt with him, who had come up to the metropolis—

"what is the latest news you have heard in London?" "The latest news, and the best news I have ever heard," was the quick reply, "is that Jesus Christ came into the world to save sinners." "Tom," says he, "I think you are mad." "William," said Tom, "I know you are. I only wish you were cured of your insanity as, by the grace of God, I have been." Oh! that we did but all of us know Jesus Christ in his beauty, and could, every one of us, rejoice in him, as those do that are charmed by the sight. If you have not your eyes opened, you cannot see the King in his beauty. But if they are opened now, so that you greet Jesus as your King and see beauty in him, then, whatever your former life may have been, its sins are forgiven—they are blotted out.

Your Savior's sacrifice, that offered such satisfaction to God for your sins, shall give sweet solace to your conscience. By the gracious help of the Holy Spirit, you shall start a fresh career and begin a new life. Be it so; and you will henceforth shut your eyes from seeing, stop your ears from hearing, shake your hands from all iniquity, and turn aside your feet from it, to live the life you live in the flesh by the faith of the Son of God, to his honor and glory. So shall your eyes, poor sinner—weeping, sorrowing, mournful eyes as they may now be—your eyes shall see the King in his beauty. The Lord grant that we, all of us, may have a present earnest and a future fruition of this delightful promise, for his name's sake. Amen.

The Earnest of Heaven

~∙∞∙~

Delivered on Sunday morning, February 3, 1861, at Exeter Hall, Strand. No. 358.

> *That holy Spirit of promise, which is the earnest of our inheritance.*
> —EPHESIANS 1:13–14

So then, heaven, with all its glories, is an *inheritance*! Now, an inheritance is not a thing which is bought with money, earned by labor, or won by conquest. If any man has an inheritance, in the proper sense of that term, it came to him by birth. It was not because of any special merit in him, but simply because he was his father's son that he received the property of which he is now possessed. So is it with heaven. The man who shall receive this glorious heritage will not obtain it by the works of the law, nor by the efforts of the flesh; it will be given to him as a matter of most gracious right, because he has been "begotten again unto a lively hope, by the resurrection of Jesus Christ from the dead"; and has thus become an heir of heaven by blood and birth.

They who come unto glory are sons; for is it not written, "The captain of our salvation brings many sons unto glory"? They come not there as servants; no servant has any right to the inheritance of his master; let him be ever so faithful, yet he is not his master's heir. But because you are sons—sons by God's adoption, sons by the Spirit's regeneration—because by supernatural energy you have been born again—you become inheritors of eternal life, and you enter into the many mansions of our Father's house above. Let us always understand, then, when we think of heaven, that it is a place which is to be ours, and a state which we are to enjoy as the result of birth—not as the result of work. "Except a man be born again, he cannot see the kingdom of God," that kingdom being an inheritance, but until he has the new birth, he can have no claim to enter it.

But is it possible for us, provided that heaven be our inheritance, and we are God's sons—is it possible for us to know anything whatever of that land beyond the flood? Is there power in human intellect to fly into the land of the hereafter and reach those islands of the happy, where God's people rest in the bosom of their God eternally? We are met at the outset with a rebuff which staggers us. "Eye hath not seen, nor ear heard, neither hath entered into the heart of man, the things which God hath prepared for them that love him." If we paused here we might give up all idea of beholding from our houses of clay that goodly land and Lebanon, but we do not pause, for like the apostle, we go on with the text, and we add "But he hath revealed it unto us by his Spirit." It *is* possible to look within the veil; God's Spirit *can* turn it aside for a moment, and bid us take a glimpse, though it be but a distant one, at that unutterable glory. There are Pisgahs even now on the surface of the earth, from the top of which the celestial Canaan can be beheld; there are hallowed hours in which the mists and clouds are swept away, and the sun shines in his strength, and our eye, being freed from its natural dimness, beholds something of that land which is very far off, and sees a little of the joy and blessedness which is reserved for the people of God hereafter.

Our text tells us that the Holy Spirit is the earnest of the inheritance, by which I understand, that he is not only the pledge, for a pledge is given for security, but when the thing pledged is given, then the pledge itself is restored—but he is an earnest, which is a pledge and something more. An earnest is a part of the thing itself; it is not only a pledge of the thing, for security, but it is a foretaste of it for present enjoyment. The word in the Greek has a stronger force than our word "pledge." Again I repeat it: if I promise to pay to a man somewhat, I may give him land or property in pledge, but if instead thereof I pay him a part of the sum which I have promised, that is a pledge, but it is more—it is *an earnest*, because it is a part of the thing itself. So the Holy Spirit is a pledge to God's people. Inasmuch as God has given them the graces of the Spirit, he will give them the glory that results therefrom.

But he is more: he is a foretaste—he is a sweet antepast of heaven, so that they who possess the Spirit of God possess the first tastes of heaven; they have reaped the firstfruits of the eternal harvest; the first drops of a shower of glory have fallen upon them; they have beheld the first beams of the rising sun of eternal bliss; they have not merely a pledge for security—they have an earnest, which is security and foretaste combined. Understand, then, for this is what I am about to speak of this morning: by the Holy Spirit there is given to the people of God even now, experiences, joys, and feelings, which prove that they shall be in heaven—which do more, which *bring heaven down to them, and make them already able to guess in some measure what heaven must be.* When I have enlarged upon that theme, I shall take the black side of the picture, and remark that *it is possible for men on earth to have both a pledge and an earnest of those eternal pains which are reserved for the impenitent:* a dark subject, but may God grant it may be for our profit and arousing.

1. First, then, *there are some works of the Spirit which are peculiarly an earnest to the child of God, of the blessings of heaven.*

And, first, *heaven is a state of rest.* It may be because I am constitutionally idle, that I look upon heaven in the aspect of rest with greater delight than under any other view of it, with but one exception. To let the head which is so continually exercised, for once lie still—to have no care, no trouble, no need to labor, to strain the intellect, or vex the limbs! I know that many of you, the sons of poverty and of toil, look forward to the Sabbath day, because of the enjoyments of the sanctuary, and because of the rest which it affords you. You look for heaven as Watts did in his song:

> *There shall I bathe my weary soul*
> *In seas of heavenly rest,*
> *And not a wave of trouble roll*
> *Across my peaceful breast.*

"There remains therefore a rest to the people of God." 'Tis not a rest of sleep, but yet a rest as perfect as though they slept; it is a rest which puts from them all carking [burdensome] care, all harrowing remorse, all thoughts of tomorrow, all straining after a something which they have not as yet. They are runners no more—they have reached the goal; they are warriors no more—they have achieved the victory; they are laborers no more—they have reaped the harvest. "'They rest,' saith the Spirit, 'they rest from their labors, and their works do follow them.'" My beloved, did you ever enjoy on certain high days of your experience, a state of perfect rest? You could say you had not a wish in all the world ungratified; you knew yourself to be pardoned, you felt yourself to be an heir of heaven, Christ was precious to you; you knew that you walked in the light of your Father's countenance; you had cast all your worldly care on him, for he cared for you. You felt at that hour that if death could smite away your dearest friends, or if calamity should remove the most valuable part of your possessions on earth, yet you could say, "The Lord gave, and the Lord hath taken away, blessed be the name of the Lord." Your spirit floated along the stream of grace without a struggle; you were not as the swimmer, who breasts the billows and tugs and toils for life. Your soul was made to lie down in green pastures, beside the still waters. You were passive in God's hands; you knew no will but his. Oh! that sweet day!

> *That heavenly calm within the breast,*
> *Was the sure pledge of glorious rest,*

Which for the church of God remains,
The end of cares, the end of pains.

No, it was more than a pledge; it was a part of the rest itself. It was a morsel taken from the loaf of delights; it was a sip out of the wine vats of immortal joy; it was silver spray from the waves of glory. So, then, whenever we are quiet and at peace—"For we which have believed do enter into rest," and have ceased from our own works, as God did from his—when we can say, "O God, my heart is fixed, my heart is fixed; I will sing and give praise"— when our spirit is full of love within us, and our peace is like a river, and our righteousness like the wave of the sea—then we already know, in some degree, what heaven is. We have but to make that peace deeper, and yet more profound, lasting, and more continual; we have but to multiply it eternally, and we have obtained a noble idea of the rest which remains for the people of God.

But, second, there is a passage in the book of Revelation which may sometimes puzzle the uninstructed reader, where it is said concerning the angels that "they rest not day and night," and as we are to be as the angels of God, it must undoubtedly be true in heaven, that in a certain sense, they rest not day nor night. They always rest, so far as ease and freedom from care is concerned; they never rest, in the sense of indolence or inactivity. In heaven, spirits are always on the wing; their lips are always singing the eternal *hallelu-jahs* unto the great *Jehovah* that sits upon the throne; their fingers are never divorced from the strings of their golden harps; their feet never cease to run in obedience to the eternal will; they rest, but they rest on the wing; as the poet pictured the angel as he flew—not needing to move his wings, but rest-ing, and yet darting swiftly through the ether, as though he were a flash shot from the eye of God.

So shall it be with the people of God eternally, ever singing—never hoarse with music; ever serving—never wearied with their service. "They rest not day and night." Have there never been times with you, when you have had both the pledge and the earnest of this kind of heaven? Yes, when we have preached once, and again and again and again, in one day, and some have said, "But the constitution will be destroyed, the mind will be weakened, such toil as this will bring the man low." But we have been able to reply, "We do not feel it; for the more toil has been cast upon us, the more strength has been given." Have you ever known what it is to have the pastor's work in revival times, when he has to sit hour after hour, seeing convert after convert—when the time for one meal is past, and he has forgotten it, and the time for another meal has come and gone, and he has forgotten that, for he has been so busy and so happy with his feast of ingatherings, that he has been like his Master, and has forgotten to eat bread, and positively did not hunger and did not thirst, because the joy of the service had taken away all fatigue?

Just at this hour, our missionaries are engaged throughout Jamaica, in a sweltering sun, preaching the Word. Perhaps there has never been a more glorious revival than that which God has sent to that island—an island which has often been blessed, but which now seems to have received a sevenfold portion. One missionary, in writing home, says that he had not been in bed one night for a week, and he had been preaching all day and all night long; and I do not doubt but his testimony to you would be, that, at least during the first part of the labor, it seemed not to be labor. He could sleep on the wing; he could rest while he worked; the joy of success took away from him the feeling of lassitude; the blessed prospect of seeing so many added to the church of God had made him forget even to eat bread. Well, then, at such a time as that, he had a foretaste of the rest, and the service too, which remains for the people of God. Oh, do not doubt, if you find comfort in serving God—and such comfort that you grow not weary in his service—do not doubt, I say, but that you shall soon join that hallowed throng, who "day without night circle his throne rejoicing," who rest not, but serve him day and night in his temple! These feelings are foretastes, and they are pledges too. They give some inklings of what heaven must be, and they make your title to heaven clear.

But let us pass on. Heaven is a place of *communion* with all the people of God. I am sure that in heaven they know each other. I could not perhaps just now prove it in so many words, but I feel that a heaven of people who did not know each other, and had no fellowship, could not be heaven because God has so constituted the human heart that it loves society, and especially the renewed heart is so made that it cannot help communing with all the people of God. I always say to my Strict Baptist brethren who think it a dreadful thing for baptized believers to commune with the unbaptized, "But you cannot help it. If you are the people of God, you must commune with all saints, baptized or not. You may deny them the outward and visible sign, but you cannot keep from them the inward and spiritual grace." If a man be a child of God, I do not care what I may think about him—if I be a child of God, I *do* commune with him, and I must, for we are all parts of the same body, all knit to Christ, and it is not possible that one part of Christ's body should ever be in any state but that of communion with all the rest of the body. Well, in glory I feel I may say we know we shall converse with each other. We shall talk of our trials on the way there—talk most of all of him who by his faithful love and his potent arm has brought us safely through. We shall not sing solos, but in chorus shall we praise our King. We shall not look upon our fellows there like men in the iron mask, whose name and character we do not know; for there we shall know even as we are known. You shall talk with the prophets, you shall have conversation with the martyrs, you shall sit again at the feet of the great reformers and all your brethren in faith who have fallen before you, or who have rather entered into rest before; these shall be your companions on the other side the grave. How sweet must that be! How blessed—that holy converse, that happy union, that general assembly and church of the Firstborn whose names are written in heaven!

Have we anything on earth like this? Yes, that we have, in miniature. We have the pledge of this; for if we love the people of God, we may know that we shall surely be with them in heaven. We have the *earnest* of it; for how often has it been our privilege to hold the highest and sweetest fellowship with our fellow Christians? Why, you and I have often said, "Did not our hearts burn within us, while we talked together by the way, and Christ was with us both?" When we have been together and the doors have been shut, has not the Master said, "Peace be unto you"? When love has gone from heart to heart, and we have all felt knit together as one man, when party names were all forgotten, when all jealousies and bickerings were driven out of doors, and we felt that we were one family, and all did bear the same one name, having "one Lord, one faith, and one baptism," then it was that we had the earnest, the foretaste, the first drinking of that well of Bethlehem which is on the other side the pearly gate of the Celestial City.

I have to be brief on each of these points, for there are so many to mention. Part of the bliss of heaven will consist *in joy over sinners saved.* The angels look down from the battlements of the city which has foundations, and when they see prodigals return they sing. Jesus calls together his friends and his neighbors, and he says unto them, "Rejoice with me, for I have found the sheep which was lost." The angels begin the theme; the sacred fire runs through the host, and all the saints above take up the strain. Hark, how they sing before the throne, for it has just been whispered there of some Saul, "Behold, he prays!" Hark how their songs get a new inspiration—how their eternal Sabbath seems to be sabbatized afresh, and "the rest" becomes more joyous far, while they sing of newborn sons added to the family, and new names written in the register of the church below!

Part of the joy of heaven, and no mean part of it, will be to watch the fight on earth, to see the conqueror as he marches on, and to behold the trophies of his grace, and the spoils which his hands shall win. Is there anything like this on earth? Yes, that there is, when the Spirit of God gives to *us joy* over sinners saved. The other evening, when some of us sat in church meeting, what joy was there, when one after another, those who had been plucked from the deepest hell of sin made avowal of their faith in Christ! Some of us look back upon those church meetings as the gladdest nights we ever spent; when first one and then another has said, "*I* have been plucked as a brand from the burning," and the tale of grace has been told; and a third has stood up and said, "And I, too, was once a strange wandering far from God, and Jesus sought me." Why, we have some of us gone home and felt that it was heaven below to have been there. We have felt more joy over the conversion of others, we have sometimes thought, than even over our own. It has been such bliss while we have taken the hand of the convert, and the tear has been in both eyes, when the word of gratitude has been spoken, and Jesus Christ has been magnified by lips that once blasphemed him.

My brothers and sisters, though the whole world should censure me, I cannot help it; I must tell it, to the praise of God's free grace and boundless love. There are hundreds here that are the most wonderful trophies of grace that ever lived on earth. My heart has been gladdened, and your hearts have been gladdened too. I must not keep it back; I *will* not. It was my Master's work, it is to his honor, it is to his praise. We will tell *that* on earth which we will sing in heaven. They *have* washed their robes and made them white in the blood of the Lamb; and I do believe that the joy we felt when sinners have been converted has been an earnest and a pledge that we shall be partakers of the like joy in heaven.

But to proceed. Here is another earnest of heaven, which is rather a personal matter than one which is drawn from others. Did you ever get a knotty passage in Scripture which repeated itself in your mind so many times that you could not get rid of it? You borrowed some commentaries; you opened them, and you found that you might inquire within, but get no information whatever upon the particular subject you wished most to be informed about. Commentaries generally are books which are written to explain those parts of Scripture which everybody understands, and to make these that are dark more mysterious than they were before. At any rate, if that was the aim of the different authors, they have most of them admirably succeeded. I do not believe in great commentaries upon the whole Bible; no one man can write such a book so that all of it shall be valuable. When a man gives his whole lifetime to some one book, that one is worth reading. When a man has taken up, as some have done, the Epistle to the Romans, or the book of Genesis, and gone on year after year toiling through it, then such a book has been a monument of labor, and has been valuable to the Christian student, but, generally, large commentaries give little information where most it is needed. Well, disappointed, you have gone back to your Bible, and have said, "I must not meddle with this text, it is above me." But it has repeated itself in your ears; you could not make it out; it has followed you—dogged your steps—it would not go away from you. At last you thought, "There was a message from God in that text to you." You prayed over it; while you were praying, some one word in the text seemed to lift itself right out of the connection and shone upon you like a star, and in the light of that one word you could see the meaning of all the words that preceded and followed, and you rose up from your knees, feeling that you knew the mind of the Spirit there, and had got a step forward in scriptural knowledge.

You remember the day, some of you, when you first learned the doctrines of grace. When we were first converted, we did not know much about them. We did not know whether God had converted us, or we had converted ourselves, but we heard a discourse one day in which some sentences were used, which gave us the clue to the whole system, and we began at once to see how God the Father planned, and God the Son carried out, and God the Holy Spirit applied, and we found ourselves on a sudden brought into the midst of a system of truths, which we might perhaps have believed before, but which we could not have clearly stated and did not understand. Well, the joy of that advance in knowledge was exceedingly great. I know it was to me. I can remember well the day and hour when first I received those truths in my own soul—when they were burned into me, as John Bunyan says—burned as with a hot iron into my soul; and I can recollect how I felt I had grown on a sudden from a babe into a man—that I had made progress in scriptural knowledge, from having got a hold once for all of the clue to the truth of God. Well, now, in that moment when God the Holy Spirit increased your knowledge and opened the eyes off your understanding, you had the earnest that you shall one day see, not through a glass darkly, but face to face, and by and by you shall know the whole truth, even as you are known.

But further than this—to put two or three thoughts into one, for brevity's sake: whenever, Christian, you have achieved a victory over your lusts—whenever after hard struggling you have laid a temptation dead at your feet—you have had in that day and hour a foretaste of the joy that awaits you, when the Lord shall shortly tread Satan under your feet. That victory in the first skirmish is the pledge and the earnest of the triumph in the last decisive battle. If you have overcome *one* foe, you shall overthrow them all. If the walls of Jericho

have been dismantled, so shall every fort be carried, and you shall go up a conqueror over the ruins thereof; and when, believer, you have known your security in Christ—when you have been able to say, "I *know* that my Redeemer
lives, and I am persuaded that he is able to keep that which I have committed
to him"—when you felt sure that earth and heaven might reel, but *his* love
could never pass away—when you have sung out the strong lines of Toplady,

> *My name from the palms of his hands*
> *Eternity will not erase;*
> *Impress'd on his heart it remains*
> *In marks of indelible grace;*

when you could put your foot upon a rock and feel that you stood securely,
knowing that you were safe in him, and because he lived, you must live also,
in that hour you had the pledge and the foretaste of that glorious security
which should be yours, when you are beyond gunshot of the infernal fiend,
beyond even the howling of the infernal dog. O Christian, there are many windows to heaven, through which God looks down on you; and there are some
windows through which you may look up to him. Let these *past* enjoyments
be guarantees of your future bliss, let them be to you as the grapes of Eshcol
were to the Jews in the wilderness; they were the fruit of the land, and when
they tasted them, they said, "It *is* a land that flows with milk and honey."
These enjoyments are the products of Canaan; they are handfuls of heavenly
flowers thrown over the wall; they are bunches of heaven's spices, brought to
times by angel hands across the stream. Heaven is full of joys like these. You
have but a few of them; heaven is shown with them. There your golden joys
are but as stones, and your most precious jewels are as common as the pebbles
of the brook. *Now* you drink drops and they are so sweet that your palate does
not soon forget them; but there you shall put your lips to the cup and drink
but never drain it dry; there you shall sit at the wellhead and drink as much as
you can draw and draw as much as you can desire. Now you see the glim-
merings of heaven as a star twinkling from leagues of distance. Follow that
glimmering and you shall see heaven no more as a star, but as the sun which
shines in its strength.

Permit me to remark yet once more, there is one foretaste of heaven
which the Spirit gives, which it were very wrong for us to omit. And now, I
shall seem, I dare say, to those who understand not spiritual mysteries, to be
as one that dreams. There are moments when the child of God has real fellowship with the Lord Jesus Christ. You know what fellowship between man
and man means. There is as real a fellowship between the Christian and

Christ. Our eyes can look on *him*. I say not that these human optics can behold the very flesh of Christ, but I say that the eyes of the soul can here on earth more truly see Christ, after a spiritual sort, than ever eyes of man saw him when he was in the flesh on earth. Today, your head may lean upon the Savior's bosom; today, he may be your sweet companion, and with the spouse you may say, "Let him kiss me with the kisses of his mouth, for his love is better than wine." I pray you, think not that I rave now. I speak what I do know, and testify what I have seen, and what many of you have seen and known too. There are moments with the believer, when, whether in the body or out of the body, he cannot tell—God knows—but this he knows, that Christ's left hand is under his head, and his right hand does embrace him. Christ has shown to him his hands and his side. He could say, with Thomas, "My Lord and my God," but he could not say much more. The world recedes, it disappears. The things of time are covered with a pall of darkness; Christ only stands out before the believer's view. I have known that some believers, when they have been in this state, could say with the spouse, "Stay me with apples, comfort me with flagons, for I am sick of love." Their love of Christ and Christ's love to them had overcome them. Their soul was something in the state of John, whom we described last Lord's Day morning: "When I saw *him*, I fell at his feet as dead." A sacred faintness overcomes my soul, I die—I die to prove the fullness of redeeming love, the love of Christ to me. Oh, these seasons! Talk not of feasts, you sons of mirth; tell us not of music, you who delight in melodious sound; tell us not of wealth and rank and honor and the joys of victory. One hour with Christ is worth an eternity of all earth's joys. May I but see *him*, may I but see *his* face, but behold *his* beauties—come winds, blow away all earthly joys I have—this joy shall well content my soul. Let the hot sun of tribulation dry up all the water brooks; but this fresh spring shall fill my cup full to the brim—yes, it shall make a river of delight, wherein my soul shall bathe. To be with Christ on earth is the best, the surest, the most ecstatic foretaste and earnest of the joys of heaven. Forget not this, Christian! If you have ever known Christ, heaven is yours; and when you have enjoyed Christ, you have learned a little of what the bliss of futurity shall be.

I do not doubt, also, that on dying beds men get foretastes of heaven which they never had in health. When death begins to pull down the old clay house he knocks away much of the plaster, and then the light shines through the chinks. When he comes to deal with our rough garment of clay, he pulls it to rags first; and then it is we begin to get a better view of the robes of righteousness, the fair white linen of the saints, with which we are always covered though we know it not. The nearer to death, the nearer to heaven, with the believer; the more sick, the nearer he is to health. The darkest part of his night is indeed the dawning of the day; just when he shall think he dies, he shall begin to live; and when his flesh drops from him, then is he prepared to be clothed upon with his house which is from heaven. Children of God in dying have said wonderful things which it were scarcely lawful for us to utter here. It needs the stillness of the room; the solemn silence of the last hour; the failing eye, the chinked utterance, the pale thin hand, to put a soul into their utterances. I remember when a Christian brother, who had often preached with me the gospel, was sorely sick and dying, he was suddenly smitten with blindness, which was a first monition of the approach of death, and he said to me—

> *And when ye see my eye-strings break,*
> *How sweet my moments roll;*
> *A mortal paleness on my cheek,*
> *But glory in my soul.*

And said it with such emphasis, as a man who, but two or three minutes after, stood before his God, that I can never read those lines without feeling how well the poet must have foreseen a death like his. Yes, there are mystic syllables that have dropped from the lips of dying men that have been priceless as the richest pearls. There have been sights of heaven seen in the midst of Jordan which these eyes cannot see, until this breast shall be chilled in the dread and cold stream. All these things that we have mentioned are the fruits of "that Holy Spirit of promise, which is the earnest of our inheritance until the redemption of the purchased possession."

2. A few minutes only—and, O God, do help us!—with all solemnity, I utter a few sentences upon *the black reverse of the joyous picture I have presented to you.*

There is another world for the wicked, as well as for the righteous. They who believe not in Christ are no more annihilated than those who do believe in him. Immortality awaits us all. We die, but we die not; we live *forever*; and if we fear not God, that immortality is the most frightful curse that ever fell on creature—

> *To linger in eternal death,*
> *Yet death forever fly.*

Can we tell what that world of woe is? In vain do we talk to you about the pit that is bottomless, and the fire that never can be quenched, and the worm that dies not. These are but images, and images which are used so often that we fear they are almost threadbare in your estimation, and you will scarcely give an ear to them. Listen, then. If you be this day without God and without Christ in the world, you have in yourself a few sparks of that eternal fire; you have already been singed by the vehement heat of that furnace which to some men has been so hot that even when they have passed it on earth, like Nebuchadnezzar's mighty men, they have fallen down, smitten by the heat thereof, before they came within its flames. Ungodly, unconverted men have an uneasiness of spirit; they are never contented, They want something; if they have that, they will want something more. They do not feel happy; they see through the amusements which the world presents to them; they are wise enough to see that they are hollow; they understand that the fair cheek is painted; they know that its beauty is but mere pretense; they are not befooled, God has awakened them. They are sensible enough to know that this world cannot fill a man's heart; they know that an immortal spirit is never to be satisfied with mortal joys. They are uneasy; they wish to kill time; it hangs heavy on their hands. They wish they could sleep three and twenty hours out of the four and twenty, or drink half the day. They try if they cannot find some pleasure that may wake up their energies—some new device, some novelty, even though it were novelty of sin, which might give a little excitement to a palate that has lost all power to be pleased. Now when a man gets into that uneasy state, he may make a guess of what hell will be. It will be that uneasiness intensified, magnified to the extreme: to wander through dry places, seeking rest and finding none, always thirsting, but never having a drop of water to cool that thirst; hungering, but feeding upon wind and hungering still; longing, yearning, groaning, sighing, conscious of misery, sensible of emptiness, feeling poverty, but never getting anything whereby that poverty may be made rich, or that hunger may be stayed. Ah! you uneasy ones, may your uneasiness bring you to Christ!

But unconverted men without Christ have another curse, which is a sure foretaste to them of hell. They are uneasy about death. I have my mind now upon a person who trembles like an aspen leaf during a thunderstorm, and I know another man who could bear a storm very well, but if there be the slightest thing the matter with him, if he has a cough, he fears his lungs are affected—if he feels a little hoarse, he is sure he will have bronchitis and die, and that thought of dying, he cannot bear. He will hear you talk about it, and crack a joke over it, merely for the sake of covering up his own dismay. He fancies you cannot see through him; but you can plainly discover that he is as afraid of dying as ever he can be. I know at this moment a family where the governess was instructed, when she took the situation, never to mention the subject of death to the children, or else she would be instantly discharged. That fear of dying which haunts some men! Not when their blood boils and they are excited—then they could rush to the cannon's mouth, but when they are cool and steady and look at it—when it is not the sword's point and glory, but dying, mere dying, then they shiver. Oh, how these strong men start and how they quail! Full many an infidel has recanted his infidelity then—given it all up when he has come to deal with the awful mysteries of death. But those already of death are but the foreshadows of that darker gloom which must gather round your spirit, except you believe in Christ. With some men it has even gone further than this. When a man has long resisted the invitations of the gospel, long gone from bad to worse, from sin to sin, a horror, an unspeakable horror, will seize hold upon him at times, especially if he be a man who is given to intoxication. Then a delirium will come upon him, mingled with a remorse, which will make his life intolerable. It has been my unhappy lot to see one or two such cases of persons who have been ill, and have been vexed with fears, fears of a most hideous caste, which you could not remove. You speak to them about Christ, they say, "What have I to do with him? I have cursed him hundreds of times." You speak to them about faith in Christ. "Faith in Christ," they say, "what is the use of that to me? I am past hope, I am given up, and I do not care about it either." And then they collapse—go back again into that dull despair which is the sure advance guard of damnation itself. With these men one may pray; they bid you pray for them, and then they say, "Get up, sir, it is of no use; God will never hear you for me." They will ask you to go home and pray, but assure you that it will be useless to do so. You read the Bible to them. "Don't read the Scriptures," say they; "every text cuts me to the quick, for I have neglected the Word of God, and all my time now is past." You tell them that

> While the lamp holds out to burn,
> The vilest sinner may return.

No, no, *they* cannot. You may tell them that there is hope—that Jesus Christ calls many at the eleventh hour; you picture to them the thief on the cross. No, no, they put far from them all hope, and choose their own delusions and perish. Now, such men give the gravest picture of what hell must be, in these forebodings of the wrath to come. I saw one man, now in eternity, and where he is, God knows. I could not describe to you what I saw that day of him. He said he would not die and walked up and down as long as there was life in him, under the notion, as he said, that if he could walk about he knew he should not die. He would not die, he said, he would live, he *must* live. "I cannot die," said he, "for I must be damned if I die; I feel I must," and that poor wretch, sometimes giving ear to your admonitions, then cursing you to your face, bidding you pray, and then blaspheming—dying with hell commenced, with all the horrors of perdition just beginning—a sort of infant perdition strangling to be born within him! Oh! may God deliver you from ever knowing this vilest premonition of destruction! And how shall you be delivered, but by this? "Believe in the Lord Jesus Christ, and you shall be saved; for he that believeth and is baptized shall be saved"—so says the Scripture—"he that believeth not shall be damned." Trust Christ and you are saved, be you who you may. Come to the foot of the cross, and cast yourself where his blood is dropping, and you are saved. Give your heart to him, believe in him, repose your confidence in him. May the Spirit of God enable you to do this! May he help you to repent of sin, and having repented, may he bring you to Christ, as the sin propitiator! And may you go away this day, saying, "I do believe in Christ; my soul rests in him!" And if you can say that, the joy and peace in believing, which must follow a simple faith in Christ, shall be to you the work of "the Holy Spirit of promise and the earnest of our inheritance, until the redemption of the purchased possession."

Foretastes of the Heavenly Life

Intended for Reading on Lord's Day, January 29, 1899 (C. H. Spurgeon Memorial Sabbath); delivered early in the year 1857, at New Park Street Chapel, Southwark. No. 2607.

> *And they took of the fruit of the land in their hands, and brought it down unto us, and brought us word again, and said, "It is a good land which the* LORD *our God doth give us."* —DEUTERONOMY 1:25

You remember the occasion concerning which these words were written. The children of Israel sent twelve men as spies into the land of Canaan, and they brought back with them the fruit of the land, among the rest a bunch of grapes from Eshcol too heavy to be borne by one man, and which, therefore. two of them carried on a staff between them. I shall not say much, at this time, concerning the Israelites; but I want to show you that, as they learned something of what Canaan was like by the fruit of the land brought to them by the spies, so you and I, even while we are on earth, if we are the Lord's chosen people, may learn something of what heaven is—the state to which we are to attain hereafter—by certain blessings which are brought to us even while we are here.

The Israelites were sure that Canaan was a fertile land when they saw the fruit of it which was brought by their brethren, and when they ate thereof. Perhaps there was but little for so many, and yet those who did eat were made at once to understand that it must have been a goodly soil that produced such fruit. In like manner, beloved, we who love the Lord Jesus Christ have had clusters of the grapes of a bettor Eshcol; we have had some of the fruits of heaven even while we have been on earth, and by them we are able to judge of the richness of the soil of paradise which brings forth such rare and choice delights.

I shall, therefore, present to you a series of views of heaven in order to give you some idea how it is that the Christian on earth enjoys a foretaste of the blessings that are yet to be revealed. Possibly, there are scarcely two Christians who have exactly the same ideas concerning heaven; though they all expect the same heaven, yet the most prominent feature in it is different to each mind according to its constitution.

1. Now, I will confess to you what is to me the most prominent feature of heaven, judging at the present moment. At another time, I may love heaven better for another thing; but, just lately, I have learned to love heaven as *a place of security*.

We have been greatly saddened as we have seen some professors dishonoring their profession—yes, and worse still, some of the Lord's own beloved committing grievous faults and slips, which have brought disgrace upon their character and injury to their souls; and we have learned to look up to heaven as a place where we shall never, never sin—where our feet shall be fixed firmly upon the rock—where there is neither tripping nor slipping—where faults shall be unknown—where we shall have no need to keep watch against an indefatigable enemy, because there is no foe that shall annoy us—where we shall not be on our guard day and night watching against the incursion of foes, for "there the wicked cease from troubling; and there the weary are at rest." We have looked upon heaven as the land of complete security, where the garment shall be always white, where the face shall be always anointed with fresh oil, where there is no fear of our turning away from our Lord, for there we shall stand fast forever. And I ask you, if that be a true view of heaven—and I am sure it is one feature of it—do not the saints, even on earth, in this sense enjoy some fruits of paradise? Do we not, even in these huts and villages below, sometimes taste the joys of blissful security? The doctrine of God's Word is that all who are in union with the Lamb are safe, that all believers must hold on their way, that those who have committed their souls to the keeping of Christ shall find him a faithful and immutable keeper. Believing this doctrine, we enjoy security even on earth; not that high and glorious security which renders us free from every slip and trip; but, nevertheless, a security well-nigh as great, because it secures us against ultimate ruin and renders us certain that we shall attain to eternal felicity.

And, beloved, have you never sat down and reflected on the doctrine of the perseverance of the saints? I am sure you have, and God has brought home to you a sense of your security in the person of Christ; he has told you that your name is graven on his hand; he has whispered in your ear the promise, "Fear thou not, for I am with thee." You have been led to look upon the great surety of the covenant as faithful and true, and, therefore, bound and engaged to present you, the weakest of the family, with all the chosen race, before the throne of God; and in such a sweet contemplation I am sure you have been drinking some of the juice of his spiced pomegranates, you have had some of the choice fruits of paradise, you have had some of the enjoyments which the perfect saints above have in a sense of your complete and eternal security in Christ Jesus. Oh, how I love that doctrine of the perseverance of the saints! I shall at once renounce the pulpit when I cannot preach it, for any other form of teaching seems to me to be a blank desert and a howling wilderness, as unworthy of God as it would be beneath even my acceptance, frail worm as I am. I could never either believe or preach a gospel which saves me today and rejects me tomorrow—a gospel which puts me in Christ's family one hour, and makes me a child of the devil the next—a gospel which first justifies and then condemns me—a gospel which pardons me, and afterward casts me down to hell. Such a gospel is abhorrent to reason itself, much more is it contrary to the mind of the God whom we delight to serve. Every true believer in Jesus can sing, with Toplady—

> My name from the palms of his hands
> Eternity will not erase;
> Impressed on his heart it remains
> In marks of indelible grace:
> Yes, I to the end shall endure,
> As sure as the earnest is given;
> More happy, but not more secure,
> The glorified spirits in heaven.

Yes, beloved, we do enjoy a sense of perfect security even as we dwell in this land of wars and fightings. As the spies brought to their brethren in the wilderness bunches of the grapes of Canaan, so, in the security we enjoy, we have a foretaste and earnest of the bliss of paradise.

2. In the next place, most probably the greater part of you love to think of heaven under another aspect, as *a place of perfect rest*.

Son of toil, you love the sanctuary because it is there you sit to hear God's Word and rest your wearied limbs. When you have wiped the hot sweat from your burning brow, you have often thought of heaven as the place where your labors shall be over, and you have sung, with sweet emphasis—

> There shall I bathe my weary soul
> In seas of heavenly rest,
> And not a wave of trouble roll
> Across my peaceful breast.

Rest, rest, rest, this is what you want, and to me also this idea of heaven is exceedingly beautiful. Rest I know I never shall have beneath this sky while

Christ's servants continue to be so unreasonable as they are. I have served them to the utmost of my power, yet I am well-nigh hounded to my grave by Christian ministers perpetually wanting me to do impossibilities that they know no mortal strength can accomplish. Willing am I to labor till I drop, but I cannot do more than I am doing; yet I am perpetually assailed on this side and the other, till, go where I may, there seems no rest for me till I slumber in my grave; and I do look forward to heaven, with great happiness, because there I shall rest from labors constant and arduous, though much loved.

And you, too, dear Christian friend, who have been toiling long to gain an object you have eagerly sought, you will be glad when you get to heaven. You have said that if you could attain your desire, you would gladly lie down and rest. You have longed to lay up a certain amount of riches. You have said that, if you could once gain a competence, you would then make yourself at ease; or, you have been laboring long to secure a certain position, and you have said that if you could only reach it, you would rest. Yes, but you have not reached it yet; and you love to think of heaven because it is the goal to the racer, the target of the arrow of existence; the couch of repose for time's tired toilers; yes, an eternal rest for the poor weary struggler upon earth. You love it because it is a place of rest; and do we never enjoy a foretaste of heaven upon earth in that sense? Oh yes, beloved! Blessed be God, "we which have believed do enter into rest." Our peace is like a river and our righteousness like the waves of the sea. God does give rest to his people even here: "there remaineth therefore a rest to the people of God." We have stormy trials and bitter troubles in the world, but we have learned to say, "Return unto your rest, O my soul; for the Lord has dealt bountifully with you." Did you never, in times of great distress, climb up to your closet and there on your knees pour out your heart before God? Did you never feel, after you had so done, that you had, as it were, bathed yourself in rest, so that—

> *Let cares like a wild deluge come,*
> *And storms of sorrow fall,*

you cared not one whit for them? Though wars and tumults were raging around you, you were kept in perfect peace, for you had found a great protecting shield in Christ; you were able to remain restful and calm, for you had looked upon the face of God's Anointed. Ah Christian! that rest, so placid and serene, without a billow of disturbance, which in your deepest troubles you have been enabled to enjoy upon the bosom of Christ, is to you like a bunch from the vintage of heaven, one grape of the heavenly cluster of which you shall soon partake in the land of the hereafter. Thus, again, you see, we can have a foretaste of heaven, and realize what it is even while we are here upon earth.

That idea of heaven as a place of rest will just suit some indolent professors, so I will turn the subject round, and show you that the very opposite idea is also true, and may be more useful to certain people. I do believe that one of the worst sins of which a man can be guilty is to be idle; I could almost forgive a drunkard, rather than a lazy man; he who is idle has as good reason to be penitent before God as David had when he was an adulterer; indeed, David's adultery probably resulted from his idleness. It is an abominable thing to let the grass grow up to your knees and do nothing toward making it into hay. God never sent a man into the world to be idle; and there are some who make a profession of being Christians who do nothing to serve the Lord from one year's end to the other.

3. A true idea of heaven is, that it is *a place of uninterrupted service.*

It is a land where they serve God day and night in his temple, and never know weariness and never require to slumber. Do you know, dear friends, the deliciousness of work? Although I must complain when people expect impossibilities of me, it is the highest enjoyment of my life to be busily engaged for Christ. Tell me the day when I do not preach, I will tell you the day in which I am not happy; but the day in which it is my privilege to preach the gospel, and labor for God, is generally the day of my peaceful and quiet enjoyment after all. Service is delight. Praising God is pleasure. Laboring for him is the highest bliss a mortal can know. Oh, how sweet it must be to sing his praises and never feel that the throat is dry! Oh, how blessed to flap the wing forever and never feel it flag! Oh, what sweet enjoyment to fly upon his errands evermore, to circle round the throne of God in heaven while eternity shall last, and never once lay the head on the pillow, never once feel the throbbing of fatigue, never once the pangs that admonish us that we need to cease, but to keep on forever like eternity's own self—a broad river rolling on with perpetual floods of labor! Oh, that must be enjoyment! That must be heaven, to serve God day and night in his temple! Many of you have served God on earth and have had foretastes of that bliss.

I wish some of you knew more of the sweets of labor, for although labor breeds sweat, it breeds sweets too—more especially labor for Christ. There is a satisfaction before the work; there is a satisfaction in the work; there is a satisfaction after the work; and there is a satisfaction in looking for the fruits of the work; and a great satisfaction when we get the fruits. Labor for Christ is, indeed, the robing room of heaven; if it be not heaven itself, it is one of the most blissful foretastes of it. Thank God, Christian, if you can do anything for your Master. Thank him if it is your privilege to do the least thing for him; but remember, in so doing, he is giving you a taste of the grapes of Eshcol. But you indolent people do not get the grapes of Eshcol because you are too lazy to carry that big bunch. You would like them to come into your mouths without the trouble of gathering them. You do not care to go forth and serve God. You sit still and look after yourselves, but what do you do for other people? You go to your place of worship; you talk about your Sunday school and sick visitation society, yet you never teach in the Sunday school, and you never visit a sick person; you take a great deal of credit to yourself while you do nothing at all. You cannot expect to know much of the enjoyments of heavenly glory until you have experienced a little of the delight of working in the kingdom of heaven on earth.

4. Another view of heaven is, that it is *a place of complete victory and glorious triumph.*

This is the battlefield; there is the triumphal procession. This is the land of the sword and the spear; that is the land of the wreath and the crown. This is the land of the garment rolled in blood and of the dust of the fight; that is the land of the trumpet's joyful sound, that is the place of the white robe and of the shout of conquest. Oh, what a thrill of joy shall shoot through the hearts of all the blessed when their conquests shall be complete in heaven, when death itself, the last of foes, shall be slain, when Satan shall be dragged captive at the chariot wheels of Christ, when Jesus shall have overthrown sin and trampled corruption as the mire of the streets, when the great song of universal victory shall rise from the hearts of all the redeemed! What a moment of pleasure shall that be! But, dear brethren, you and I have foretastes of even that joy. We know what conflicts, what soul battles we have even here; did you never struggle against unbelief and at last overcome it? Oh, with what joy did you lift your eyes to heaven, the tears flowing down your cheeks, and say, "Lord, I bless you that I have been able to vanquish that sin." Did you ever meet a strong temptation and wrestle hard with it, and know what it was to sing with great joy, "My feet well-nigh slipped; but thy mercy held me up"? Have you, like Bunyan's Christian, fought with old Apollyon, and have you seen him flap his dragon wings and fly away? There you had a foretaste of heaven; you had just a hint of what the ultimate victory will be. In the death of that one Philistine, you saw the destruction of the whole army; that Goliath who fell through your sling and stone was but one out of the multitude who must yield their bodies to the fowls of heaven. God gives you partial triumphs that they may be the earnest of ultimate and complete victory. Go on and conquer, and let each conquest, though a harder one and more strenuously contested, be to you as a grape of Eshcol, a foretaste of the joys of heaven!

5. Furthermore, without doubt, one of the best views we can ever give of heaven is, that it is *a state of complete acceptance with God,* recognized and felt in the conscience.

I suppose that a great part of the joy of the blessed saints consists in a knowledge that there is nothing in them to which God is hostile; that their peace with God has not anything to mar it; that they are so completely in union with the principles and thoughts of the most High, that his love is set on them, that their love is set on him, and they are one with him in every respect. Well, beloved, and have we not enjoyed a sense of acceptance here below? Blotted and blurred by many doubts and fears, yet there have been moments when we have known ourselves as truly accepted as we shall know ourselves to be even when we stand before the throne. There have been bright days with some of us, when we could set to our seal that God was true; and when, afterward, feeling that "the Lord knows them that are his," we could say, "And we know that we are his, too." Then have we known the meaning of Dr. Watts when he sang—

> When I can say, "My God is mine,"
> When I can feel thy glories shine,
> I tread the world beneath my feet,
> And all that earth calls good or great.
>
> While such a scene of sacred joys
> Our raptured eyes and souls employ,
> Here we could sit and gaze away
> A long, an everlasting day.

We had such a clear view of the perfection of Christ's righteousness that we felt that God had accepted us, and we could not be otherwise than happy; we had such a sense of the efficacy of the blood of Christ that we felt sure our sins were all pardoned and could never be mentioned against us forever. And, beloved, though I have spoken of other joys, let me say, this is the cream of all of them, to know ourselves accepted in God's sight. Oh, to feel that I, a guilty worm, am now at rest in my Father's bosom; that I, a lost prodigal, am now feasting at his table with delight; that I, who once heard the voice of his anger, now listen to the notes of his love! This is a joy that is worth more than all worlds. What more can they know up there than that? And were it not that our sense of it is so imperfect, we might bring heaven down to earth, and might at least dwell in the suburbs of the Celestial City, if we could not be privileged to go within the gates, So you see, again, we can have, in that sense, bunches of the grapes of Eshcol. Seeing that heaven is a state of acceptance, we, too, can know and feel that acceptance, and rejoice in it.

6. And again, heaven is *a state of great and glorious manifestations*.

As you look forward to your experience in heaven, you sing—

> *Then shall I see, and hear, and know*
> *All I desired or wished below;*
> *And every power find sweet employ*
> *In that eternal world of joy.*

You are now looking at it darkly, through a glass; but there you shall see face to face. Christ looks down on the Bible, and the Bible is his looking glass. You look into it and see the face of Christ as in a mirror, darkly; but soon you shall look upon him face to face. You expect heaven to be a place of peculiar manifestations; you believe that there Jesus will unveil his face to you; that—

> *Millions of years your wondering eyes*
> *Shall o'er your Savior's beauties rove.*

You are expecting to see his face and never, never sin. You are longing to know the secrets of his heart. You believe that, in that day, you shall see him as he is, and shall be like him in the world of spirits. Well, beloved, though Christ does not manifest himself to us as he does to the bright ones there, have we not had blessed manifestations even while we have been in this vale of tears? Speak, believer; let your heart speak; have you not had visions of Calvary? Has not your Master sometimes touched your eyes with eye salve and let you see him on his cross? Have you not said—

> *"Sweet the moments, rich in blessing,*
> *Which before the cross I spend,*
> *Life, and health, and peace possessing,*
> *From the sinner's dying friend.*
>
> *Here I'll sit forever viewing*
> *Mercy's streams, in streams of blood;*

Precious drops! my soul bedewing,
Plead and claim my peace with God."?

Have you not wept both for joy and for grief when you beheld him nailed
to the tree for your sakes and saw him bleeding out his life for you? Oh yes! I
know you have had such manifestations of him. And have you not seen him
in his risen glories? Have you not beheld him there exalted on his throne?
Have you not, by faith, beheld him as the Judge of the quick and the dead, and
as the Prince of the kings of the earth? Have you not looked through the dim
future and seen him with the crown of all kingdoms on his head, with the
diadems of all monarchs beneath his feet, and the scepters of all thrones in his
hand? Have you not anticipated the moment of his most glorious triumphs,
when—

"He shall reign from pole to pole,
With illimitable sway."?

Yes, you have, and therein you have had foretastes of heaven. When Christ
has thus revealed himself to you, you have looked within the veil, and, therefore, you have seen what is there; you have had some glimpses of Jesus while
here: those glimpses of Jesus are but the beginning of what shall never end.
Those joyous melodies of praise and thanksgiving are but the preludes of the
songs of paradise.

7. Last, the highest idea of heaven is, that it is *a place of most hallowed and blissful communion.*

I have not given you even half that I might have told you of the various
characteristics of heaven, as described in God's Word, but communion is the
best. Communion! That word so little spoken of, so seldom understood.
Blessed word, "communion"! Dearly beloved, you hear us say, "And the communion of the Holy Ghost be with you all"; but there are many of you who
do not know the meaning of that sweet heaven in a word—communion! It is
the flower of language; it is the honeycomb of words—communion! You like
best to talk of corruption, do you not? Well, if you like that ugly word, you
are very willing to meditate upon it. I do so when I am forced to do it; but
communion seems to me to be a far sweeter word than that. You like to talk
a great deal about affliction, do you not? Well, if you love that black word, you
may have reason to love it; and if you care to be happy about it, you may do
so; but give me for my constant text and for my constant joy, communion, and

I will not choose which kind of communion it shall be. Sweet Master, if you give me communion with you in your sufferings, if I have to bear reproach and shame for your name's sake, I will thank you; if I may have fellowship with you in it, and if you will give me to suffer for your sake, I will call it an honor, that so I can be a partaker of your sufferings; and if you give me sweet enjoyments, if you do raise me up, and make me to sit with you in heavenly places in Christ, I will bless you. I will bless God for ascension communion—communion with Christ in his glories. Do you not say the same? And for communion with Christ in death; have you died unto the world, as Christ did die unto it himself? Then, have you had communion with him in resurrection? Have you been raised to newness of life, even as he was raised from the grave? And have you had communion with him in his ascension, so that you know yourself to be an heir to a throne in glory? If so, you have had the best earnest you can receive of the joys of paradise. To be in heaven is to lean one's head upon the breast of Jesus; have you not done that on earth? Then you know what heaven is. To be in heaven is to talk to Jesus, to sit at his feet, to let our heart beat against his heart. If you have had that bliss on earth, you have already tasted some of the grapes of heaven.

Cherish, then, these foretastes of whatever kind they may have been in your individual case. Differently constituted, you will all look at heaven in a different light. Keep your foretaste just as God gave it to you. He has given each of you a separate experience of it which is most suitable to your own condition. Treasure it up; think much of it; but think more of your Master, for, remember, it is, "Christ in you, the hope of glory," that is your best foretaste of heaven; and the more you realize that blessed truth, the more fully prepared shall you be for the bliss of the joyous ones in the land of the happy.

Heaven Above and Heaven Below

꧁⚬꧂

Delivered on Lord's Day morning, February 2, 1890, at the Metropolitan Tabernacle, Newington. No. 2128.

They shall hunger no more, neither thirst any more, neither shall the sun light on them, nor any heat. For the Lamb which is in the midst of the throne shall feed them, and shall lead them unto living fountains of waters.
—REVELATION 7:16–17

They shall not hunger nor thirst; neither shall the heat nor sun smite them for he that hath mercy on them shall lead them, even by the springs of water shall he guide them. —ISAIAH 49:10

Jordan is a very narrow stream. It made a sort of boundary for Canaan; but it hardly sufficed to divide it from the rest of the world, since a part of the possessions of Israel was on the eastern side of it. Those who saw the Red Sea divided, and all Israel marching through its depths, must have thought it a small thing for the Jordan to be dried up and for the people to pass through it to Canaan. The greatest barrier between believers and heaven has been safely passed. In the day when we believed in the Lord Jesus Christ, we passed through our Red Sea, and the Egyptians of our sins were drowned. Great was the marvel of mercy! To enter fully into our eternal inheritance, we have only to cross the narrow stream of death; and scarcely that, for the kingdom of heaven [is on this side of the] river as well as on the other. I start by reminding you of this, because we are very apt to imagine that we must endure a kind of purgatory while we are on earth, and then, if we are believers, we may break loose into heaven after we have shuffled off this mortal coil. But it is not so. Heaven must be in us before we can be in heaven; and while we are yet in the wilderness, we may spy out the land, and may eat of the clusters of Eshcol. There is no such gulf between earth and heaven as gloomy thoughts suggest. Our dreams should not be of an abyss, but of a ladder whose foot is on the earth, but whose top is in glory. There would not be one hundredth part so much difference between earth and heaven if we did not live so far below our privileges. We live on the ground, when we might rise as on the wings of eagles. We are all too conscious of this body. Oh, that we were oftener where Paul was when he said, "Whether in the body or out of the body, I cannot tell: God knows"! If not caught up into paradise, yet may our daily life be as the garden of the Lord.

Listen a while, you children of God; for I speak to you and not to others. To unbelievers, what can I say? They know nothing of spiritual things and will not believe them, though a man should show them unto them. They are spiritually blind and dead: the Lord quicken and enlighten them! But to you that are begotten again unto a lively hope by the resurrection of Jesus Christ from the dead, I speak with joy. Think of what you are by grace, and remember that what you will be in glory is already outlined and foreshadowed in your life in Christ. Being born from above, you are the same men that will be in heaven. You have within you the divine life—the same life which is to enjoy eternal immortality. "He that believeth on the Son hath everlasting life": it is your possession now. As the quickened ones of the Holy Spirit, the life which is to last on forever has begun in you. At this moment you are already, in many respects, the same as you ever will be. I might almost repeat this passage in Revelation concerning some of you at this very hour: "What are these? and whence came they? These are they that came out of great tribulation, and have washed their robes and made them white in the blood of the Lamb." I might even go on to say, "Therefore are they before the throne of God"—for you abide in close communion with the King—"and serve him day and night in his temple: and he that sitteth on the throne shall dwell among them." I am straining no point when I thus speak of the sanctified.

Beloved, you are now "elect according to the foreknowledge of God," and you are "the called according to his purpose." Already you are as much forgiven as you will be when you stand without fault before the throne of God. The Lord Jesus has washed you whiter than snow, and none can lay anything to your charge. You are as completely justified by the righteousness of Christ as you ever can be; you are covered with his righteousness, and heaven itself cannot provide a robe more spotless. "Beloved, now are we the sons of God." "He hath made us accepted in the beloved." Today we have the spirit of adoption, and enjoy access to the throne of the heavenly grace; yes, and today by faith we are raised up in Christ, and made to sit in the heavenlies in him. We are now united to Christ, now indwelt by the Holy Ghost: are not these great things, and heavenly things? The Lord has brought us out of darkness into his marvelous light. Although we may, from one point of view, lament the dimness of the day, yet, as compared with our former darkness, the light is marvelous; and, best of all, it is the same light which is to brighten from dawn into midday. What is grace but the morning twilight of glory?

Look you, beloved: the inheritance that is to be yours tomorrow is, in very truth, yours today; for in Christ Jesus you have received the inheritance, and you have the earnest of it in the present possession of the Holy Spirit, who dwells in you. It has been well said, that all the streets of the New Jerusalem begin here. See, here is the High Street of Peace, which leads to the central palace of God; and now we set our foot on it. "Being justified by faith, we have peace with God." The heavenly street of Victory, where are the palms and the harps, surely we are at the lower end of it here; for "this is the victory that overcomes the world, even our faith." Everything that is to be ours in the home country is, in measure, ours at this moment. As sleeps the oak within the acorn, so slumbers heaven within the first cry of "Abba, Father!" Yes, and the hallelujahs of eternity lie hidden within the groans of penitence. "God be merciful to me a sinner" has in its bowels the endless "We praise you, O Lord." O saints, little do you know how much you have in what you have!

If I could bring believers consciously nearer to the state of glory by their more complete enjoyment of the privileges of the state of grace, I should be exceedingly glad. Beloved, you will never have a better God: and "this God is our God forever and ever." Delight yourselves in him this day. The richest saint in glory has no greater possession than his God: and even I also can say, in the words of the psalm, "Yea, mine own God is he."

Despite your tribulation, take full delight in God, your exceeding joy this morning, and be happy in him. They in heaven are shepherded by the Lamb of God, and so are you: he still carries the lambs in his bosom, and does gently lead those that are with young. Even here he makes us to lie down in green pastures: what would we have more? With such a God, and such a Savior, all you can want is that indwelling Spirit, who shall help you to realize your God, and to rejoice in your Savior; and you have this also; for the Spirit of God dwells with you and is in you: "know you not that you are the temple of God?" God the Holy Ghost is not far away, neither have we to entreat his influence as though it were rays from a far-off star; for he abides in his people evermore.

I will not say that heavenly perfection is not far superior to the highest state that we ever reach on earth; but the difference lies more in our own failure than in the nature of things. Grace, if realized to its full, would brighten off into glory. When the Holy Spirit fully possesses our being, and we yield ourselves to his power, our weakness is strength, and our infirmity is to be gloried in. Then is it true, that on earth God is with us; and there is but a step between us and heaven, where we are with God.

Thus I have conducted you to my two texts, which I have put together as an illustration of what I would teach. In the New Testament text we have the heavenly state above; and in the Old Testament text we have the state of the Lord's flock while on the way to their eternal rest. Very singular, to my mind, is the sameness of the description of the flock in the fold, and the flock feeding in the ways. The verses are almost word for word the same. When John would describe the white-robed host, he can say no more of them than Isaiah said of the pilgrim band, led by the God of mercy.

1. First, *let us consider the heavenly state above*. The beloved John tells us what he heard and saw.

The first part of the description assures us of *the supply of every need*. "They shall hunger no more, neither thirst anymore." In heaven no need is unsatisfied, and no desire ungratified. They can have no want as to their bodies, for they are as the angels of God. Children of poverty, your straitness of bread will soon be ended, and your care shall end in plenty. The worst hunger is that of the heart; and this will be unknown above. There is a ravenous hunger, fierce as a wolf, which possesses some men: all the world cannot satisfy their greed. A thousand worlds would be scarce a mouthful for their lust. Now, in heaven there are no sinful and selfish desires. The ravening of covetousness or of ambition enters not the sacred gate. In glory there are no desires which should not be, and those desires which should be are all so tempered or so fulfilled that they can never become the cause of sorrow or pain; for "they shall hunger no more." Even the saints need love, fellowship, rest: they have all these in union to God, in the communion of saints, and in the rest of Jesus. The unrenewed man is always thirsting; but Christ can stay this even now, for he says, "He that drinketh of the water that I shall give him shall never thirst." Be you sure, then, that from the golden cup of glory we shall drink that which will quench all thirst forever. There is not, in all the golden streets of heaven, a single person who is desiring what he may not have, or wanting what he cannot obtain, or even wishing for that which he has not to his hand. Oh, happy state! Their mouth is satisfied with good things; they are filled with all the fullness of God.

And as there is in heaven a supply for every need, so is there *the removal of every ill*. Thus says the Spirit, "Neither shall the sun light on them, nor any heat." We are such poor creatures that excess of good soon becomes evil to us. I love the sun: if you have ever seen it shining in the clear blue heavens, you would not wonder that I speak with emphasis. Life, joy, and health stream from it in lands where it is enough of pleasure to bask in its beams. But too much of the sun overpowers us; his warmth makes men faint, his stroke destroys them. Too great a blessing may prove too heavy a cargo for the ship of life. Hence we need guarding from dangers which, at the first sight, look as if they were not perilous. In the beatific state, if these bodies of flesh and blood were still our dwelling place, we could not live under the celestial conditions. Even here, too much of spiritual joy may prostrate a man and cast him into a swoon. I would like to die of the disease; but still, a sickness comes upon one to whom heavenly things are revealed in great measure and enjoyed with special vividness. One of the saints cried out in an agony of delight, "Hold, Lord, hold! Remember I am but an earthen vessel and can contain no more!" The Lord has to limit his revelations because we cannot bear them now. I have heard of one who looked upon the sun imprudently and was blinded by the light. The very sunlight of divine revelation, favor, and fellowship could readily prove too much for our feeble vision, heart, and brain. Therefore, in the glorious state, flesh and blood shall be removed, and the raised body shall be strengthened to endure that fierce light which beats about the throne of Deity. As for us, as we now are, we might well cry, "Who among us shall dwell with the devouring fire?" But when the redemption of the body has come about, and the soul has been strengthened with all might, we shall be able to be at home with our God, who is a consuming fire. "Neither shall the sun light on them, nor any heat." May God grant us to enjoy the anticipation of that happy period when we shall behold his face, when his secret shall be with us, and we shall know even as we are known! Oh, for that day when we shall enter into the holiest and shall stand before the presence of his glory; and yet, so far from being afraid, shall be filled with exceeding joy!

But, further, the description of the heavenly life has this conspicuous feature—*the leading of the Lamb*. "The Lamb which is in the midst of the throne shall feed them, and shall lead them." It is heaven to be personally shepherded by him who is the great sacrifice. In this present state, we have earthly shepherds; and when God graciously feeds us by men after his own heart, whom he himself instructs, we prize them much. Those whom the Lord ordains to feed his flock we love, and their faith we follow, for the Lord makes them of great service to us; but still, they are only underlings, and we do not forget their imperfections, and their dependence upon their Lord. But in the glory land, "that great shepherd of the sheep" will himself personally minister to us. Those dear lips that are as lilies, dropping sweet-smelling myrrh, shall speak directly to each one of our hearts. We shall hear his voice; we shall behold his face; we shall be fed by his hand; we shall follow at his heel. How gloriously will he "stand and feed"! How restfully shall we lie down in green pastures!

He shall feed us in his dearest character. As the Lamb he revealed his greatest love, and as the Lamb will he lead and feed us forever. The Revised Version wisely renders the passage, "The Lamb in the midst of the throne shall be their shepherd." We are never fed so sweetly by our Lord himself as when he reveals to us most clearly his character as the sacrifice for sin. The atoning sacrifice is the center of the sun of infinite love, the light of light. There is no truth like it for the revelation of God. Christ in his wounds and bloody sweat is Christ indeed. "He his own self bore our sins in his own body on the tree." With this truth before us, his flesh is meat indeed, and his blood is drink indeed. In heaven we shall know him far better than we do now as the Lamb slain from before the foundation of the world, the Lamb of God's Passover, "the Lamb of God, which taketh away the sin of the world." That deep peace, that eternally unbroken rest which we shall derive from a sight of the great sacrifice, will be a chief ingredient in the bliss of heaven. "The Lamb shall feed them."

But though we shall see our Lord as a lamb, it will not be in a state of humiliation, but in a condition of power and honor. "The Lamb which is in the midst of the throne shall feed them." Heaven will largely consist of expanded views of King Jesus and nearer beholdings of the glory which follows upon his sacrificial grief. Ah brethren, how little do we know his glory! We scarce know who he is that has befriended us. We hold the doctrine of his deity tenaciously; but in heaven we shall perceive his Godhead in its truth so far as the finite can apprehend the infinite. We have known his friendship to us, but when we shall behold the King in his beauty in his own halls, and our eyes shall look into his royal countenance, and his face, which outshines the sun, shall beam ineffable affection upon each one of us, then shall we find our heaven in his glory. We ask no thrones; his throne is ours. The enthroned Lamb himself is all the heaven we desire.

Then the last point of the description is full of meaning. *The drinking at the fountain* is the secret of the ineffable bliss. "The Lamb which is in the midst of the throne shall feed them, and lead them unto living fountains of waters." We are compelled to thirst at times, like the poor flock of slaughter which we see driven through our London streets; and, alas, we stop at the very puddles by the way, and would refresh ourselves at them if we could. This will never happen to us when we reach the land where flows the river of the water of life. There the sheep drink of no stagnant waters or bitter wells, but they are satisfied from living fountains of waters. Comfort is measurably to be found in the streams of providential mercies, and therefore they are to be received with gratitude; but yet common blessings are unfilling things to souls quickened by grace. Corn can fill the barn, but not the heart. Of the wells of earth we may say, "Whosoever drinketh of this water shall thirst again"; but when we go beyond temporal supplies, and live upon God himself, then the soul receives a draft of far truer and more enduring refreshment; even as our Lord Jesus said to the woman at the well, "He that drinketh of the water that I shall give him shall never thirst; but the water that I shall give him shall be in him a well of water springing up into everlasting life." In heaven the happy ones live not on bread, which is the staff of life, but on God, who is life itself. The second cause is passed over, and the first cause alone is seen.

In the home country souls have no need of the means of grace, for they have reached the God of grace. The means of grace are like conduit pipes which bring down the living water to us: but we have found them fail us; and at times we have used them in so faulty a way that the water has lost its freshness, or has even been made to taste of the pipe through which it flowed. Fruit is best when gathered fresh from the garden: the fingering of the market destroys the bloom. We have too much of this in our ministries. Brethren, we shall soon drink living water at the wellhead, and gather the golden fruit from him who is "as the apple tree among the trees of the wood." We shall have no need of baptisms and breakings of bread, nor of churches and pastors. We shall not need the golden chalices or the earthen vessels which now serve our turn so well, but we shall come to the river's source, and drink our fill. "He shall lead them unto living fountains of water."

At times, alas, we know what it is to come to the pits and find no water; and then we try to live on happy memories. We sing and sigh; or sigh and sing—

> *What peaceful hours I once enjoyed,*
> *How sweet their memory still!*
> *But they have left an aching void*
> *The world can never fill.*

A cake made of memories will do for a bite now and then, but it makes poor daily bread. We want the present enjoyment of God. We need still to go to the fountain for new supplies; for water which stands long in the pitcher loses its cool and refreshing excellence. Happy is the man that is not living upon the memories of what he used to enjoy, but is even now in the banqueting house! The present and perpetual renewal of first love and first delight in God is heaven.

Heaven is to know the substance and the secret of the divine life, not to hold a cup, but to drink of the living water. The doctrine is precious, but it is far better to know the thing about which the doctrine speaks. The doctrine is the salver of silver, but the blessing itself is the apple of gold. Blessed are they that are always fed on the substance of the truth, the verity of verities, the essence of essential things.

"He shall lead them unto fountains." There the eternal source is unveiled: they not only receive the mercy, but they see how it comes, and whence it flows: they not only drink, but they drink with their eye upon the glorious well-head. Did you ever see a boy on a hot day lie down, when he has been thirsty, and put his mouth down to the top of the water at the brim of the well? How he draws up the cool refreshment! Drink away, poor child! He has no fear that he will drink the well dry, nor have we. How pleasant it is to take from the inexhaustible! That which we drink is all the sweeter because of the measureless remainder. Enough is not enough: but when we have God for our all in all, then are we content. When I am near to God and dwell in the overflowing of his love, I feel like the cattle on a burning summer's day when they take to the brook which ripples around them up to their knees, and there they stand, filled, cooled, and sweetly refreshed. O my God, in you I feel that I have not only all that I can contain, but all that contains me. In you I live and move with perfect content. Such is heaven! We shall have bliss within and bliss around us; we ourselves drinking at the source, and dwelling by the well forever. The fact is, that heaven is God fully enjoyed. The evil that God hates will be wholly cast out; the capacity which God gives will be enlarged and prepared for full fruition, and our whole being will be taken up with God, the ever blessed, from whom we came, and to whom it will be heaven to return. Who knows God knows heaven. The source of all things is our fountain of living waters.

Thus I could occupy all the morning with my first head; but I must not tarry, or I shall miss my aim, which is to show you that, even here, we may outline glory and in the wilderness we may have the pattern of things in the heavens. This you will see by carefully referring to the second text.

2. Let us consider the heavenly state below.

I think I have heard you saying, "Ah! this is all about heaven; but we have not yet come to it. We are still wrestling here below." Well, well, if we cannot go to heaven at once, heaven can come to us. The words which I will now read refer to the days of earth, the times when the sheep feed in the ways, and come from the north and from the south at the call of the Shepherd. "They shall not hunger nor thirst; neither shall the heat nor sun smite them: for he that hath mercy on them shall lead them, even by the springs of water shall he guide them."

Look at the former passage and at this. The whole description is the same. When I noticed this parallel, I stood amazed. John, you are a great artist; I entreat you, paint me a picture of heaven! Isaiah, you also have a great soul; draw me a picture of the life of the saintly ones on earth when their Lord is with them! I have both pictures. They are masterpieces. I look at them, and they are so much alike that I wonder if there be not some mistake. Surely they are depicting the same thing. The forms, the lights and shades, the touches and the tones are not only alike, but identical. Amazed, I cry, "Which is heaven, and which is the heavenly life on earth?" The artists know their own work, and by their instruction I will be led. Isaiah painted our Lord's sheep in his presence on the way to heaven, and John drew the same flock in the glory with the Lamb; and the fact that the pictures are so much alike is full of suggestive teaching. Here are the same ideas in the same words. Brethren, may you and I as fully believe and enjoy the second passage as we hope to realize and enjoy the first Scripture when we get home to heaven.

First, here is a promise that *every want shall be supplied.* "They shall not hunger nor thirst." If we are the Lord's people and are trusting in him, this shall be true in every possible sense. Literally, "your bread shall be given you, your water shall be sure." You shall have no anxious thought concerning what you shall eat, and what you shall drink. But, mark you, if you should know the trials of poverty, and should be greatly tried, and brought very low in temporal things, yet the Lord's presence and sensible consolations shall so sustain you that spiritually and inwardly you shall know neither hunger nor thirst. Many saints have found riches in poverty, ease in labor, rest in pain, and delight in affliction. Our Lord can so adapt our minds to our circumstances that the bitter is sweet and the burden is light. Paul speaks of the saints "as sorrowful, yet always rejoicing." Note well that the sorrow has an "as" connected with it; but the rejoicing is a fact. "They shall not hunger nor thirst." If you live in God, you shall have no ungratified desire. "Delight thyself also in the Lord, and he shall give thee the desires of thine heart." There may be many things that you would like to have, and you may never have them; but then you will prefer to be without them, saying, "Nevertheless, not as I will, but as you will." If Christ be with you, you will be so happy in him that wanton, wandering wishes will be like the birds which may fly over your head but dare not make their nests in your hair. You will be without a peevish craving or a pining ambition or a carking care. "Oh," says a believer, "I wish I could reach that state." You may reach it: you are on the way to it. Only love Christ more, and be more like him, and you shall be satisfied with favor, and sing, "All my springs are in you"; "My soul, wait only upon God; for my expectation is from him."

I do not mean that the saints find a full content in this world's goods, but that they find such content in God, that with them or without them they live in wealth. A man's life consists not in the abundance of that which he possesses; and many a man who has had next to nothing that could be seen with eyes or handled with hands, has been a very millionaire for true wealth in possessing the kingdom of the most High. The Lord has brought some of us into that state in which we have all things in him; and it is true to us, "They shall not hunger nor thirst."

Then, next, there is such a thing as having *every evil removed* from you while yet in this wilderness. "Neither shall the heat nor sun smite them." Suppose God favors you with prosperity; if you live near to God you will not be rendered proud or worldly minded by your prosperity. Suppose you should become popular because of your usefulness; you will not be puffed up if Christ Jesus is your continual leader and Shepherd. If you live near to him, you will be lowly. If your days are spent in sunlight, and you go from joy to joy, yet still no sunstroke shall smite you. If still you dwell in God, and your heart is full of Christ, and you are led as a sheep by him, no measure of heat shall overpower you. It is a mistake to think that our safety or our danger is according to our circumstances; our safety or our danger is according to our nearness to God or our distance from him. A man who is near to God can stand on the pinnacle of the temple, and the devil may tempt him to throw himself down, and yet he will be firm as the temple itself. A man that is without God may be in the safest part of the road, and traverse a level way, and yet he will stumble. It is not the road, but the Lord that keeps the pilgrim's foot. O heir of heaven, commit your way unto God, and make him your all in all, and rise above the creature into the Creator, and then shall you hunger no more, neither thirst anymore, neither shall the heat nor the sun smite you.

Further, it is said, that on earth we may enjoy *the leading of the Lord*. See how it is put: "For he that hath mercy on them shall lead them." Here we have not quite the same words as in Revelation, for there we read, "The Lamb that is in the midst of the throne shall lead them." Yet the sense is but another shade of the same meaning. Oh, but that is a sweet, sweet name, is it not? "He that hath mercy on them." He has saved them, and so has had mercy on them. Yes, that is very precious, but the word is sweeter still—"he that hath mercy on them," he that is always having mercy on them, he that follows them with mercy all the days of their lives, he that continually pardons, upholds, supplies, strengthens, and thus daily loads them with benefits: "He that hath mercy on them shall lead them."

Do you know, beloved friends, what it is to be led of the Lord? Many are led by their own tastes and fancies. They will go wrong. Others are led by their own judgments. But these are not infallible, and they may go wrong. More are led by other people; these may go right, but it is far from likely that they will. He that is led of God, he is the happy man, he shall not err. He shall be conducted providentially in a right way to the city of habitations. Commit your way unto the Lord: trust also in him, and he will bring it to pass. It may be a rough way, but it must be a right way if we follow the track of the Lord's feet. The true believer shall be led by the Spirit of God in sacred matters: "He will guide you into all truth." He that has mercy on us in other things will have mercy on us by teaching us to profit. We shall each one sing, "He leadeth me in the paths of righteousness for his name's sake." We shall be led into duty and through struggles; we shall be led to happy attainments and gracious enjoyments; we shall go from strength to strength.

In the case of the gracious soul, earth becomes like heaven because he walks with God. He that has mercy on him visits him, communes with him, and manifests himself to him. A shepherd goes before his flock, and the true sheep follow him. Blessed are they who follow the Lamb whithersoever he goes. They have a love to their Lord, and therefore they only want to know which way he would have them go, and they feel drawn along it by the cords of love and the bands of a man. If they can get a glance from their Lord's eye, it suffices them: as it is written, "I will guide thee with mine eye." Every day they stand anxiously attentive to do the King's commandment, be it what it may. They yield themselves and their members to him to be instruments of righteousness, vessels fit for the Master's use. Beloved, this is heaven below. If you have ever tried it, you know it is so. If you have never fully tried it, try it now, and you will find a new joy in it. Jesus says to you, "Take my yoke upon you, and learn of me, and ye shall find rest unto your souls."

I do not know anything more delightful than to be such a fool, as the world will call you, as to yield your intellect to the teaching of the Lord; and to be so weak that you cannot judge but accept his will; and so incapable that even to will and to do must be worked in you of the Lord. Oh, to be so unselfed as to take anything from Christ far more gladly than you would choose of your own accord! If your Lord puts his hand into the bitter box, you will think the potion sweet; and if he scourge, you will thank him for being so kind as to think of you at all. When you get to that point, that you are as a sheep to whom God himself is the Shepherd, it is well with you. Then you will realize, even in the pastures of the wilderness, how the rain from heaven drops upon the inheritance of the Lord and refreshes it when it is weary. "The peace of God, which passeth all understanding, shall keep your hearts and minds through Christ Jesus." God give you to know it, dear friends! I can speak experimentally of it: it is not only the antepast of heaven, but a part of the banquet itself.

But now the last touch is *the drinking at the springhead*. We were not surprised to find, in our description of heaven, that the Lamb led them to the fountains of waters; but we are delighted to find that, here below, "even by the springs of water shall he guide them." Beloved, covet earnestly this drinking at the springs. It is not all who profess to be Christians who will know what I am talking about this morning: they will think I have got into the way of the mystics, and am dreaming of things unpractical. I will not argue with them; let me speak to those who understand me.

Beloved in the Lord, you can even now live upon God himself, and there is no living comparable to it. You can get beyond all the cisterns and come to the river of the water of life, even as they do in heaven. To live by second causes is a very secondary life: to live on the First Cause is the first of living. I exhort you to do this with regard to the inspired Word. This is a day of man's opinions, views, judgments, criticisms. Leave them all, good, bad, and indifferent, and come to this Book, which is the pure fount of inspiration undefiled. When you study the Word of God, live upon it as his Word. I am not going to defend it; it needs no defense. I am not going to argue about its inspiration; if you know the Lord aright, his Word is inspired to you, if to no one else. You know not only that it was inspired when it was written, but that it is inspired still; and, moreover, its inspiration affects you in a way in which no other writings can ever touch you. It breathes upon you; it breathes *life* into you and makes you to speak words *for* God which prove to be words *from* God to other souls. Oh, it is wonderful, if you read the Word of God in a little company, morning by morning—simply read it and pray over it, what an effect it may have upon all who listen! I speak what I do know. If you read the inspired words themselves, and look up to him who spoke them, their spiritual effect will be the witness of their inspiration. This is a miracle-working Book: it may be opposed, but never conquered; it may be buried under unbelief, but it must rise again. Blessed are they to whom the Word is meat and drink. They quit the cistern of man for the fountain of God; and they do well. "By the springs of water shall he guide them."

Yet I would exhort you not even to tarry at the letter of God's Word, but believingly and humbly advance to drink from the Holy Ghost himself. He will not teach you anything which is not in the Bible, but he will take of the things of Christ and will show them unto you. A truth may be like a jewel in the Word of God, and yet we may not see its brilliance until the Holy Spirit holds it up in the light and bids us mark its luster. The Spirit of God brings up the pearl from the deeps of revelation, and sets it where its radiance is perceived by the believing eye. We are such poor scholars that we learn little from the Book till "the Interpreter, one of a thousand," opens our heart to the Word, and opens the Word to our heart. The Holy Ghost who revealed truth in the Book must also personally reveal it to the individual. If ever you get a hold of truth in that way, you will never give it up. A man who has learned truth from one minister may unlearn it from another minister; but he that has been taught it of the Holy Ghost has a treasure which no man takes from him.

Beloved, we would exhort you to drink of the springs of living water while you are here. Be often going back to fundamental doctrines. Especially get back to the consideration of covenant engagements. Whence come all the deeds of mercy from God our Father, and from our Lord Jesus Christ? Come they not from eternal purposes and from that covenant, "ordered in all things, and sure," made ere the earth was, between the Father and the ever-blessed Son? Get you often to the well of the covenant. I know of nothing that can make you so happy as to know in your very soul how the Father pledged himself by oath to the Son, and the Son pledged himself to the eternal Father concerning the great mystery of our redemption. Eternal love and covenant faithfulness: these are ancient wells. Do not hesitate to drink deep at the fountain of electing love. The Lord himself chose you, having loved you with an everlasting love. Everything comes to the saints "according as he hath chosen us in him before the foundation of the world." The Philistines have stopped this well full many a time, but they cannot prevent its waters bubbling up from among the stones which they have cast into it. There it stands. "I have loved thee with an everlasting love: therefore with loving-kindness have I drawn thee." Get you back to the love that had no cause but the First Cause, to the love that knows no change, to the love that knows no limit, no hesitancy, no diminution, the love that stands, like the Godhead itself, eternal and immovable. Drink from eternal springs; and if you do so, your life will be more and more "as the days of heaven upon the earth." God grant us to get away from the deceitful brooks to "the deep which lieth under," and with joy may we draw water.

Christ's presence and fountain drinking—give me these two things, and I ask no more. The Lamb to feed me and the fountain to supply me; these are enough. Lord, whom have I in heaven but thee? Come poverty, come sickness, come shame, come casting out by brethren; yes, come death itself, nothing can I want, and nothing can harm me if the Lamb be my Shepherd and the Lord my fountain.

Before another Sunday some of us may be in heaven. Before this month has finished, some of us may know infinitely more about the eternal world than the whole assembly of divines could tell us. Others of us may have to linger here a while. Yet are we not in banishment. Here we dwell with the King for his work. We will endeavor to keep close to our Master, and if we may serve him and see his face, we will not grudge the glorified their fuller joys.

You that know nothing about these things, God grant you spiritual sense to know that you do not know, and then give you further grace to pray to him, "Lord, lead me to the living fountains." There is an inner life; there is a heavenly secret; there is a surpassing joy—some of us know it—we wish that you, also, had it. Cry for it. Jesus can give it to you at once. Believe in the Lord Jesus Christ, and you shall live forever. The new birth goes with faith in Christ. May he give it to you this morning, and may you begin to be heavenly here, that you may be fit for heaven hereafter. The Lord bless you, dear friends, for Jesus' sake! Amen.

Saints in Heaven and Earth, One Family

Delivered on Lord's Day morning, August 8, 1875, at the Metropolitan Tabernacle, Newington. No. 1249.

The whole family in heaven and earth. —EPHESIANS 3:15

Bereavements are among the sorest griefs of this mortal life. We are permitted by God to love those whom he gives to us, and our heart eagerly casts its tendrils around them, and therefore when suddenly the beloved objects are withdrawn by death, our tenderest feelings are wounded. It is not sinful for us to lament the departure of friends, for Jesus wept; it would be unnatural and inhuman if we did not mourn for the departed—we should be less feeling than the beasts of the field. The Stoic is not a Christian and his spirit is far removed from that of the tenderhearted Jesus.

The better the friend, the greater our regret at his loss, although there also lie within that fact more abundant sources of consolation. The mourning for Josiah was very sore because he was so good a prince. Because Stephen was so full of the Holy Ghost, and so bold for the faith, devout men carried him to his burial and made great lamentation over him. Dorcas was wept for and bewailed because of her practical care for the poor. Had they not been true saints, the mourning had not been so great; and yet, had they been wicked, there had been graver cause for woe. Brethren, we cannot but sorrow this day, for the Lord has taken away a sister, a true servant of the church, a consecrated woman who'll be honored above many, and to whom he gave many crowns of rejoicing; and we cannot but sorrow all the more, because so loving a mother in Israel has fallen asleep, so useful a life has come to a close, and so earnest a voice is hushed in silence. I have this day lost from my side one of the most faithful, fervent, and efficient of my helpers, and the church has lost one of her most useful members.

Beloved, we need comfort. Let us seek it where it may be found. I pray that we may view this source of grief, not with our natural, but with our spiritual eyes. The things external are for the natural eye, and from that eye they force full many a tear, for in his natural life man is the heir of sorrow; but there is an inward and spiritual life which God has given to believers, and this life has an inner eye, and to this inner eye there are other scenes presented than the senses can perceive. Let that spiritual vision indulge itself now. Close your eyes as much as your tears will permit you to the things which are seen, for they are temporal and shadowy and look to the eternal, secret, underlying truths, for these are realities. Take a steady look into the invisible, and the text, I think, sets before us something to gaze upon which may minister comfort to us. The saints in heaven, though apparently sundered from us, are in reality one with us; though death seems to have made breaches in the church of God, it is in fact perfect and entire; though the inhabitants of heaven and believers on earth might seem to be two orders of beings, yet in truth they are "one family."

> Let all the saints terrestrial sing,
> With those to glory gone;
> For all the servants of our King
> In earth and heaven, are one.

So sings the poet. The text tells us that there is a "whole family"; it speaks not of a broken family, nor of two families, but of "the whole family in heaven and earth." It is one undivided household still, notwithstanding all the graves which crowd the cemetery. To this thought I shall call your attention, hoping that thereby you may enter into that "one communion," in which saints above are bound up with saints below. I invite you to consider the ties which bind us to those who have gone before, and the indissoluble kinship in Christ which holds us as much as ever in one sacred unity.

1. First, let us think of *the points of this great family union.*

In what respects are the people of our God in heaven and earth our family? We answer, in very many; for their family relationship is so ancient, so certain, and so paramount, that it may be seen in a vast variety of ways.

Let us note, first, concerning those in heaven and earth whom the Lord loves that their names are all *written in our family register.* That mystical roll which eye has not seen contains all the names of his chosen. They are born by degrees, but they are chosen at once; by one decree set apart from the rest of mankind, by one declaration, "They shall be mine," separated forever as hallowed things unto the most High. "Blessed be the God and Father of our Lord Jesus Christ, who hath blessed us with all spiritual blessings in heavenly places in Christ: according as he hath chosen us in him before the foundation of the world, that we should be holy and without blame before him in love: having predestinated us unto the adoption of children by Jesus Christ to himself, according to the good pleasure of his will, to the praise of the glory of his grace, wherein he hath made us accepted in the beloved." We like to keep our own family registers; we are pleased to look back to the place where our parents recorded our names with those of our brothers and sisters. Let us gaze by faith upon that great book of life where all the names of the redeemed stand indelibly written by the hand of everlasting love, and as we read those beloved names let us remember that they make but one record. The faithful of modern times are on the same page with the saints of the Old Testament, and the names of the feeblest among us are written by the same hand which inscribed the apostles and the martyrs. We confidently believe that Mrs. Bartlett's name is found in the same roll which contains yours, my sister, though you may be the most obscure of the Lord's daughters. "Even as ye are called in one hope of your calling," so were you all comprehended in one election of grace.

The saints above and below are also *one family in the covenant*, "ordered in all things and sure," made with them in the person of their one great federal Head, the Lord Jesus Christ. Sadly one are all the members of the human race in our first father, Adam, for in Adam we all fell. We realize that we are one family by the common sweat of the face, the common tendency to sin, the common liability to death: but there is a second Adam, and all whom he represented are most surely one family beneath his blessed headship. What the Lord Jesus has accomplished was achieved for all his people; his righteousness is theirs, his life is theirs, his resurrection is the pledge of their resurrection, his eternal life is the source and guarantee of their immortal glory.

> With him, their Head, they stand or fall—
> Their life, their surety, and their all.

Let us think how close we are together then, for we are in very truth nearer to the saints in heaven than we are to the ungodly with whom we dwell. We are in one covenant headship with just men made perfect, but not with the unregenerate. We are fellow citizens with the glorified, but we are strangers and foreigners among worldlings. Christ Jesus represented us even as he represented the glorified ones in the old eternity, when the covenant was signed, and in that hour when the covenant stipulations were fulfilled upon the bloody tree, and he represents us with the glorified ones still as he takes possession of the inheritance in the names of all his elect and dwells in the glory which he is preparing for his one church.

It is sweet to remember that all the saints in heaven and earth have *the covenant promises secured to them by the selfsame seal*. You know the seal of the covenant; your eyes delight to dwell upon it; it is the sacrifice of the bleeding Lamb. And what, my brethren, is the ground of the security of the saints above, but the covenant of divine grace, sealed and ratified by the blood of the Son of God? We are rejoiced to see that, in the Epistle to the Hebrews, in connection with the spirits of just men made perfect, the Holy Spirit mentions Jesus the mediator of the new covenant, and the blood of sprinkling, which speaks better things than that of Abel. The promise and the oath of God, those two immutable things, in which it is impossible for God to lie, are given to all the heirs of promise whether they be militant or triumphant, and to them all has the Lord said, "I will be to them a God, and they shall be to me a people." Glory be to his name, the blood which is the ground of our hope of heaven guarantees to the perfected that they shall abide in their bliss. They are there as the "redeemed from among men," which we also are this day. That same blood which has made white their robes has also cleansed us from all sin.

The family in heaven and earth, again, will be plainly seen to be one if you remember that they are *all born of the same Father*, each one in process of time. Every soul in heaven has received the new birth, for that which is born of the flesh cannot inherit a spiritual kingdom, and therefore even babes snatched away from the womb and before yet they had fallen into actual sin, have entered heaven by regeneration. All there, whether they lived to old age or died in childhood, have been begotten again into a lively hope by the resurrection of Jesus Christ from the dead, and are born as to their heavenly state, not of blood, nor of the will of the flesh, nor of the will of man, but of God.

The nature of all regenerate persons is the same, for in all it is the living and incorruptible seed which lives and abides forever. The same nature is in the saints above as in the saints below. They are called the sons of God and so are we; they delight in holiness and so also do we; they are of the church of the firstborn and so are we; their life is the life of God and so is ours; immortality pulses through our spirits as well as through theirs. Not yet, I grant, is the body made immortal, but as to our real life we know who has said, "Whosoever liveth and believeth in me shall never die." Is it not written, "Ye are made partakers of the divine nature, having escaped the corruption which is in the world through lust"? I know there is no higher nature than the divine, and this is said to have been bestowed upon the saints below. The new life in heaven is more developed and mature; it has also shaken off its dust, and has put on its beautiful garments, yet it is the same. In the sinner born to God but yesterday there is a spark of the same fire which burns in the breasts of the glorified above. Christ is in the perfected and the same Christ is in us, for we are "all of one" and he calls us all brethren. Of the same Father begotten, into the same nature born, with the same life quickening us, are we not one family? Oh, it needs but little alteration in the true saint below to make him a saint above. So slight the change that in an instant it is accomplished. "Absent from the body and present with the Lord." The work has proceeded so far that it only remains for the Master to give the last touch to it, and we shall be meet for glory and shall enter into the heavenly rest with capacities of joy as suitable for heaven as the capacities of those who have been there these thousand years.

We are one yet further brethren, because all saints, whether in heaven or earth, are *partakers in the same divine love*. "The Lord knoweth them that are his," not merely those in heaven but those below. The poor struggling child of God in poverty is as well known by God as you bright songster who walks the golden streets. "The eyes of the Lord are upon the righteous, and his ears are open to their cry." I tell you, timid, trembling woman, humbly resting on your Savior, that you are as truly beloved of God as Abraham, Isaac, and Jacob, who sit down at his table in glory. The love of God toward his children is not affected by their position, so that he loves those in heaven better and those on earth less. God forbid. You, being evil, are not so partial as to bestow all your love upon a son who has prospered in the world, and give none of it to another who is bearing the burden of poverty. Our great Father loves the world of his elect with love surpassing thought and has given himself to each one of them to be the portion of each individual forever. What more can he do for those in heaven? What less has he done for us? Jesus has engraved the names of all the redeemed upon his hands and heart, and loves them all unto perfection. If then they all dwell in the bosom of God as the dearly beloved of his soul, are they not indeed one family?

As they all receive the same love so are they all *heirs of the same promises* and the same blessed inheritance. I am bold to say that as a believer in Christ, heaven is as much mine as it is Paul's or Peter's; they are there to enjoy it, and I am waiting to obtain it, but I hold the same title deeds as they do, and as an heir of God, and joint heir with Jesus Christ, my heritage is as broad and as sure as theirs. Their only right to heaven lay in the grace of God which brought them to believe in Jesus; and if we also have been brought by grace to believe in Jesus, our title to eternal glory is the same as theirs. O child of God, do not think that the Lord has set apart some very choice and special blessings for a few of his people—all things are yours. The land is before you, even the land which flows with milk and honey, and the whole of it is yours, though you may be less than the least of all saints. The promise is sure to all the seed, and all the seed have an interest in it. Remember that blessed passage. "If children, then heirs, heirs of God, joint heirs with Jesus Christ"—not if full-grown children, not if well-developed children, not if strong, muscular children, but "if children," and that is all; regeneration proves you to be heirs, and alike heirs, for there can be no difference in the heirship if they are all heirs of God and joint heirs with Jesus Christ. Will you think of this, you who are little in Israel? You who rank with the Benjamites, will you sit down and think of this? You are one of the same family as those bright spirits who shine as the stars forever and ever, and their inheritance is also yours, though as yet you have not come of age, and like a minor must wait till you have been trained under tutors and governors and educated for heaven. You are a prince, though as yet an infant; one of the Redeemer's kings and priests, as yet uncrowned; waiting, waiting, but still secure of the inheritance; tarrying till the day breaks and the shadows flee away, but sure that in the morning the crown of life so long reserved will be brought forth, and you also shall sit with Jesus on his throne.

So might I continue showing the points in which the saints above and the saints below are akin, but this last must suffice.

They are all members of one body, and are necessary to the completion of one another. In the Epistle to the Hebrews we are told concerning the saints above that "they without us cannot be made perfect." We are the lower limbs as it were of the body, but the body must have its inferior as well as its superior members. It cannot be a perfect body should the least part of it be destroyed. Hence it is declared that in the dispensation of the fullness of time, he will gather together in one all things in Christ, both which are in heaven and which are on earth. The saints above with all their bliss must wait for their resurrection until we also shall have come out of great tribulation; like ourselves they are waiting for the adoption, to wit, the redemption of the body. Until all who were predestinated to be conformed to the image of the First-born shall have been so conformed, the church cannot be complete. We are linked to the glorified by bonds of indispensable necessity. We think that we cannot do without them, and that is true; but they also cannot do without us. "As the body is one and has many members, and all the members of that one body, being many are one body, so also is Christ." How closely this brings us together. Those for whom we sorrow cannot be far away, since we are all "the body of Christ and members in particular." If it be dark, my hand knows that the head cannot be far off, nor can the foot be far removed: eye, ear, foot, hand, head, are all comprised within the limits of one body; and so if I cannot see my beloved friend, if I shall not again hear her pathetic voice on earth, nor see her pleading tears, yet am I sure she is not far away, and that the bond between us is by no means snapped, for we are members of our Lord's body, of which it is written, "not a bone of him shall be broken." Thus have I according to my ability set forth some of the points of this family union; may the Holy Spirit give us to know them for ourselves.

2. Let us now speak upon *the inseparableness of this union.*

"The whole family in heaven and earth," not the two families nor the divided family, but the whole family in heaven and earth. It appears at first sight as if we were very effectually divided by the hand of death. Can it be that we are one family when some of us labor on and others sleep beneath the greensward? There was a great truth in the sentence which Wordsworth put into the mouth of the little child when she said, "O master, we are seven."

> *"But they are dead: those two are dead!*
> *Their spirits are in heaven!"*
> *'Twas throwing words away, for still*
> *The little maid would have her will,*
> *And said "Nay, we are seven."*

Should we not thus speak of the divine family, for death assuredly has no separating power in the household of God. Like the apostle, we are persuaded that death cannot separate us from the love of God. The breach caused by the grave is only apparent; it is not real, the family is still united: for if you think of it, when there is a loss in a family, the father is bereaved, but you cannot conceive of our heavenly Father's being bereaved. Our Father which are in heaven, you have lost none of your children. We wept and went to the grave, but you did not, for your child is not dead; rather had your child come closer unto your bosom to receive a sweeter caress, and to know more fully the infinity of your love! When a child is lost from a family, the elder brother is a mourner, for he has lost one of his brethren. But our Elder Brother is not bereaved; Jesus has lost none of his; no, has he not rather brought home to himself his own redeemed? Has he not rejoiced exceedingly to see his good work perfected in one whom he loved? There is no break toward the Father, and no break toward the Elder Brother, and therefore it must be our mistake to fancy that there is any break at all. It cannot be that death divides our Israel; were not the tribes of Reuben and Gad and Manasseh one with the rest of Israel, though the Jordan rolled between? It is a *whole* family, that redeemed household in heaven and in earth.

How little death prevents actual intercourse it is impossible for us to tell. Some attractive, but worthless, books have been written pretending to unfold to us the connection between departed spirits and ourselves, but I trust you will not be led into such idle speculations. God has not revealed these things to us, and it is not for us to go dreaming about them, for we may dream ourselves into grievous errors if we once indulge our fancies. We know nothing about the commerce of the glorified with earth, but we do know that all departed saints are supremely blessed, and that they are with Christ; and if they be with Christ, and we are with Christ, we cannot be far from each other. We meet all the saints of every age whenever we meet with God in Christ Jesus. In fellowship with Jesus you are come unto the city of the living God, the heavenly Jerusalem, and to an innumerable company of angels, to the general assembly and church of the Firstborn, whose names are written in heaven, and to the spirits of just men made perfect. It is impossible to restrict our communion with the people of God by the bounds of sect, race, country, or time, for we are vitally one with them all. Come, brethren, let us join our hands with those who have gone before, and let us with equal love join hands with those below, who before long will be numbered with the selfsame company. Death has removed part of the family to an upper room, but we are one family still: there may be two brigades, but we are one army; we may feed in two pastures, but we are only one flock; we may dwell awhile in separate habitations, but one homestead will before long receive us all.

As a matter which grows out of death, it may be well to say that *space* makes no inroads into the wholeness of the Lord's family. So far as spirits are limited to place, there must be a vast distance between the saint in heaven and the saint on earth; but we ought to remember that space, which seems vast to us, is not vast relatively, either as to God or to spiritual beings. Space is but the house of God; no, God comprehends all space, and space, therefore, is but the bosom of the Eternal. Space also is scarcely to be reckoned when dealing with spiritual beings. We can love and commune with those who are across the Atlantic with as much ease as we can have fellowship with those in the next house. Our friends in Australia, though on the other side of the world, are by no means too distant for our spiritual embrace. Thought flies more swiftly than electricity; spirits defy space and annihilate distance; and we, in spirit, still meet with the departed in our songs of praise, rejoicing with them in our Lord Jesus Christ. Space does not divide: there are many mansions, but they are all in our Father's house.

And, dear brethren, it is such a great mercy that sin, that greatest of all separators, does not now divide us; for we are made near by the blood of Christ. When we think of those bright spirits before the throne, they seem to be of a superior race to us, and we are half tempted to bow at their feet; but this feeling is rebuked in us, as it was in John, by the voice which said, "See thou do it not; I am of thy fellow servants, the prophets: worship God." They are one with us, after all; for they have washed their robes and made them white in the blood of the Lamb, and that is exactly what we have done. Beloved in Christ, we are already justified and accepted in the beloved as much as the glorified. The veil is rent for us as well as for them, the dividing mountains of sin are overturned for us as well as for them. Sinners as we are, we have access to God by the blood of Jesus, and with joy we draw near the throne. They have attained to perfectness, and we are following after: they see the Lord face to face, but we also who are pure in heart have grace given us to see God. The atoning blood has removed the middle wall, and we are one in Christ Jesus.

Neither do *errors* and failures of understanding divide the family of God; if, indeed, they did, who among us could be of the same family as those who know even as they are known? The little child makes a thousand mistakes, and his elder brethren smile sometimes, but they do not deny that he is their brother because he is so ignorant and childish. Even so, dear brothers and sisters, we know very little now; like the apostle we may each one say, "I spoke as a child, I understood as a child, I thought as a child." For now we see through a glass darkly, and only know in part, but this does not disprove our kinship with those who see "face to face." We are of the same school, though on a lower form, and it is written, "All thy children shall be taught of the Lord." What they know they learned at those same feet at which we also sit.

Neither can *sorrow* separate us. Ah, they know no tears, their griefs are ended and their toils, but we must abide awhile in the stern realities of life's battle, to wrestle, and to suffer; but it is evident that we are not divided from them, for we are all spoken of in one sentence, as "These are they that are coming out of great tribulation," for so the translation may run. Those who are already arrived and those who are on the way are described as one company. The sick child is of the same family as his brother in perfect health; soldiers who are enduring the brunt of the battle are of the same army as those who have gained their laurels. To deny that your warring soldier is a part of the host would be a great mistake; to say that he is not of the army because he is in the midst of the conflict would be cruel and false. The saints militant are of the same host as the triumphant; those who are suffering are of the same company as the beatified. None of these things part us—we are still one family in Christ Jesus. Who shall separate us?

ʃ deep interest now comes before us—*the present display
on.*

ʃe have been speaking of our being one family, but perhaps it appears to
ˌ ˌ to be only a pleasing theory, and therefore we will notice certain points in
which our unity practically appears.

I like to think, first, that the *service* of those who have departed blends
with ours. I do not mean that they can descend to earth to preach and teach
and labor, but I do mean this, that they being dead, yet speak; their service projects itself beyond this life. A good man is not dead as to his influential life and
real service for God as soon as the breath leaves his body; his work has a
momentum in it which makes it roll on: his influence abides. "Even in their
ashes live their wonted fires." A very large part of the power which the Holy
Spirit gives to the church is found in the form of influence derived from the
testimonies and examples of departed saints. Today the church of God feels
the influence of Paul and Peter; at this very moment the work of the apostles
is telling upon the nations. Is it not certain that the energetic souls of Luther
and Calvin have left vital forces behind them which throb and pulsate still?
Perhaps the Reformers are doing as much today as they did when they were
alive. So each man, according to his talent and grace, leaves behind him not
merely his arrow and his bow, his sword and his shield, for other hands to use;
but the arrows which he shot before he died are still flying through the air, and
the javelin which he hurled before his hand was paralyzed in death is yet piercing through the bucklers of the foe. The influence of my dear sister, Mrs.
Bartlett, will operate upon some of you as long as you live; and you will trans-
mit it to your successors. You Christians will be the more intense because of
her glowing example; and you sinners will find it the harder to live in sin
when you remember her tearful warnings. Some of you, I do not doubt, will
be her posthumous children, born unto her after she has entered into her rest.
Do not let the living think that they are the sole champions in this holy war,
for, to all intents and purposes, the spirits of the just made perfect stand side
by side with them; and the battle is being carried on, in no small measure, by
cannon which they cast and weapons which they forged. Though the builders
be absent in body, yet the gold, silver, and precious stones which they built
their Lord will establish forever.

Then again, we are one family in heaven and earth, and that very visibly,
because the influence of *the prayers* of those in heaven still abides with us. Do
not mistake me, I am no believer in the intercession of the saints above. I

believe that they pray, but I believe it to be a damnable error to urge anyone to seek their intercession. What I mean is very different. I mean that prayers offered while they were here, and unanswered in their lifetime, still remain in the church's treasury of prayer. Many a mother dies with her children unsaved, but the prayers she continually offered for them will prevail after her death. Many a minister, and many a private member, pleads with God for blessing on the church, and perhaps does not see it; but prayer must be answered, and fifty years afterward it is possible that the church will reap the result of those supplications. Is not Scotland today the better and the holier for the prayers of John Knox? Is not England the brighter for the prayers of Latimer and Ridley? The august company of the glorified have ceased to kneel with us in person, but in effect they do so. They have gone to other work, but the incense which they kindled when they were below still perfumes the chambers of the church of God.

Further, the unity of the church will be seen in this, that their *testimony* from above blends with ours. The church is ordained to be a witness. My brethren, we try to witness as God helps us to the truth as it is in Jesus, even as those who are above once witnessed with us here in life and in death. What a sweet witness dying Christians often bear when they cannot speak, in the gleam of the eye, in the perfect rest of soul, which others may well envy, enjoyed just in the moment when pain was most severe, and the flesh was failing. But now that these spirits have entered within the veil, do they cease their testimony? No. Hear them. They bear witness to the Lamb, saying, "for thou wast slain and hast redeemed us to God by thy blood." They make known to angels and principalities and powers in heavenly places the manifold wisdom of God, according to the eternal purpose which he purposed in Christ Jesus our Lord. We are engaged with them in revealing the abundant mercy and all-sufficiency of the Lord. You are comrades with us, you shining ones; you are fellow witnesses for Jesus, and therefore you are one with us. The main employment of saints above is *praise*. Beloved, what is ours but praise too? Is it not well put by our poet?

> They sing the Lamb in hymns above,
> And we in songs below.

Their music is sweeter than ours, freer from discord, and from all that is cold or wandering, but still the theme is the same, and the song springs from the same motive and was wrought in the heart by the same grace. I think I shall never praise my Lord in heaven more sincerely than I often praise him now, when my mouth cannot speak for the overfloodings of my soul's delight and joy in my God, who has taken me up out of the horrible pit and out of the miry clay, and set my feet upon a rock, and established my goings, and put a new song into my mouth. The deep obligations of every day overwhelm me with indebtedness; I cannot but praise my God, when I think of dire necessities perpetually supplied, multiplied sin continually pardoned, wretched infirmity graciously helped. Yes, we are one family, because when holy worship goes up into the ear of the Eternal, our praise blends with the praise of those who are glorified above, and we are one.

Brethren, I believe we are one in some other points as well. Do you not rejoice over sinners? Is it not one of our holidays on earth when the prodigal returns? "Verily I say unto you, there is joy in the presence of the angels of God over one sinner that repenteth." Do you ever cry out against sin and groan because of the power of error in the land? Know you not that the souls under the altar also cry with the selfsame indignation, "O Lord, how long! Wilt thou not judge and avenge thine own elect?" Do you not expect each day the coming of your Lord, and look for it with rapture? They also do the same. They say there is no hope in heaven, but who told them so? The saints, like ourselves, are looking for the blessed hope, the glorious appearing of our Lord and Savior Jesus Christ. Your joy, your desire, your hope, are not these the same as theirs before the throne?

Towering over all is the fact that *the Well Beloved [One] is the common joy of saints in heaven and on earth.* What makes *their* heaven? Who is the object of all their worship? Who is the subject of all their songs? In whom do they delight themselves all the day long? Who leads them to living fountains of waters and wipes all tears from their eyes? Beloved, he is as much all in all to us as he is to them. Jesus, *we* know you, and *they* know you; Jesus, we love you, and they love you; Jesus, we embrace you, and they embrace you; Jesus, we are oftentimes lost in you, and they are lost in you—you Sun of our soul, you Life of our life, you Light of our delight, you are that to us which you are to them, and herein we are all one.

4. Last of all, there is to come, before long, *a future manifestation of this family union,* much brighter than anything we have as yet seen.

We are one family, and we shall meet again. If they cannot come to us, we shall go to them by and by. It does not often happen that we carry to the grave one who is known to all this congregation, but seldom does a week pass but what one or other of our number, and frequently two or three, are taken home. I have to look upon you and upon myself as so many shadows, and when I meet you, how often does the question occur to me, "Who will go next?" Naturally, I think of some of you who have grown gray in your Master's service, and have passed your threescore years and ten. You must go soon, my brethren and my sisters; and I know you are not grieved at the prospect. Yet the young as well as the old are taken home, and men in middle life, with the marrow moist in their bones, are removed, even as those who lean upon their staff for very age.

Who knows but what I may leave you soon? My brother, who knows but that you may be called away? Well, in that blessed day when we leave the earth, we shall perceive that as we were free of the church below, we are citizens of the church above. Whenever some of us enter an assembly of believers, they recognize and welcome us: the like reception awaits us above! We shall be quite at home in heaven, when we get there. Some of you have more friends in heaven than on earth. How few are left of your former friends, compared with the many who have gone above. In the day when you enter into heaven, you will perceive that the church is one family, for they will welcome you heartily and recognize in you a brother, and a friend, and so, together with them, you shall adore your Lord.

Remember there is coming another day in which the family union of the church will be seen, and that is when the trumpet shall sound and the dead shall be raised. It may be that we shall all be of the company of those who sleep, and if so, when the trumpet sounds, the dead in Christ shall rise first, and we shall have our share in the first resurrection. Or, if our Lord should come before we die, we shall be "alive and remain"; but we shall undergo a change at the same moment as the dead are raised, so that this corruptible shall put on incorruption. What a family we shall be when we all rise together, and all the changed ones stand with us, all of one race, all regenerate, all clothed in the white robe of Jesus' righteousness! What a family! What a meeting it will be!

> *How loud shall our glad voices sing,*
> *When Christ his risen saints shall bring*
> *From beds of dust, and silent clay,*
> *To realms of everlasting day.*

Beloved, I cannot dwell upon what glory will follow on earth, but if our Lord shall live and reign on earth a thousand years, and if there shall be set up a great empire, which shall outshine all other monarchies as much as the sun outshines the stars, we shall all share in it, for he will make us all kings and priests unto God, and we shall reign with him upon the earth. Then, when comes the end, and he shall deliver up the kingdom to God, even the Father, and God shall be all in all, we shall forever be with the Lord. My soul anticipates that grandest of all family meetings, when all the chosen shall assemble around the throne of God. It is but a little while and it shall come; it is but the twinkling of an eye and it shall all be matter of fact. We talk of time as though it were a far-reaching thing; I appeal to you gray heads who know what seventy years mean; are they not gone as a watch in the night? Well, let the waiting be prolonged for ten thousand years, if the Lord pleases; the ten thousand years will end, and then forever and forever we shall be as one family where Jesus is. This hope should cheer us. Death, where is your sting? Grave, where is your victory? Cheered by the prospect of an everlasting reunion, we defy you to sadden us! Encouraged by the glory which God has decreed, we laugh at your vain attempts to make breaches in the ranks of the one and indivisible family of the living God!

The practical point is—*do we belong to that family?* I will leave that naked question to work in every heart. Do I belong to that family? Am I born of God? Am I a believer in Jesus? If not, I am an heir of wrath and not in the family of God.

If we do belong to the family, *let us show our relationship* by loving all the members of it. I should not like a brother to be gone to heaven and to reflect that I was unkind to him; I should not like to think that I might have smoothed his pathway, and I did not; or I might have cheered him and refused. Dear brethren, we shall live together in heaven forever; let us love each other now with a pure heart fervently. Help your poor brethren, cheer your desponding sisters; let no man look only on his own things, but every man also on the things of others. Brother, be brotherly; sister, be a true sister. Let us not love in word only, but in deed and in truth, for we shall soon be at home together in our Father's house on high.

Heavenly Rest

⁂

Delivered on Sabbath morning, May 24, 1857, at the Music Hall, Royal Surrey Gardens. No. 133.

There remaineth therefore a rest to the people of God. —HEBREWS 4:9

The apostle proved, in the former part of this and the latter part of the preceding chapter, that there was a rest promised in Scripture called the rest of God. He proved that Israel did not attain that rest; for God swore in his wrath, saying, "They shall not enter into my rest." He proved that this did not merely refer to the rest of the land of Canaan; for he says that after they were in Canaan, David himself speaks again in after ages concerning the rest of God, as a thing which was yet to come. Again he proves, that "seeing those to whom it was promised did not enter in, because of unbelief, and it remaineth that some must enter in, therefore," says he, "there remaineth a rest to the people of God."

"*My* rest," says God: the rest of God! Something more wonderful than any other kind of rest. In my text it is (in the original) called the *Sabbatism*—not the Sabbath, but the rest of the Sabbath—not the outward ritual of the Sabbath, which was binding upon the Jew, but the inward spirit of the Sabbath, which is the joy and delight of the Christian. "There remaineth therefore"—because others have not had it, because some are to have it—"there remaineth therefore a rest to the people of God."

Now, this rest, I believe, is partly enjoyed on earth. "We that have believed do enter into rest," for we have ceased from our own works, as God did from his. But the full fruition and rich enjoyment of it remains in the future and eternal state of the beatified on the other side the stream of death. Of that it shall be our delightful work to talk a little this morning. And oh! if God should help me to raise but one of his feeble saints on the wings of love to look within the veil and see the joys of the future, I shall be well contented to have made the joy bells ring in one heart at least, to have set one eye flashing with joy, and to have made one spirit light with gladness. The rest of heaven! I shall try first to *exhibit it* and then to *extol it*.

all try to *exhibit* the rest of heaven; and in doing so
>it it, first by way of contrast, and then by way of
1.

To begin then, I shall try to exhibit heaven *by way of contrast*. The rest of
the righteous in glory is now to be contrasted with certain other things.

We will contrast it, first, *with the best estate of the worldling and the sinner.*
The worldling has frequently a good estate. Sometimes his vats overflow, his
barns are crammed, his heart is full of joy and gladness, there are periods with
him when he flourishes like a green bay tree, when field is added to field, and
house to house, when he pulls down his barns and builds greater, when the
river of his joy is full, and the ocean of his life is at its flood with joy and
blessedness. But ah! beloved, the state of the righteous up there is not for a
moment to be compared with the joy of the sinner; it is so infinitely superior,
so far surpassing it, that it seems impossible that I should even try to set it in
contrast. The worldling, when his corn and his wine are increased, has a glad
eye and a joyous heart; but even then he has the direful thought that *he may
soon leave his wealth.* He remembers that death may cut him down, that he
must then leave all his fair riches behind him, and sleep like the meanest of the
land in a narrow coffin, six feet of earth his only heritage. Not so the righteous
man: he has obtained an inheritance which is "undefiled, and that fadeth not
away." He knows that there is no possibility of his losing his joys—

> *He is securely blessed,*
> *Has done with sin, and care, and woe,*
> *And doth with Jesus rest.*

He has no dread of dissolution, no fear of the coffin or the shroud, and so
far the life of heaven is not worthy to be put in comparison with the life of the
sinner. But the worldling, with all his joys, always has *a worm at the root* of
them. You votaries of pleasure! The blush upon your cheek is frequently but
a painted deception. Ah! you sons and daughters of gaiety! The light foot of
your dance is not in keeping with the heavy woe of your miserable spirits. Do
you not confess that if by the excitement of company you for a while forget
the emptiness of your heart, yet silence, and the hour of midnight, and the
waking watches of your bed, bid you sometimes think that there must be
something more blessed than the mere wanderings of gaiety in which you
now are found? You are trying the world, some of you; speak then! Do you not

find it empty? Might it not be said of the world, as an old philosopher said of it when he represented a man with it in his hands smiting it and listening to its ringing? Touch it, touch it! Make it ring again; it is empty. So it is with the world. You know it is so; and if you know it not as yet, the day is coming when after you have plucked the sweets, you shall be pricked with the thorn, and when you shall find that all is unsatisfactory that does not begin and end with God.

Not so the Christian in heaven. For him there are no nights; and if there be times of solitude and rest, he is ever filled with ecstatic joy. His river flows ever full of bliss, without one pebble of sorrow over which it ripples; he has no aching conscience, no "aching void the world can never fill." He is supremely blessed, satisfied with favor, and full with the goodness of the Lord.

And you know, you worldlings, that your best estates often bring you great anxiety, *lest they should depart from you*. You are not so foolish yet as to conceive that riches endure forever. You men of business are frequently led to see that riches take to themselves wings and fly away. You have accumulated a fortune; but you find it is harder to retain than it is to get. You are seeking after a competence; but you find that you grasp at shadows that flit away—that the everlasting vicissitudes of business and the constant changes of mankind are causes of prudent alarm to you, for you fear that you shall lose your gods, and that your gourd shall be eaten by the worm, and fall down, and your shadow shall be taken away.

Not so the Christian. He lives in a house that can never hasten to decay; he wears a crown, the glister of which shall never be dim; he has a garment which shall never wax old; he has bliss that never can depart from him, nor he from it. He is now firmly set, like a pillar of marble in the temple of God. The world may rock, the tempest may sway it like the cradle of a child; but there, above the world, above the perpetual revolution of the stars, the Christian stands secure and immovable; his rest infinitely surpasses yours. Ah, if you shall go to all the fabled luxuries of eastern monarchs, and see their dainty couches and their luscious wines—behold the riches of their pleasantry! How charming is the music that lulls them to their sleep! How gently moves the fan that wafts them to their slumber! But ah!

> I would not change my blessed estate
> For all the world calls good or great;
> And whilst my faith can keep her hold
> I envy not the sinner's gold.

I reckon that the richest, highest, noblest condition of a worldly man is not worthy to be compared with the joy that is to be revealed hereafter in the breasts of those who are sanctified. O you spendthrift mortals, that for one merry dance and a giddy life will lose a world of joys! O fools that catch at bubbles and lose realities! O ten thousand times mad men, that grasp at shadows and lose the substance! What! Sirs, do you think a little round of pleasure, a few years of gaiety and merriment, just a little time of the tossing about, to and fro, of worldly business, is a compensation for eternal ages of unfading bliss? Oh! how foolish will you conceive yourselves to be, when you are in the next state, when cast away from heaven you will see the saints blessed! I think I hear your mournful soliloquy, "Oh! how cheaply did I sell my soul! What a poor price did I get for all I have now lost! I have lost the palace and the crown, and the joy and bliss forever, and am shut up in hell! And for what did I lose it? I lost it for the lascivious wanton kiss. I lost it for the merry drunken song; I lost it for just a few short years of pleasures, which, after all, were only painted pleasures!" Oh! I think I see you in your lost estates, cursing yourselves, rending your hair, that you should have sold heaven for counters [mere change] and have traded away eternal life for pitiful farthings, which were spent quickly and which burned your hand in the spending of them! Oh! that you were wise, that you would weigh those things, and reckon that a life of the greatest happiness here is nothing compared with the glorious hereafter: "There remaineth a rest to the people of God."

Now let me put it in *more pleasing contrast*. I shall contrast the rest of the believer above with the miserable estate of the believer sometimes here below. Christians have their sorrows. Suns have their spots, skies have their clouds, and Christians have their sorrows too. But oh! how different will the state of the righteous be up there, from the state of the believer here! Here the Christian has to suffer anxiety. He is anxious to serve his Master, to do his best in his day and generation. His constant cry is—"Help me to serve you, O my God," and he looks out, day after day, with a strong desire for opportunities of doing good. Ah! if he be an active Christian, he will have much labor, much toil, in endeavoring to serve his Master; and there will be times when he will say, "My soul is in haste to be gone; I am not wearied of the labor; I am wearied in it. To toil thus in the sun, though for a good Master, is not the thing that just now I desire." Ah! Christian, the day shall soon be over, and you shall no longer have to toil; the sun is nearing the horizon; it shall rise again with a brighter day than you have ever seen before. There, up in heaven, Luther has no more to face a thundering Vatican; Paul has no more to run from city to city, and

continent to continent; there Baxter has no more to toil in his pulpit, to preach
with a broken heart to hard-hearted sinners; there no longer has Knox to "cry
aloud and spare not" against the immoralities of the false church; there no
more shall be the strained lung and the tired throat and the aching eye; no
more shall the Sunday school teacher feel that his Sabbath is a day of joyful
weariness; no more shall the tract distributor meet with rebuffs. No, there,
those who have served their country and their God, those who have toiled for
man's welfare, with all their might, shall enter into everlasting rest. Sheathed
is the sword; the banner is furled; the fight is over; the victory won; and they
rest from their labors.

Here, too, the Christian is always *sailing onward*; he is always in motion;
he feels that he has not yet attained. Like Paul he can say, "Forgetting the
things that are behind, I press forward to that which is before." But there his
weary head shall be crowned with unfading light. There the ship that has been
speeding onward shall furl its sails in the port of eternal bliss. There he who
like an arrow has sped his way shall be fixed forever in the target. There we
who like fleeting clouds were driven by every wind shall gently distill in one
perennial shower of everlasting joy. There is no progress, no motion there;
they are at rest; they have attained the summit of the mountain; they have
ascended to their God and our God. Higher they cannot go; they have reached
the *Ultima Thule*; there are no fortunate islands beyond; this is life's utmost end
of happiness; and they furl their sails, rest from their labors, and enjoy themselves forever. There is a difference between the progress of earth and the perfect fixity of the rest of heaven.

Here, too, the believer is often the subject of *doubt and fear*. "Am I his or
am I not?" is often the cry. He trembles lest he should be deceived; at times he
almost despairs and is inclined not to put his name down as one of the children of God. Dark insinuations are whispered into his ears; he thinks that
God's mercy is clean gone forever, and that he will not be mindful of him any
more. Again, his sins sometimes upbraid him, and he thinks God will not have
mercy on him. He has a poor fainting heart; he is like Ready-to-Halt—he has
to go all his way on crutches; he has a poor feeble mind, always tumbling
down over a straw and fearing one day he shall be drowned in a cart rut.
Though the lions are chained he is as much afraid of them as if they were
loose. Hill Difficulty often frightens him, going down into the Valley of
Humiliation is often troublesome work to him. But there, there are no hills to
climb, no dragons to fight, no foes to conquer, no dangers to dread. Ready-to-
Halt, when he dies, will bury his crutches, and Feeble-Mind will leave his fee-
bleness behind him; Fearing will never fear again; poor Doubting-Heart will

learn confidently to believe. Oh, joy above all joys! The day is coming when I shall "know as I am known," when I shall not want to ask whether I am his or not, for in his arms encircled, there shall be no room for doubt. O Christian, you think there are slips between your lips and that cup of joy, but when you grasp the handle of that cup with your hand and are drinking drafts of ineffable delight, then you will have no doubt or fear.

> *There you shall see his face,*
> *And never, never sin.*
> *There from the rivers of his grace,*
> *Drink endless pleasures in.*

Here, too, on earth, the Christian has to suffer; here he has the aching head and the pained body; his limbs may be bruised or broken, disease may rack him with torture; he may be an afflicted one from his birth, he may have lost an eye or an ear or he may have lost many of his powers; or if not, being of a weakly constitution, he may have to spend the most of his days and nights upon the bed of weariness.

Or if his body be sound, yet what suffering he has in his mind! Conflicts between depravity and gross temptations from the evil one, assaults of hell, perpetual attacks of diverse kinds, from the world, the flesh, and the devil. But there, no aching head, no weary heart; there, no palsied arm, no brow plowed with the furrows of old age; there, the lost limb shall be recovered, and old age shall find itself endowed with perpetual youth; there, the infirmities of the flesh shall be left behind, given to the worm and devoured by corruption. There, they shall flit, as on the wings of angels, from pole to pole, and from place to place, without weariness or anguish; there, they shall never need to lie upon the bed of rest, or the bed of suffering, for day without night, with joy unflagging, they shall circle God's throne rejoicing, and ever praise him who has said, "The inhabitants there shall never be sick."

There, too, they shall be free from persecution. Here Sicilian Vespers and St. Bartholomew and Smithfield are well-known words; but there, shall be none to taunt them with a cruel word or touch them with a cruel hand. There, emperors and kings are not known, and those who had power to torture them cease to be. They are in the society of saints; they shall be free from all the idle converse of the wicked, and from their cruel jeers set free forever. Set free from persecution! You army of martyrs, you were slain; you were torn asunder; you were cast to wild beasts; you wandered about in sheepskins and goatskins, destitute, afflicted, and tormented. I see you now, a mighty host. The habiliments [clothes] you wear are torn with thorns; your faces are scarred with sufferings; I see you at your stakes, and on your crosses; I hear your words of submission on your racks; I see you in your prisons; I behold you in your pillories, but—

Now ye are arrayed in white,
Brighter than the noonday sun,
Fairest of the sons of light,
Nearest the eternal throne.

These are they, who "for their Master died, who love the cross and crown"; they waded through seas of blood in order to obtain the inheritance; and there they are, with the bloodred crown of martyrdom about their heads, that ruby brightness, far excelling every other. Yes, there is no persecution there. "There remaineth a rest for the people of God." Alas! In this mortal state, the child of God is also subject to sin; even he fails in his duty and wanders from his God; even he does not walk in all the law of his God blameless, though he desires to do it. Sin now troubles him constantly; but there, sin is dead; there, they have no temptation to sin, from without or from within, but they are perfectly free to serve their Master. Here, the child of God has sometimes to weep repentingly of his backslidings; but there, they never shed tears of penitence, for they have never cause to do so.

And last of all, here, the child of God has to wet the cold ashes of his relatives with *tears*; here, he has to bid adieu to all that is lovely and fair of mortal race; here it is he hears, "earth to earth, and dust to dust, and ashes to ashes," while the solemn music of the dust upon the coffin lid beats doleful time to those words. Here, is the mother buried, the child snatched away, the husband rent from the bosom of a loving wife, the brother parted from the sister. The plate upon the coffin, the last coat of arms of earth, earth's last emblems are here ever before our eyes. But there, never once shall be heard the toll of the funeral bell; no hearse with plumes has ever darkened the streets of gold; no emblems of sorrow have ever intruded into the homes of the immortal; they are strangers to the meaning of death; they cannot die— they live forever, having no power to decay, and no possibility of corruption. O rest of the righteous, how blessed are you, where families shall again be bound up in one bundle, where parted friends shall again meet to part no more, and where the whole church of Christ united in one mighty circle, shall together praise God and the Lamb throughout eternal ages.

Brethren, I have tried thus to set the rest of the righteous in the way of contrast; I feel I have failed. Poor are the words I can utter to tell you of immortal things. Even holy Baxter himself, when he wrote of the *Saints' [Ever-*

lasting] Rest, paused, and said, "But these are only tinklings compared with the full thunders of heaven." I cannot tell you, dear friends, nor can mortal tell, what God has prepared for them that love him.

And now I shall try very briefly to exhibit this contrast *in the way of comparison*. The Christian has some rest here, but nothing compared with the rest which is to come.

There is the *rest of the church*. When the believer joins the church of God, and becomes united with them, he may expect to rest. The good old writer of *The Pilgrim's Progress* says, that when the weary pilgrims were once admitted to the house Beautiful, they were shown to sleep in a chamber called "peace," or "rest." The church member at the Lord's table has a sweet enjoyment of rest in fellowship with the saints; but ah! up there the rest of church fellowship far surpasses anything that is known here; for there are no divisions there, no angry words at the church meetings, no harsh thoughts of one another, no bickerings about doctrine, no fightings about practice. There, Baptist and Presbyterian and Independent and Wesleyan and Episcopalian, serving the same Lord, and having been washed in the same blood, sing the same song and are all joined in one. There pastors and deacons never look coolly on each other; no haughty prelates there, no lofty-minded ministers there, but all meek and lowly, all knit together in brotherhood; they have a rest which surpasses all the rest of the church on earth.

There is, again, a rest of *faith* which a Christian enjoys; a sweet rest. Many of us have known it. We have known what it is, when the billows of trouble have run high, to hide ourselves in the breast of Christ and feel secure. We have cast our anchor deep into the rocks of God's promise; we have gone to sleep in our chamber and have not feared the tempest; we have looked at tribulation and have smiled at it; we have looked at death himself and have laughed him to scorn; we have had much trust by Christian faith that, dauntless and fearless, nothing could move us. Yes, in the midst of calumny, reproach, slander, and contempt, we have said, "I shall not be moved, for God is on my side." But the rest up there is better still—more unruffled, more sweet, more perfectly calm, more enduring, and more lasting than even the rest of faith.

And, again, the Christian sometimes has the blessed rest of *communion*. There are happy moments when he puts his head on the Savior's breast— when, like John, he feels that he is close to the Savior's heart, and there he sleeps. "God giveth his beloved sleep"; not the sleep of unconsciousness, but the sleep of joy. Happy, happy, happy are the dreams we have had on the couch of communion; blessed have been the times, when, like the spouse in

Solomon's song, we could say of Christ, "His left hand was under my head, and with his right hand did he embrace me."

> But sweeter still the fountainhead,
> Though sweet may be the stream.

When we shall have plunged into a very bath of joy, we shall have found the delights even of communion on earth to have been but the dipping of the finger in the cup, but the dipping of the bread in the dish, whereas heaven itself shall be the participation of the whole of the joy, and not the mere antepast of it. Here, we sometimes enter into the portico of happiness; there, we shall go into the presence chamber of the King; here, we look over the hedge and see the flowers in heaven's garden; there, we shall walk between the beds of bliss and pluck fresh flowers at each step; here, we just look and see the sunlight of heaven in the distance, like the lamps of the thousand-gated cities shining afar off, but there, we shall see them in all their blaze of splendor; here, we listen to the whisperings of heaven's melody, borne by winds from afar; but there, entranced, amid the grand oratorio of the blessed, we shall join in the everlasting hallelujah to the great Messiah, the God, the I AM. Oh! again I say, do we not wish to mount aloft and fly away, to enter into the rest which remains to the people of God?

2. And now, yet more briefly, and then we shall have done. I am to endeavor to *extol* this rest, as I have tried to *exhibit* it.

I would extol this rest for many reasons; and oh! that I were eloquent, that I might extol it as it deserves! Oh! for the lip of angel and the burning tongue of cherub, to talk now of the bliss of the sanctified and of the rest of God's people!

It is, first, a *perfect* rest. They are wholly at rest in heaven. Here, rest is but partial. I hope in a little time to cease from everyday labors for a season, but then the head will think, and the mind may be looking forward to prospective labor, and while the body is still, the brain will yet be in motion. Here, on Sabbath days a vast multitude of you sit in God's house, but many of you are obliged to stand and rest but little except in your mind, and even when the mind is at rest, the body is wearied with the toil of standing. You have a weary mile, perhaps many miles, to go to your homes on the Sabbath day. And let the Sabbatarian say what he will, you may work on the Sabbath day, if you work for God; and this Sabbath day's work of going to the house of God is work for God, and God accepts it. For yourselves you may not labor; God commands you to rest, but if you have to toil these three, these four, these five, these six miles, as many of you have done, I will not and I must not blame you. "The priests in the sanctuary profane the Sabbath, and are blameless." It is toil and labor, it is true, but it is for a good cause—for your Master. But there, my friends, the rest is perfect; the body there rests perpetually, the mind too always rests; though the inhabitants are always busy, always serving God, yet they are never weary, never toilworn, never exhausted; they never fling themselves upon their couches at the end of the day, and cry, "Oh! when shall I be away from this land of toil?" They never stand up in the burning sunlight and wipe the hot sweat from their brow; they never rise from their bed in the morning, half refreshed, to go to laborious study. No, they are perfectly at rest, stretched on the couch of eternal joy. They know not the semblance of a tear; they have done with sin, and care, and woe, and with their Savior rest.

Again, it is a *seasonable* rest. How seasonable it will be for some of you! You sons of wealth, you know not the toils of the poor; the callous-handed laborer, perhaps, you have not seen, and you know not how he has to tug and to toil. Among my congregation I have many of a class upon whom I have always looked with pity, poor women who must rise tomorrow morning with the sun and begin that everlasting "stitch, stitch" that works their finger to the bone. And from Monday morning till Saturday night, many of you, my members, and multitudes of you, my hearers, will not be able to lay aside your needle and your thread, except when, tired and weary, you fall back on your chair and are lulled to sleep by your thoughts of labor! Oh! how seasonable will heaven's rest be to you! Oh! how glad will you be, when you get there, to find that there are no Monday mornings, no more toil for you, but rest, eternal rest! Others of you have hard manual labor to perform; you have reason to thank God that you are strong enough to do it, and you are not ashamed of your work; for labor is an honor to a man. But still there are times when you say, "I wish I were not so dragged to death by the business of London life." We have but little rest in this huge city; our day is longer, and our work is harder than our friends in the country. You have sometimes sighed to go into the green fields for a breath of fresh air; you have longed to hear the song of the sweet birds that used to wake you when you were lads; you have regretted the bright blue sky, the beauteous flowers, and the thousand charms of a country life. And perhaps you will never get beyond this smoky city, but remember, when you get up there, "sweet fields arrayed in living green" and "rivers of delight" shall be the place where you shall rest; you shall have all the joys you can conceive of in that home of happiness. And though worn and weary, you come to your grave, tottering on your staff; having journeyed through the wilderness of life like a weary camel, which has only stopped on the Sabbath to sip its little water at the well, or to be baited at the oasis, there you will arrive at your journey's end, laden with gold and spices, and enter into the grand caravansary of heaven, and enjoy forever the things you have wearily carried with you here.

And I must say, that to others of us who have not to toil with our hands, heaven will be a seasonable rest. Those of us who have to tire our brain day after day will find it no slight boon to have an everlasting rest above. I will not boast of what I may do; there may be many who do more; there may be many who are perpetually and daily striving to serve God and are using their mind's best energies in so doing. But this much I may say, that almost every week I have the pleasure of preaching twelve times, and often in my sleep do I think of what I shall say next time. Not having the advantage of laying out my seven shillings and sixpence in buying manuscripts, it costs me hard diligent labor to find even something to say. And I sometimes have a difficulty to keep the hopper full in the mill; I feel that if I had not now and then a rest I should have no wheat for God's children. Still it is on, on, on, and on we must go; we hear the chariot wheels of God behind us, and we dare not stop; we think that eternity is drawing nigh, and we must go on. Rest to us now is more than labor; we want to be at work; but oh! how seasonable it shall be, when to the minister it shall be said—

> *Servant of God, well done!*
> *Rest from thy loved employ;*
> *The battle fought, the victory won,*
> *Enter thy Master's joy.*

It will be seasonable rest. You that are weary with state cares, and have to learn the ingratitude of men; you that have sought honors, and have got them to your cost, you seek to do your best, but your very independence of spirit is called servility, while your servility would have been praised! You who seek to honor God, and not to honor men, who will not bind yourselves to parties, but seek in your own independent and honest judgment to serve your country and your God; you, I say, when God shall see fit to call you to himself, will find it no small joy to have done with parliaments, to have done with states and kingdoms, and to have laid aside your honors, to receive honors more lasting among those who dwell forever before the throne of the most High.

One thing, and then once more, and then farewell. This rest, my brethren, ought to be extolled, because it is *eternal*. Here, my best joys bear "mortal" on their brow; here, my fair flowers fade; here, my sweet cups have dregs and are soon empty; here, my sweetest birds must die, and their melody must soon be hushed; here, my most pleasant days must have their nights; here, the flowings of my bliss must have their ebbs; everything does pass away, but there, everything shall be immortal; the harp shall be unrusted, the crown unwithered, the eye undimmed, the voice unfaltering, the heart unwavering, and the being wholly consolidated unto eternity. Happy day, happy day, when mortality shall be swallowed up of life, and the mortal shall have put on immortality!

And then, last, this glorious rest is to be best of all commended for its *certainty.* "There remaineth a rest to the people of God." Doubting one, you have often said, "I fear I shall never enter heaven." Fear not, all the people of God shall enter there; there is no fear about it. I love the quaint saying of a dying man, who, in his country brogue, exclaimed, "I have no fear of going home; I have sent all before me. God's finger is on the latch of my door, and I am ready for him to enter." "But," said one, "are you not afraid lest you should miss your inheritance?" "No," said he, "no, there is one crown in heaven that the angel Gabriel could not wear; it will fit no head but mine. There is one throne in heaven that Paul the apostle could not fill; it was made for me, and I shall have it. There is one dish at the banquet that I must eat, or else it will be untasted, for God has set it apart for me." O Christian, what a joyous thought! Your portion is secure! "There remaineth a rest." "But cannot I forfeit it?" No, it is entailed. If I be a child of God, I shall not lose it. It is mine as securely as if I were there.

> Come, Christian, mount to Pisgah's top,
> And view the landscape o'er.

See you that little river of death, glistening in the sunlight, and across it do you see the pinnacles of the eternal city? Do you mark the pleasant suburbs and all the joyous inhabitants? Turn your eye to that spot. Do you see where that ray of light is glancing now? There is a little spot there; do you see it? That is your patrimony; that is yours. Oh, if you could fly across, you would see written upon it: "This remains for such a one, preserved for him only. He shall be caught up and dwell forever with God." Poor doubting one, see your inheritance; it is yours. If you believe in the Lord Jesus, you are one of the Lord's people; if you have repented of sin, you are one of the Lord's people; if you have been renewed in heart, you are one of the Lord's people, and there is a place for you, a crown for you, a harp for you. No one else shall have it but yourself, and you shall have it before long. Just pardon me one moment if I beg of you to conceive of yourselves as being in heaven. Is it not a strange thing to think of—a poor clown in heaven? Think, how will you feel with your crown on your head? Weary matron, many years have rolled over you. How changed will be the scene when you are young again. Ah, toilworn laborer, only think when you shall rest forever. Can you conceive it? Could you but think for a moment of yourself as being in heaven now, what a strange surprise would seize you. You would not so as much say, "What! Are these streets of gold? What! Are these walls of jasper?" "What, am I here? In white? Am I here, with a crown on my brow? Am I here singing, that was always groaning? What! I praise God that once cursed him? What! I lift up my voice in his honor? Oh, precious blood that washed me clean! Oh, precious faith that set me free! Oh, precious Spirit that made me repent, else I had been cast away and been in hell! But oh! what wonders! Angels! I am surprised. I am enraptured! Wonder of wonders! Oh! gates of pearls, I long since heard of you! Oh! joys that never fade, I long since heard tell of you! But I am like the Queen of Sheba, the half has not yet been told me. Profusion, oh profusion of bliss! Wonder of wonders! Miracle of miracles! What a world I am in! And oh! that I am here, this is the topmost miracle of all!" And yet 'tis true, 'tis true; and that is the glory of it. It is true. Come, worm, and prove it; come, pall; come shroud; come, and prove it. Then come, wings of faith, come, leap like a seraph; come, eternal ages, come, and you shall prove that there are joys that the eye has not seen, which the ear has not heard, and which only God can reveal to us by his Spirit. Oh! my earnest prayer is that none of you may come short of this rest, but that you may enter into it, and enjoy it forever and ever. God give you his great blessing, for Jesus' sake! Amen.

The Good Man's Life and Death

—◦◦◦—

Delivered on Sabbath morning, August 16, 1857, at the Music Hall, Royal Surrey Gardens. No. 146.

For to me to live is Christ, and to die is gain. —Philippians 1:21

How ominously these words follow each other in the text—"live," "die." There is but a comma between them, and surely as it is in the words so is it in reality. How brief the distance between life and death! In fact there is none. Life is but death's vestibule, and our pilgrimage on earth is but a journey to the grave. The pulse that preserves our being beats our death march, and the blood which circulates our life is floating it onward to the deeps of death. Today we see our friends in health; tomorrow we hear of their decease. We clasped the hand of the strong man, but yesterday and today we close his eyes. We rode in the chariot of comfort but an hour ago, and in a few more hours the last black chariot must convey us to the home of all living.

Oh, how closely allied is death to life! The lamb that sports in the field must soon feel the knife. The ox that lows in the pasture is fattening for the slaughter. Trees do but grow that they may be felled. Yes, and greater things than these feel death. Empires rise and flourish; they flourish but to decay, they rise to fall. How often do we take up the volume of history and read of the rise and fall of empires. We hear of the coronation and the death of kings. Death is the black servant who rides behind the chariot of life. See life! And death is close behind it. Death reaches far throughout this world and has stamped all terrestrial things with the broad arrow of the grave. Stars die perhaps; it is said that conflagrations have been seen far off in the distant ether, and astronomers have marked the funerals of worlds, the decay of those mighty orbs that we had imagined set forever in sockets of silver to glisten as the lamps of eternity. But blessed be God; there is one place where death is not life's brother, where life reigns alone; "to live," is not the first syllable which is to be followed by the next, "to die." There is a land where death knells are never tolled, where winding sheets are never woven, where graves are never dug. Blessed land beyond the skies! To reach it we must die. But if after death we obtain a glorious immortality, our text is indeed true: "to die is gain."

If you would get a fair estimate of the happiness of any man, you must judge him in these two closely connected things, his life and his death. The heathen Solon said, "Call no man happy until he is dead; for you know not what changes may pass upon him in life." We add to that—Call no man happy until he is dead; because the life that is to come, if that be miserable, shall far outweigh the highest life of happiness that has been enjoyed on earth. To estimate a man's condition we must take it in all its length. We must not measure that one thread which reaches from the cradle to the coffin. We must go further; we must go from the coffin to the resurrection, and from the resurrection on throughout eternity. To know whether acts are profitable, I must not estimate their effects on me for the hour in which I live, but for the eternity in which I am to exist. I must not weigh matters in the scales of time; I must not calculate by the hours, minutes, and seconds of the clock, but I must count and value things by the ages of eternity.

Come, then, beloved; we have before us the picture of a man, the two sides of whose existence will both of them bear inspection; we have his life, we have his death: we have it said of his life, *"to live is Christ,"* of his death, *"to die is gain"*; and if the same shall be said of any of you, oh! you may rejoice! You are among that thrice-happy number whom the Lord has loved, and whom he delights to honor.

We shall now divide our text very simply into these two points, *the good man's life* and *the good man's death*.

1. As to *his life,* we have that briefly described thus: "For me to live is Christ."

The believer did not always live to Christ. When he was first born into this world, he was a slave of sin and an heir of wrath, even as others. Though he may have afterward become the greatest of saints, yet until divine grace has entered his heart, he is "in the gall of bitterness and in the bonds of iniquity." He only begins to live to Christ when God the Holy Spirit convinces him of his sin and of his desperate evil nature, and when by grace he is brought to see the dying Savior making a propitiation for his guilt. From that moment when by faith he sees the slaughtered victim of Calvary, and casts his whole life on him, to be saved, to be redeemed, to be preserved, and to be blessed by the virtue of his atonement and the greatness of his grace, from that moment the man begins to live to Christ.

And now shall we tell you as briefly as we can what living to Christ means. It means, first, that *the life of a Christian derives its parentage from Christ.* "For me to live is Christ." The righteous man has two lives. He has one which he inherited from his parents; he looks back to an ancestral race of which he is the branch, and he traces his life to the parent stock; but he has a second life, a life spiritual, a life which is as much above mere mental life, as mental life is above the life of the animal or the plant; and for the source of this spiritual life he looks not to father or mother, nor to priest nor man, nor to himself, but he looks to Christ. He says, "O Lord Jesus, the everlasting Father, the Prince of peace, you are my spiritual parent; unless your Spirit had breathed into my nostrils the breath of a new, holy, and spiritual life, I had been to this day 'dead in trespasses and sins.' I owe my third principle, my spirit, to the implantation of your grace. I had a body and a soul by my parents; I have received the third principle, the spirit from you, and in you I live, and move, and have my being. My new, my best, my highest, my most heavenly life, is wholly derived from you. To you I ascribe it. My life is hid with Christ in God. It is no longer I that live, but Christ that lives in me."

And so the Christian says, "For me to live is Christ," because for me to live is to live a life whose parentage is not of human origin, but of divine, even of Christ himself. Again he intended to say, that *Christ was the sustenance of his life*, the food his newborn spirit fed upon. The believer has three parts to be sustained. The body, which must have its proper nutriment; the soul, which must have knowledge and thought to supply it; and the spirit which must feed on Christ. Without bread I become attenuated to a skeleton, and at last I die; without thought my mind becomes dwarfed and dwindles itself until I become the idiot, with a soul that has just life, but little more. And without Christ my newborn spirit must become a vague shadowy emptiness. It cannot live unless it feeds on that heavenly manna which came down from heaven. Now the Christian can say, "The life that I live is Christ," because Christ is the food on which he feeds and the sustenance of his newborn Spirit.

The apostle also meant that *the fashion of his life was Christ*. I suppose that every man living has a model by which he endeavors to shape his life. When we start in life, we generally select some person, or persons, whose combined virtues shall be to us the mirror of perfection. "Now," says Paul, "if you ask me after what fashion I mold my life, and what is the model by which I would sculpture my being, I tell you, it is Christ. I have no fashion, no form, no model by which to shape my being, except the Lord Jesus Christ. Now, the true Christian, if he be an upright man, can say the same. Understand, however, what I mean by the word "*upright*." An upright man means a straight-up man—a man that does not cringe and bow and fawn to other men's feet; a man that does not lean for help on other men, but just stands with his head heavenward, in all the dignity of his independence, leaning nowhere except on the arm of the Omnipotent. Such a man will take Christ alone to be his model and pattern.

This is the very age of conventionalities. People dare not now do a thing unless everybody else does the same. You do not often say, "Is a thing right?" The most you say is, "Does So-and-So do it?" You have some great personage or other in your family connection who is looked upon as being the very standard of all propriety; and if he do it, then you think you may safely do it. And oh! what an outcry there is against a man who dares to be singular, who just believes that some of your conventionalities are trammels and chains, and kicks them all to pieces and says, "I am free!" The world is at him in a minute; all the bandogs of malice and slander are at him, because he says, "I will not follow your model! I will vindicate the honor of my Master and not take your great masters to be forever my pattern."

Oh! I would to God that every statesman, that every minister, that every Christian were free to hold that his only form, and his only fashion for imitation, must be the character of Christ. I would that we could scorn all superstitious attachments to the ancient errors of our ancestors; and while some would be forever looking upon age and upon hoary antiquity with veneration, I would we had the courage to look upon a thing, not according to its age, but according to its rightness, and so weigh everything, not by its novelty, or by its antiquity, but by its conformity to Christ Jesus and his holy gospel; rejecting that which is not, though it be hoary with years, and believing that which is, even though it be but the creature of the day, and saying with earnestness, "For me to live is not to imitate this man or the other, but 'for me to live is Christ.'"

I think, however, that the very center of Paul's idea would be this: *the end of his life is Christ*. You think you see Paul land upon the shores of Philippi. There, by the riverside, were ships gathered and many merchant men. There you would see the merchant busy with his ledger and overlooking his cargo, and he paused and put his hand upon his brow, and said as he gripped his money bag, "For me to live is gold." And there you see his humbler clerk, employed in some plainer work, toiling for his master, and he, perspiring with work, mutters between his teeth, "For me to live is to gain a bare subsistence." And there stands for a moment to listen to him, one with a studious face and a sallow countenance, and with a roll full of the mysterious characters of wisdom. "Young man," he says, "for me to live is learning." "Aha, aha!" says another, who stands by, clothed in mail, with a helmet on his head, "I scorn your modes of life; for me to live is glory." But there walks one, a humble tentmaker, called Paul; you see the lineaments of the Jew upon his face, and he steps into the middle of them all and says, "For me to live is Christ." Oh! how they smile with contempt upon him, and how they scoff at him, for having chosen such an object! "For me to live is Christ." And what did he mean? The learned man stopped and said, "Christ! Who is he? Is he that foolish, mad fellow, of whom I have heard, who was executed upon Calvary for sedition?" The meek reply is, "It is he who died, Jesus of Nazareth, the King of the Jews." "What?" says the Roman soldier, "and do you live for a man who died a slave's death? What glory will you get by fighting his battles?" "What profit is there in your preaching?" chimes in the trader. Ah! and even the merchant's clerk thought Paul mad, for he said, "How can he feed his family? How will he supply his wants if all he lives for is to honor Christ?" Yes, but Paul knew what he was at. He was the wisest man of them all. He knew which way was right for heaven, and which would end the best. But, right or wrong, his soul was wholly possessed with the idea—"For me to live is Christ."

Brethren and sisters, can you say, as professing Christians, that you live up to the idea of the apostle Paul? Can you honestly say that for you to live is Christ? I will tell you my opinion of many of you. You join our churches; you are highly respectable men; you are accepted among us as true and real Christians; but in all honesty and truth, I do not believe that for you to live is Christ. I see many of you whose whole thoughts are engrossed with the things of earth; the mere getting of money, the amassing of wealth, seems to be your only object. I do not deny that you are liberal; I will not dare to say that you are not generous, and that your checkbook does not often bear the mark of some subscription for holy purposes, but I dare to say, after all, that you cannot in honesty say that you live wholly for Christ. You know that when you go to your shop or your warehouse, you do not think, in doing business, that you are doing it for Christ; you dare not be such a hypocrite as to say so. You must say that you do it for self-aggrandizement and for family advantage. "Well!" says one, "and is that a mean reason?" By no means; not for you, if you are mean enough to ask that question, but for the Christian it is. He professes to live for Christ; then how is it he dares to profess to live for his Master, and yet does not do so, but lives for mere worldly gain?

Let me speak to many a lady here. You would be shocked if I should deny your Christianity. You move in the highest circles of life, and you would be astonished if I should presume to touch your piety, after your many generous donations to religious objects; but I dare to do so. You—what do you do? You rise late enough in the day: you have your carriage out, and call to see your friends or leave your card by way of proxy. You go to a party in the evening; you talk nonsense, and come home and go to bed. And that is your life from the beginning of the year to the end. It is just one regular round. There comes the dinner or the ball, and the conclusion of the day; and then, amen, so be it, forever. Now you don't live for Christ. I know you go to church regularly, or attend at some dissenting chapel; all well and good. I shall not deny your piety, according to the common usage of the term, but I deny that you have got to anything like the place where Paul stood when he said, "For me to live is Christ."

I, my brethren, know that with much earnest seeking I have failed to realize the fullness of entire devotion to the Lord Jesus. Every minister must sometimes chasten himself and say, "Am I not sometimes a little warped in my utterances? Did I not in some sermon aim to bring out a grand thought instead of stating a home truth? Have I not kept back some warning that I ought to have uttered because I feared the face of man?" Have we not all good need to chasten ourselves because we must say that we have not lived for Christ as we should have done? And yet there are, I trust, a noble few, the elite of God's elect, a few chosen men and women on whose heads there is the crown and diadem of dedication, who can truly say, "I have nothing in this world I cannot give to Christ—I have said it, and mean what I have said—

> 'Take my soul and body's powers,
> All my goods and all my hours,
> All I have and all I am.'

Take me, Lord, and take me forever." These are the men who make our missionaries; these are the women to make our nurses for the sick; these are they that would dare death for Christ; these are they who would give of their substance to his cause; these are they who would spend and be spent, who would bear ignominy and scorn and shame if they could but advance their Master's interest. How many of this sort have I here this morning? Might I not count many of these benches before I could find a score? Many there are who do in a measure carry out this principle; but who among us is there (I am sure he stands not here in this pulpit) that can dare to say he has lived wholly for Christ, as the apostle did? And yet, till there be more Pauls and more men dedicated to Christ, we shall never see God's kingdom come, nor shall we hope to see his will done on earth, even as it is in heaven.

Now this is the true life of a Christian, its source, its sustenance, its fashion, and its end, all gathered up in two words, Christ Jesus; and, I must add, its happiness, and its glory, is all in Christ. But I must detain you no longer.

2. I must go to the second point, *the death of the Christian.*

Alas, alas, that the good should die; alas, that the righteous should fall! Death, why do you not hew the deadly upas [tropical Asian tree]? Why do you not mow the hemlock? Why do you touch the tree beneath whose spreading branches weariness has rest? Why do you touch the flower whose perfume has made glad the earth? Death, why do you snatch away the excellent of the earth, in whom is all our delight? If you would use your ax, use it upon the cumber-grounds, the trees that draw nourishment but afford no fruit; you might be thanked then. But why will you cut down the cedars, why will you fell the goodly trees of Lebanon? O death, why do you not spare the church? Why must the pulpit be hung in black; why must the missionary station be filled with weeping? Why must the pious family lose its priest and the house its head? O death, what are you at? Touch not earth's holy things; your hands are not fit to pollute the Israel of God. Why do you put your hand upon the hearts of the elect? Oh, stay you, stay you; spare the righteous, death, and take the bad!

But no, it must not be; death comes and smites the goodliest of us all; the most generous, the most prayerful, the most holy, the most devoted must die. Weep, weep, weep, O church, for you have lost your martyrs; weep, O church, for you have lost your confessors, your holy men are fallen. Howl, fir tree, for the cedar has fallen, the godly fail, and the righteous are cut off. But stay awhile; I hear another voice. Say you thus unto the daughter of Judah, Spare your weeping. Say you thus unto the Lord's flock, Cease, cease your sorrow; your martyrs are dead, but they are glorified; your ministers are gone, but they have ascended up to your Father and to their Father; your brethren are buried in the grave, but the archangel's trumpet shall awake them, and their spirits are ever now with God.

Hear you the words of the text, by way of consolation, "to die is gain." Not such gain as you wish for, you son of the miser; not such gain as you are hunting for, you man of covetousness and self-love; a higher and a better gain is that which death brings to a Christian.

My dear friends, when I discoursed upon the former part of the verse, it was all plain. No proof was needed; you believed it, for you saw it clearly. "To live is Christ" has no paradox in it. But "to die is gain" is one of the gospel riddles which only the Christian can truly understand. To die is not gain if I look upon the merely visible; to die is loss, it is not gain. Has not the dead man lost his wealth? Though he had piles of riches, can he take anything with him? Has it not been said, "Naked came I out of my mother's womb, and naked shall I return there"? "Dust you are, and unto dust shall you return." And which of all your goods can you take with you? The man had a fair estate and a goodly mansion; he has lost that. He can no more tread those painted halls nor walk those verdant lawns. He had abundance of fame and honor; he has lost that, so far as his own sense of it is concerned, though still the harp string trembles at his name. He has lost his wealth, and buried though he may be in a costly tomb, yet is he as poor as the beggar who looked upon him in the street in envy. That is not gain; it is loss, and he has lost his friends: he has left behind him a sorrowing wife and children, fatherless, without his guardian care; he has lost the friend of his bosom, the companion of his youth. Friends are there to weep over him, but they cannot cross the river with him; they drop a few tears into his tomb, but with him they must not and cannot go. And has he not lost all his learning, though he has toiled ever so much to fill his brain with knowledge? What is he now above the servile slave, though he has acquired all knowledge of earthly things? Is it not said,

> "Their memory and their love are lost
> Alike unknowing and unknown"?

Surely death is loss. Has he not lost the songs of the sanctuary and the prayers of the righteous? Has he not lost the solemn assembly and the great gathering of the people? No more shall the promise enchant his ear, no more shall the glad tidings of the gospel wake his soul to melody. He sleeps in the dust, the Sabbath bell tolls not for him, the sacramental emblems are spread upon the table, but not for him. He has gone to his grave; he knows not that which shall be after him. There is neither work nor device in the grave, where we all are hastening. Surely death is loss. When I look upon you, you clay-cold corpse, and see you just preparing to be the palace of corruption and the carnival for worms, I cannot think that you have gained. When I see that your eye has lost light, and your lip has lost its speech, and your ears have lost hearing, and your feet have lost motion, and your heart has lost its joy, and they that look out of the windows are darkened, the grinders have failed, and no sounds of tambourine and of harp wake up your joys, O clay-cold corpse, then have you lost, lost immeasurably. And yet my text tells me it is not so. It says, "to die is gain." It looks as if it could not be thus, and certainly it is not, so far as I can see. But put to your eye the telescope of faith—take that magic glass which pierces through the veil that parts us from the unseen. Anoint your eyes with eye salve, and make them so bright that they can pierce the ether and see the unknown worlds. Come, bathe yourself in this sea of light, and live in holy revelation and belief, and then look, and oh, how changed the scene! Here is the corpse, but there the spirit; here is the clay, but there the soul; here is the carcass, but there the seraph. He is supremely blessed; his death is gain.

Come now, what did he lose? I will show that in everything he lost, he gained far more. He lost his friends, did he? His wife, and his children, his brethren in church fellowship, are all left to weep his loss. Yes, he lost them, but, my brethren, what did he gain? He gained more friends than ever he lost. He had lost many in his lifetime, but he meets them all again. Parents, brethren and sisters who had died in youth or age, and passed the stream before him, all salute him on the further brink. There the mother meets her infant, there the father meets his children, there the venerable patriarch greets his family to the third and fourth generation, there brother clasps brother to his arms, and husband meets with wife, no more to be married or given in marriage, but to live together, like the angels of God.

Some of us have more friends in heaven than in earth. We have more dear relations in glory than we have here. It is not so with all of us, but with some it is so; more have crossed the stream than are left behind. But if it be not so, yet what friends we have to meet us there! Oh, I reckon on the day of death it were much gain if it were for the mere hope of seeing the bright spirits that are now before the throne; to clasp the hand of Abraham and Isaac and Jacob, to look into the face of Paul the apostle, and grasp the hand of Peter; to sit in flowery fields with Moses and David, to bask in the sunlight of bliss with John and Magdalene. Oh, how blessed! The company of poor imperfect saints on earth is good; but how much better the society of the redeemed. Death is no loss to us by way of friends. We leave a few, a little band below, and say to them, "Fear not, little flock," and we ascend and meet the armies of the living God, the hosts of his redeemed. "To die is gain." Poor corpse! You have lost your friends on earth; no, bright spirit, you have received a hundredfold in heaven.

What else did we say he lost? We said he lost all his estate, all his substance and his wealth. Yes, but he has gained infinitely more. Though he were rich as Croesus, yet he might well give up his wealth for that which he has attained. Were his fingers bright with pearls, and has he lost their brilliancy? The pearly gates of heaven glisten brighter far. Had he gold in his storehouse? Mark you, the streets of heaven are paved with gold, and he is richer far. The mansions of the redeemed are far brighter dwelling places than the mansions of the richest here below. But it is not so with many of you. You are not rich; you are poor. What can you lose by death? You are poor here; you shall be rich there. Here you suffer toil; there you shall rest forever. Here you earn your bread by the sweat of your brow; but there, no toil. Here wearily you cast yourself upon your bed at the week's end, and sigh for the Sabbath; but there Sabbaths have no end. Here you go to the house of God, but you are distracted with worldly cares and thoughts of suffering; but there, there are no groans to mingle with the songs that warble from immortal tongues. Death will be gain to you in point of riches and substance.

And as for the *means of grace* which we leave behind, what are they when compared with what we shall have hereafter? Oh, might I die at this hour, I think I would say something like this, "Farewell, Sabbaths; I am going to the eternal Sabbath of the redeemed. Farewell, minister; I shall need no candle, neither light of the sun, when the Lord God shall give me light and be my life forever and ever. Farewell, you songs and sonnets of the blessed; farewell, I shall not need your melodious burst; I shall hear the eternal and unceasing hallelujahs of the beatified. Farewell, you prayers of God's people; my spirit shall hear forever the intercessions of my Lord and join with the noble army of martyrs in crying, 'O Lord, how long?' Farewell, O Zion! Farewell, house of my love, home of my life! Farewell, you temples where God's people sing and pray; farewell, you tents of Jacob, where they daily burn their offering! I am going to a better Zion than you, to a brighter Jerusalem, to a temple that has foundations, whose builder and maker is God!" O my dear friends, in the thought of these things, do we not, some of us, feel as if we could die!

> *E'en now by faith we join our hands*
> *With those that went before,*
> *And greet the blood-besprinkled bands*
> *Upon th' eternal shore.*
>
> *One army of the living God,*
> *At his command we bow,*
> *Part of the host have crossed the flood,*
> *And part are crossing now.*

We have not come to the margin yet, but we shall be there soon: we soon expect to die.

And again, one more thought. We said that when men died, they lost their knowledge; we correct ourselves. Oh no, when the righteous die, they know infinitely more than they could have known on earth.

> *There shall I see and hear and know*
> *All I desired or wished below;*
> *And every power find sweet employ,*
> *In that eternal world of joy.*

"Here we see through a glass darkly, but there face to face." There, what "eye hath not seen nor ear heard" shall be fully manifest to us. There, riddles shall be unraveled, mysteries made plain, dark texts enlightened, hard providences made to appear wise. The meanest soul in heaven knows more of God than the greatest saint on earth. The greatest saint on earth may have it said of him, "Nevertheless he that is least in the kingdom of heaven is greater than he." Not our mightiest divines understand so much of theology as the lambs of the flock of glory. Not the greatest masterminds of earth understand the millionth part of the mighty meanings which have been discovered by souls emancipated from clay. Yes, brethren, "to die is gain." Take away, take away that hearse, remove that shroud; come, put white plumes upon the horses' heads and let gilded trappings hang around them. There, take away that fife, that shrill sounding music of the death march. Lend me the trumpet and the drum. O hallelujah, hallelujah, hallelujah; why weep we the saints to heaven; why need we lament? They are not dead, they are gone before. Stop, stop that mourning, refrain your tears, clap your hands, clap your hands.

> *They are supremely blessed,*
> *Have done with care and sin and woe;*
> *And with their Savior rest.*

What! Weep, weep for heads that are crowned with coronals of heaven? Weep, weep for hands that grasp the harps of gold? What, weep for eyes that see the Redeemer? What, weep for hearts that are washed from sin and are throbbing with eternal bliss? What, weep for men that are in the Savior's bosom? No, weep for yourselves, that you are here. Weep that the mandate has not come which bids *you* to die. Weep that you must tarry. But weep not for them. I see them turning back on you with loving wonder, and they exclaim, "Why weepest thou?" What, weep for poverty that it is clothed in riches? What, weep for sickness that it has inherited eternal health? What, weep for shame that it is glorified; and weep for sinful mortality that it has become immaculate? Oh, weep not, but rejoice. "If ye knew what it was that I have said unto you, and whither I have gone, ye would rejoice with a joy that no man should take from you." "To die is gain." Ah, this makes the Christian long to die—makes him say,

> *Oh, that the word were given!*
> *O Lord of hosts, the wave divide,*
> *And land us all in heaven!*

And now, friends, does this belong to you all? Can you claim an interest in it? Are you living to Christ? Does Christ live in you? For if not, your death will not be gain. Are you a believer in the Savior? Has your heart been renewed, and your conscience washed in the blood of Jesus? If not, my hearer, I weep for you. I will save my tears for lost friends; there, with this handkerchief I'd stanch my eyes forever for my best beloved that shall die, if those tears could save you. Oh, when you die, what a day! If the world were hung in sackcloth, it could not express the grief that you would feel. You *die*. O death! O death! How hideous are you to men that are not in Christ! And yet, my hearer, you shall soon die. Save me your bed of shrieks, your look of gall, your words of bitterness! Oh, that you could be saved the dread hereafter! Oh! the wrath to come! the wrath to come! the wrath to come! who is he that can preach of it? Horrors strike the guilty soul! It quivers upon the verge of death; no, on the verge of hell. It looks over, clutching hard to life, and it hears there the sullen groans, the hollow moans, and shrieks of tortured ghosts, which come up from the pit that is bottomless, and it clutches firmly to life, clasps the physician, and bids him hold, lest he should fall into the pit that burns. And the spirit looks down and sees all the fiends of everlasting punishments, and back it recoils. But die it must. It would barter all it has to gain an hour; but no, the fiend has got its grip, and down it must plunge. And who can tell the hideous shriek of a lost soul? It cannot reach heaven; but if it could, it might well be dreamed that it would suspend the melodies of angels, might make even God's redeemed weep, if they could hear the wailings of a damned soul. Ah! you men and women, you have wept; but if you die unregenerate, there will be no weeping like that, there will be no shriek like that, no wail like that. May God spare us from ever hearing it or uttering it ourselves! Oh, how the grim caverns of Hades startle, and how the darkness of night is frightened, when the wail of a lost soul comes up from the ascending flames, while it is descending in the pit.

"Turn ye, turn ye; why will ye die, O house of Israel?" Christ is preached to you. "This is a faithful saying, and worthy of all acceptation, that Christ Jesus came into the world to save sinners." Believe on him and live, you guilty, vile, perishing; believe and live. But this know—if you reject my message, and despise my Master, in that day when he shall judge the world in righteousness by that man, Jesus Christ, I must be a swift witness against you. I have told you—at your soul's peril reject it. Receive my message, and you are saved; reject it—take the responsibility on your own head. Behold, my skirts are clear of your blood. If you be damned, it is not for want of warning. O God grant you may not perish.

The Unbeliever's Unhappy Condition

Delivered on Lord's Day morning, September 24, 1871, at the Metropolitan Tabernacle, Newington. No. 1012.

He that believeth not the Son shall not see life; but the wrath of God abideth on him. —JOHN 3:36

This is a part of a discourse by John the Baptist. We have not many sermons by that mighty preacher, but we have just sufficient to prove that he knew how to lay the ax at the root of the tree by preaching the law of God most unflinchingly; and also that he knew how to declare the gospel, for no one could have uttered sentences which more clearly contain the way of salvation than those in the text before us. Indeed, this third chapter of the Gospel according to the evangelist John is notable among clear and plain Scriptures—notable for being yet clearer and plainer than almost any other. John the Baptist was evidently a preacher who knew how to discriminate—a point in which so many fail—he separated between the precious and the vile, and therefore he was as God's mouth to the people. He does not address them as all lost nor as all saved, but he shows the two classes; he keeps up the line of demarcation between him that fears God and him that fears him not.

He plainly declares the privileges of the believer; he says he has even now eternal life; and with equal decision he testifies to the sad state of the unbeliever—"he shall not see life; but the wrath of God abideth on him." John the Baptist might usefully instruct many professedly Christian preachers. Although he that is least in the kingdom of heaven is greater than John the Baptist, and ought, therefore, more clearly to bear witness to the truth, yet there are many who muddle the gospel, who teach philosophy, who preach a mingle-mangle which is neither law nor gospel; and these might well go to school to this rough preacher of the wilderness and learn from him how to cry, "Behold the Lamb of God which taketh away the sin of the world."

I desire this morning to take a leaf out of the Baptist's lesson book; I would preach as he did the gospel of the Lord Jesus, "whose shoes I am not worthy to bear." It is my earnest desire to enjoy the delight of expounding to you the deep things of God; I feel a profound pleasure in opening up the blessings of the covenant of grace and bringing forth out of its treasury things new and old. I should be happy to dwell upon the types of the Old Testament, and even to touch upon the prophecies of the New; but, while so many yet remain unsaved, my heart is never content except when I am preaching simply the gospel of Jesus Christ. My dear unconverted hearers, when I see you brought to Christ, I will then advance beyond the rudiments of the gospel; but, meanwhile, while hell is gaping wide, and many of you will certainly help to fill it, I cannot turn aside from warning you. I dare not resist the sacred impulse which constrains me to preach over and over again to you the glad tidings of salvation. I shall, like John, continue laying the ax at the root of the trees and shall not go beyond crying, "Repent ye, for the kingdom of heaven is at hand." As he did, we shall now declare the sad estate of him who believes not the Son of God.

This morning, with the burden of the Lord upon us, we shall speak upon the words of the text. Our first point shall be a discovery of *the guilty one,* "he that believeth not the Son." Next, we shall consider *his offense;* it lies in "not believing the Son"; third, we shall lay bare the *sinful causes which create this unbelief;* and, fourth, we shall show the terrible result of not believing in the Son: "he shall not see life; but the wrath of God abideth on him." May the Spirit help us in all.

1. To begin, then, who is *the guilty one?*

Who is the unhappy man here spoken of? Is he a person to be met with only once in a century? Must we search the crowds through and through to find out an individual in this miserable plight? Ah no! the persons who are here spoken of are common; they abound even in our holy assemblies; they are to be met with by thousands in our streets. Alas, alas! They form the vast majority of the world's population. Jesus has come unto his own, and his own have not received him, the Jewish race remain unbelieving; while the Gentiles, to whom he was to be a light, prefer to sit in darkness and reject his brightness. We shall not be talking this morning upon a recondite theme with only a remote relation to ourselves, but there are many here of whom we shall be speaking, and we devoutly pray that the word of God may come with power to their souls.

The persons here spoken of are those who believe not the Son of God. Jesus Christ, out of infinite mercy, has come into the world, has taken upon himself our nature, and in that nature has suffered the just for the unjust, to bring us to God. By reason of his sufferings, the gospel message is now pro-

...ned to all men, and they are honestly assured that "whosoever believeth in him shall not perish, but have everlasting life." The unhappy persons in this text will not believe in Jesus Christ—they reject God's way of mercy; they hear the gospel but refuse obedience to its command. Let it not be imagined that these individuals are necessarily avowed skeptics, for many of them believe much of revealed truth. They believe the Bible to be the Word of God; they believe there is a God; they believe that Jesus Christ is come into the world as a Savior; they believe most of the doctrines which cluster around the cross.

Alas! They may do this, but yet the wrath of God abides on them if they believe not the Son of God. It may surprise you to learn that many of these persons are very much interested in orthodoxy. They believe that they have discovered the truth, and they exceedingly value those discoveries, so that they frequently grow very warm in temper with those who differ from them. They have read much, and they are matters of argument in the defense of what they consider to be sound doctrine. They cannot endure heresy, and yet sad is the fact, that believing what they do, and knowing so much, they have not believed the Son of God. They believe the doctrine of election, but they have not the faith of God's elect: they swear by final perseverance, but persevere in unbelief. They confess all the five points of Calvinism, but they have not come to the one most needful point of looking unto Jesus, that they may be saved. They accept in creed the truths that are assuredly believed among us, but they have not received that faithful saying, worthy of all acceptance, that Christ Jesus came into the world to save sinners; at any rate, they have not received it personally and practically for their souls' salvation.

It must be admitted that not a few of these persons are blameless as to their morals. You could not, with the closest observation, find either dishonesty, falsehood, uncleanness, or malice in their outward life; they are not only free from these blots, but they manifest positive excellences. Much of their character is commendable. They frequently are courteous and compassionate, generous and gentle minded. Oftentimes they are so amiable and admirable that, while looking upon them, we understand how our Lord, in a similar case, loved the young man who asked, "What lack I yet?" The one thing needful they are destitute of—they have not believed in Christ Jesus, and loath as the Savior was to see them perish, yet it cannot be helped. One doom is common to all who believe not. They shall not see life, but the wrath of God abides on them.

In many cases these persons are, in addition to their morality, religious persons after a fashion. They would not absent themselves from the usual service of the place of worship. They are most careful to respect the Sabbath;

they venerate the Book of God; they use a form of prayer; they join in the songs of the sanctuary; they sit as God's people sit, and stand as God's people stand, but, alas, there is a worm in the center of that fair fruit; they have missed the one essential thing which, being omitted, brings certain ruin; they have not believed on the Son of God. Ah, how far a man may go, and yet, for lack of this one thing, the wrath of God may still abide upon him. Beloved of parents who are hopeful of the conversion of their boy, esteemed by Christians who cannot but admire his outward conversation, yet for all that, the young man may be under the frown of God, for "God is angry with the wicked every day." The wrath of God abides on the man, whoever he may be, that has not believed in Jesus.

Now, if our text showed that the wrath of God was resting on the culprits in our jails, most persons would assent to the statement, and none would wonder at it. If our text declared that the wrath of God abides upon persons who live in habitual unchastity and constant violation of all the laws of order and respectability, most men would say, "Amen"; but the text is aimed at another character. It is true that God's wrath does rest upon open sinners; but, O sirs, this too is true—the wrath of God abides upon those who boast of their virtues but have not believed in Jesus his Son. They may dwell in palaces; but, if they are not believers, the wrath of God abides on them. They may sit in the senate house and enjoy the acclamations of the nation; but, if they believe not on the Son, the wrath of God abides on them. Their names may be enrolled in the peerage and they may possess countless wealth, but the wrath of God abides on them. They may be habitual in their charities and abundant in external acts of devotion; but, if they have not accepted the appointed Savior, the Word of God bears witness that "the wrath of God abideth on them."

2. Now let us, with our hearts awakened by God's Spirit, try to think upon *their offense.*

What is this peculiar sin which entails the wrath of God upon these people? It is that they have not believed the Son of God. What does that amount to? It amounts to this, first of all, that they refuse to accept the mercy of God. God made a law, and his creatures were bound to respect and obey it. We rejected it and turned aside from it. It was a great display of the heart's hatred, but it was not in some respects so thoroughly and intensely wicked a manifestation of enmity to God as when we reject the gospel of grace. God has now presented not the law but the gospel to us, and he has said: "My creatures, you have broken my law, you have acted very vilely toward me. I must punish for sin, else I were not God, and I cannot lay aside my justice; but I have devised a way by which, without any injury to any of my attributes, I can have mercy upon you. I am ready to forgive the past and to restore you to more than your lost position, so that you shall be my sons and my daughters. My only command to you is, believe in my Son. If this command be obeyed, all the blessings of my new covenant shall be yours. Trust him and follow him; for, behold, I give him as a leader and commander to the people. Accept him as making atonement by his substitution, and obey him."

Now, to reject the law of God shows an evil heart of unbelief; but who shall say what a depth of rebellion must dwell in that heart which refuses not only the yoke of God but even the gift of God. The provision of a Savior for lost men is the free gift of God. By it all our wants are supplied, all our evils are removed, peace on earth is secured to us, and glory forever with God: the rejection of this gift cannot be a small sin. The all-seeing One, when he beholds men spurning the supreme gift of his love, cannot but regard such rejection as the worst proof of the hatred of their hearts against himself. When the Holy Spirit comes to convince men of sin, the special sin which he brings to light is thus described: "of sin, because they believe not on me." Not because the heathen were licentious in their habits, barbarians in their ways, and bloodthirsty in their spirit. No: "of sin, because they believe not on me." Condemnation has come upon men, but what is the condemnation? "That light is come into the world, and men love darkness rather than light, because their deeds are evil." Remember, also, that expressive text: "He that believeth not is condemned already"; and what is he condemned for? "Because he hath not believed in the name of the only begotten Son of God."

Let me remark, further, that in the rejection of divine mercy as presented in Christ, the unbeliever has displayed an intense venom against God, for observe how it is. He must either receive the mercy of God in Christ, or he must be condemned—there is no other alternative. He must trust Christ whom God has set forth to be the propitiation for sin, or else he must be driven from the presence of God into eternal punishment. The unbeliever in effect says, "I had sooner be damned than I would accept God's mercy in Christ." Can we conceive a grosser insult to the infinite compassion of the great Father? Suppose a man has injured another, grossly insulted him, and that repeatedly, and yet the injured person, finding the man at last brought into a wretched and miserable state, goes to him and, simply out of kindness to him, says, "I freely forgive you all the wrong you ever did me, and I am ready to relieve your poverty, and to succor you in your distress." Suppose the other replies, "No, I would sooner rot than take anything from you"; would not you have in such a resolve a clear proof of the intense enmity that existed in his heart? And so when a man says, and everyone of you unbelievers do practically say so, "I would sooner lie forever in hell than honor Christ by trusting him," this is a very plain proof of his hatred of God and his Christ.

Unbelievers hate God. Let me ask, for what do you hate him? He keeps the breath within your nostrils; he it is that gives you food and raiment and sends fruitful seasons. For which of these good things do you hate him? You hate him because he is good. Ah, then, it must be because you yourself are evil, and your heart very far removed from righteousness. May God grant that this great and crying sin may be clearly set before your eyes by the light of the eternal Spirit, and may you repent of it and turn from your unbelief and live this day.

But yet further, the unbeliever touches God in a very tender place by his unbelief. No doubt it was to the great Maker a joyous thing to fashion this world, but there are no expressions of joy concerning it at all equal to the joy of God in the matter of human redemption. We would be guarded when we speak of him; but, as far as we can tell, the gift of his dear Son to men, and the whole scheme of redemption, is the master work even of God himself. He is infinite in power and wisdom and love; his ways are as high above our ways as the heavens are above the earth; but Scripture, I think, will warrant me in saying—

> *That in the grace which rescued man*
> *His brightest form of glory shines;*
> *Here on the cross 'tis fairest writ,*
> *In precious blood and crimson lines.*

Now, the man who says, "There is no God," is a fool, but he who denies God the glory of redemption, in addition to his folly, has robbed the Lord of the choicest jewel of his regalia and aimed a deadly blow at the divine honor. I may say of him who despises the great salvation, that, in despising Christ, he touches the apple of God's eye. "This is my beloved Son," says God, "hear ye him." Out of heaven he says it, and yet men stop their ears and say, "We will not have him." No, they wax wrath against the cross and turn away from God's salvation. Do you think that God will always bear this? The times of your ignorance he has winked at, but "now commands all men everywhere to repent." Will you stand out against his love? His love that has been so inventive in ingenious plans by which to bless the sons of men? Shall his choicest work be utterly contemned by you? If so, it is little wonder that it is written, "The wrath of God abides on him."

I must, still further, unveil this matter by saying that the unbeliever perpetrates an offense against every person of the blessed Trinity. He may think that his not believing is a very small business, but, indeed, it is a barbed shaft shot against the Deity. Take the Persons of the blessed Trinity, beginning with the Son of God who comes to us most nearly. It is to me the most surprising thing I ever heard of, that "the Word was made flesh and dwelt among us." I do not wonder that in Hindustan the missionaries are often met with this remark: "It is too good to be true that God ever took upon himself the nature of such a thing as man!" Yet, more wonderful does it seem to be, that, when Christ became man, he took all the sorrows and infirmity of man, and, in addition, was made to bear the sin of many. The most extraordinary of all facts is this: that the infinitely Holy should be "numbered with the transgressors," and, in the words of Isaiah, should "bear their iniquities." The Lord has made him, who knew no sin, to be made sin for us. Wonder of wonders! It is beyond all degree amazing that he who distributes crowns and thrones should hang on a tree and die, the just for the unjust, bearing the punishment due to sinners for guilt. Now, knowing this, as most of you do, and yet refusing to believe, you do, in effect, say, "I do not believe that the incarnate God can save." "Oh no," you reply, "we sincerely believe that he can save." Then, it must be that you feel, "I believe he can, but I will not have him to save me." Wherein I excuse you in the first place, I must bring the accusation more heavily in the second. You answer that "you do not say you will not believe him." Why do you then remain in unbelief? The fact is, you do not trust him; you do not obey him. I pray you account for the fact. "May I believe him?" says one. Have we not told you ten thousand times over that whosoever will, may take the water of life freely. If there be any barrier, it is not with God; it is not with Christ; it is with your own sinful heart. You are welcome to the Savior now, and if you trust him now, he is yours forever. But oh, unbeliever, it appears to be nothing to you that Christ has died. His wounds attract you not. His groans for his enemies have no music in them to you. You turn your back upon the incarnate God who bleeds for men, and in so doing you shut yourselves out of hope, judging yourselves unworthy of eternal life.

Furthermore, the willful rejection of Christ is also an insult to God the Father. "He that believeth not hath made God a liar, because he hath not believed the record that God gave of his Son." God has himself often borne testimony to his dear Son. "Him hath God the Father set forth to be a propitiation for our sins." In rejecting Christ, you reject God's testimony and God's gift. It is a direct assault upon the truthfulness and loving-kindness of the gracious Father, when you trample on or cast aside his priceless, peerless gift of love.

And, as for the blessed Spirit, it is his office here below to bear witness to Christ. In the Christian ministry, the Holy Spirit daily cries to the sons of men to come to Jesus. He has striven in the hearts of many of you, given you a measure of conviction of sin, and a degree of knowledge of the glory of Christ, but you have repressed it, you have labored to your utmost to do despite to the Spirit of God. Believe me, this is no slight sin. An unbeliever is an enemy to God the Father, to God the Son, and God the Holy Ghost. Against the blessed Trinity in unity, O unbeliever, your sin is a standing insult: you are now to God's face insulting him by continuing an unbeliever.

And, I must add, that there is also in unbelief an insult against every attribute of God. The unbeliever in effect declares, "If the justice of God is seen in laying the punishment of sin upon Christ, I do not care for his justice; I will bear my own punishment." The sinner seems to say, "God is merciful in the gift of Christ to suffer in our stead; I do not want his mercy; I can do without it." Others may be guilty, and they may trust in the Redeemer, but I do not feel such guilt, and I will not sue for pardon." Unbelievers attack the wisdom of God, for, whereas the wisdom of God is in its fullness revealed in the gift of Jesus, they say, "It is a dogma, unphilosophical, and worn out." They count the wisdom of God to be foolishness, and thus cast a slight upon another of the divine attributes. I might in detail mention every one of the attributes and prerogatives of God, and prove that your nonacceptance of the Savior is an insult to every one of them, and to God himself: but the theme is too sad for us to continue upon it, and, therefore, let us pass to another phase of the subject, though I fear it will be equally grievous.

3. Third, let us consider *the causes of this unbelief.*

In a great many, unbelief may be ascribed to a careless *ignorance* of the way of salvation. Now, I should not wonder if many of you imagine that, if you do not understand the gospel, you are therefore quite excused for not believing it. But, sirs, it is not so. You are placed in this world, not as heathens in the center of Africa, but in England, where you live in the full blaze of gospel day. There are places of worship all around you, which you can without difficulty attend. The Book of God is very cheap; you have it in your houses; you can all read it or hear it read. Is it so, then, that the King has been pleased to reveal himself to you and tell you the way to salvation, and yet you, at the age of twenty, thirty, or forty, do not know the way of salvation? What do you mean, sir? What can you mean? Has God been pleased to reveal himself in Scripture and tell you how to escape from hell and fly to heaven, and yet have you been too idle to inquire into that way? Dare you say to God, "I do not think it worth my while to learn what you have revealed, neither do I care to know of the gift which you have bestowed on men." How can you think that such ignorance is an excuse for your sin? What could be a more gross aggravation of it? If you do not know, you ought to know; if you have not learned the gospel message, you might have learned it, for there are some of us whose language it is not difficult for even the most illiterate to understand, and who would, if we caught ourselves using a hard word, retract it and put it into little syllables, so that not even a child's intellect need be perplexed by our language. Salvation's way is plain in the Book; those words, "Believe and live," are in this Christian England almost as legible and as universally to be seen as though they were printed on the sky. That trust in the Lord Jesus saves the soul is well-known news. But if you still say you have not known all this, then I reply, "Dear sir, do try to know it. Go to the Scriptures, study them, see what is there. Hear, also, the gospel, for it is written, "Incline your ear to come unto me; hear, and your soul shall live." "Faith comes by hearing, and hearing by the word of God." For your soul's sake I charge you, be no longer ignorant of that which you must know, or else must perish.

In some others, the cause is *indifference*. They do not think the matter to be of any very great consequence. They are aware that they are not quite right, but they have a notion that somehow or other they will get right at last; and, meanwhile, it does not trouble them. O man, I pray you, as your fellow creature let me speak with you a word of expostulation. God declares that his wrath abides upon you as an unbeliever, and do you call that nothing? God says, "I am angry with you," and you say to him, "I do not care; it is of very small importance to me. The rise or fall of the consols [funded government securities in Great Britain] is of much more consequence than whether God is angry with me or not. My dinner being done to a turn concerns me a great deal more than whether the infinite God loves me or hates me." That is the English of your conduct, and I put it to you whether there can be a higher impertinence against your Creator, or a direr form of arrogant revolt against the eternal ruler. If it does not trouble you that God is angry with you, it ought to trouble you; and it troubles *me* that it does not trouble *you*. We have heard of persons guilty of murder, whose behavior during the trial has been cool and self-possessed. The coolness with which they pleaded "not guilty" has been all of a piece with the hardness of tears which led them to the bloody deed. He who is capable of great crime is also incapable of shame concerning it. A man who is able to take pleasure and be at ease while God is angry with him shows that his heart is harder than steel.

In certain cases, the root of this unbelief lies in another direction. It is fed by pride. The person who is guilty of it does not believe that he needs a Savior. His notion is that he will do his very best, attend the church or the meetinghouse very regularly, subscribe occasionally or frequently, and go to heaven partly by what he does, and partly by the merits of Christ. So that not believing in Christ is not a matter of any great consequence with him because he is not naked and poor and miserable; but he is rich and increased in goods [though not] in spiritual things. To be saved by faith is a religion for harlots and drunkards and thieves; but for respectable persons such as he is, who have kept the law from their youth up, he does not see any particular need of laying hold upon Christ. Such conduct reminds me of the words of Cowper—

> Perish the virtue, as it ought, abhorr'd,
> And the fool with it that insults his Lord.

God believed it needful, in order to save man, that the Redeemer should die; yet you self-righteous ones evidently think that death a superfluity: for if a man could save himself, why did the Lord descend and die to save him? If there be a way to heaven by respectability and morality without Christ, what is the good of Christ? It is utterly useless to have an expiator and a mediator, if men are so good that they do not require them. You tell God to his face that he lies unto you, that you are not so sinful as he would persuade you, that you do not need a substitute and sacrifice as he says you do. O sirs, this pride of yours is an arrogant rebellion against God. Look at your fine actions, you that are so good—your motives are base, your pride over what you have done has defiled, with black fingers, all your acts. Inasmuch as you prefer your way to God's way, and prefer your righteousness to God's righteousness, the wrath of God abides on you.

Perhaps I have not hit the reason of your unbelief, therefore let me speak once more. In many, *love of sin* rather than any boasted self-righteousness keeps them from the Savior. They do not believe in Jesus, not because they have any doubt about the truths of Christianity, but because they have an enslaving love for their favorite sin. "Why," says one, "if I were to believe in Christ, of course, I must obey him; to trust and to obey go together. Then I could not be the drunkard I am; I could not trade as I do; I could not practice secret licentiousness; I could not frequent the haunts of the ungodly, where laughter is occasioned by sin, and mirth by blasphemy. I cannot give up these my darling sins." Perhaps, this sinner hopes that one day, when he cannot any longer enjoy his sin, he will meanly sneak out of it and try to cheat the devil of his soul; but, meanwhile, he prefers the pleasures of sin to obedience to God, and unbelief to acceptance of his salvation. O sweet sin! O bitter sin! How you are murdering the souls of men! As certain serpents before they strike their prey fix their eyes upon it and fascinate it, and then at last devour it, so does sin fascinate the foolish sons of Adam; they are charmed with it, and perish for it. It yields but a momentary joy, and the wage thereof is eternal misery, yet are men enamored of it. The ways of the strange woman, and the paths of uncleanness lead most plainly to the chambers of death, yet are men attracted thereto as moths by the blaze of the candle, and so are they destroyed. Alas! that men wantonly dash against the rocks of dangerous lusts and perish willfully beneath the enchantment of sin. Sad pity it is to prefer a harlot to the eternal God, to prefer a few pence made by dishonesty to heaven itself, to prefer the gratification of the belly to the love of the Creator and the joy of being reconciled and saved. It was a dire insult to God when Israel set up a golden calf, and said, "These be thy gods, O Israel." Shall the image of an ox that eats grass supplant the living God? He that had strewn the earth with manna, had made Sinai to smoke with his presence, and the whole wilderness to tremble beneath his marchings, is he to be thrust aside by the image of a bullock that has horns and hoofs? Will men prefer molten metal to the infinitely holy and glorious Jehovah? But, surely, the preference of a lust to God is a greater insult still: to obey our passions rather than his will, and to prefer sin to his mercy; this is the crime of crimes. May God deliver us from it, for his mercy's sake.

4. We have heavy tidings in the last head of my discourse, *the terrible result* of unbelief.

"He shall not see life, but the wrath of God abideth on him." "The wrath of God!" No words can ever fully explain this expression. Holy Whitefield, when he was preaching, would often hold up his hands, and, with tears streaming down his eyes, would exclaim, "Oh, the wrath to come! the wrath to come!" Then would he pause because his emotions checked his utterance. The wrath of God! I confess I feel uneasy if anybody is angry with me, and yet one can bear the anger of foolish, hot-tempered persons with some equanimity. But the wrath of God is the anger of One who is never angry without a cause, One who is very patient and longsuffering. It takes much to bring the choler into Jehovah's face, yet is he wroth with unbelievers. He is never angry with anything because it is feeble and little, but only because it is wrong. His anger is only his holiness set on fire. He cannot bear sin; who would wish that he should?

What right-minded man would desire God to be pleased with evil? That were to make a devil of God. Because he is God, he must be angry with sin wherever it is. This makes the sting of it, that his wrath is just and holy anger. It is the anger, remember, of an omnipotent Being who can crush us as easily as a moth. It is the anger of an infinite Being, and therefore infinite anger, the heights and depths and breadths and lengths of which no man can measure. Only the incarnate God ever fully knew the power of God's anger. It is beyond all conception, yet the anger rests on you, my hearer. Alas, for you, if you are an unbeliever, for this is your state before God. It is no fiction of mine, but the word of inspired truth: "the wrath of God abideth on him."

Then notice the next word, it *"abides."* This is to say, it is upon you now. He is angry with you at this moment, and always. You go to sleep with an angry God gazing into your face; you wake in the morning, and if your eye were not dim, you would perceive his frowning countenance. He is angry with you, even when you are singing his praises, for you mock him with solemn sounds upon a thoughtless tongue; angry with you on your knees, for you only pretend to pray—you utter words without heart. As long as you are not a believer, he must be angry with you every moment. "God is angry with the wicked every day."

That the text says it abides, and the present tense takes a long sweep, for it always will abide on you. But may you not, perhaps, escape from it, by ceasing to exist? The test precludes such an idea. Although it says that you "shall not see life," it teaches that God's wrath is upon you, so that the absence of life is not annihilation. Spiritual life belongs only to believers; you are now without that life, yet you exist, and wrath abides on you, and so it ever must be. While you shall not see life, you shall exist in eternal death, for the wrath of God cannot abide on a nonexistent creature. You shall not see life, but you shall feel wrath to the uttermost. It is horror enough that wrath should be on you now; it is horror upon horrors, and hell upon hell, that it shall be upon you forever.

And notice that it must be so, because you reject the only thing that can heal you. As George Herbert says, "Whom oils and balsams kill, what salve can cure?" If Christ himself has become a savor of death unto death unto you, because you reject him, how can you be saved? There is but one door, and if you close it by your unbelief, how can you enter heaven? There is one healing medicine, and if you refuse to take it, what remains but death? There is one water of life, but you refuse to drink it; then must you thirst forever. You put from you, voluntarily, the one only Redeemer; how then shall you be ransomed? Shall Christ die again, and in another state be offered to you once more? O sirs, you would reject him then as you reject him now. But there remains no more sacrifice for sin. On the cross God's mercy to the sons of men was fully revealed, and will you reject God's ultimatum of grace, his last appeal to you? If so, it is at your own peril: Christ being raised from the dead dies no more; he shall come again, but without a sin offering unto the salvation of his people.

Remember, sirs, that the wrath of God will produce no saving or softening effect. It has been suggested that a sinner, after suffering God's wrath awhile, may repent and so escape from it. But our observation and experience prove that the wrath of God never softened anybody's heart yet, and we believe it never will: those who are suffering divine wrath will go on to harden and harden and harden; the more they suffer, the more they will hate: the more they are punished, the more will they sin. The wrath of God abiding on you will produce no good results to you, but rather you shall go from evil to evil, further and further from the presence of God.

The reason why the wrath of God abides on an unbeliever is partly because all his other sins remain on him. There is no sin that shall damn the man who believes, and nothing can save the man who will not believe. God removes all sin the moment we believe; but while we believe not, fresh cords fasten upon us our transgressions. The sin of Judah is written as with an iron pen, and graven with a point of a diamond. Nothing can release you from guilt while your heart remains at enmity with Jesus Christ your Lord. Remember that God has never taken an oath, that I know of, against any class of persons, except unbelievers. "To whom sware he that they should not enter into his rest, but to them that believed not?" Continued unbelief God never will forgive, because his word binds him not to do so. Does he swear an oath, and shall he go back from it? It cannot be. Oh, that you might have grace to relinquish your unbelief, and close in with the gospel and be saved.

Now, I hear someone object, "You tell us that certain people are under the wrath of God, but they are very prosperous." I reply, that yonder bullock will be slaughtered. Yet it is being fattened. And your prosperity, O ungodly man, is but a fattening of you for the slaughter of justice. Yes, but you say, "They are very merry, and some of those who are forgiven are very sad." Mercy lets them be merry while they may. We have heard of men who, when driven to Tyburn in a cart, could drink and laugh as they went to the gallows. It only proved what bad men they were. And so, whereas the guilty can yet take comfort, it only proves their guiltiness.

Let me ask: what ought to be your thoughts concerning these solemn truths which I have delivered to you? I know what my thoughts were; they made me go to my bed unhappy. They made me very grateful because I hope I have believed in Jesus Christ; yet they made me start in the night, and wake this morning with a load upon me. I come here to say to you, must it be so that you will always remain unbelievers and abide under the wrath of God? If it must be so, and the dread conclusion seems forced upon me, at any rate, do look it in the face, do consider it. If you are resolved to be damned, know what you are at. Take advice and consider. O sirs, it cannot need an argument to convince you that it is a most wretched thing to be now under the wrath of God. You cannot want any argument to show that it must be a blessed thing to be forgiven—you must see that. It is not your reason that wants convincing, it is your heart that wants renewing.

The whole gospel lies in this nutshell. Come, you guilty one, just as you are, and rest yourself upon the finished work of the Savior, and take him to be yours forever. Trust Jesus now. In your present position it may be done. God's Holy Spirit blessing your mind, you may at this moment say, "Lord, I believe, help thou mine unbelief." You may now confide in Jesus, and some who came in here unforgiven may make the angels sing because they go down yonder steps saved souls, whose transgressions are forgiven, and whose sins are covered. God knows one thing, that if I knew by what study and what art I could learn to preach the gospel so as to affect your hearts, I would spare no cost or pains. For the present, I have aimed simply to warn you, not with adornment of speech, lest the power should be the power of man; and now I leave my message and commit it to him who shall judge the quick and the dead. But this know, if you receive not the Son, I shall be a swift witness against you. God grant it be not so, for his mercy's sake. Amen.

Noah's Flood

Delivered on Thursday evening, March 5, 1868, at the Metropolitan Tabernacle, Newington. No. 823.

The flood came, and took them all away. —MATTHEW 24:39

We commonly say that "there is no rule without an exception," and certainly the rule that there is no rule without an exception has an exception to itself, for the rules of God are without exception. The rule that God will punish the ungodly is without an exception; the rule that all who are out of Christ shall perish is a rule without an exception; and the rule that all who are in Christ shall be saved is also without an exception.

1. I shall have to call your attention tonight to three rules that are without exception, and the first is the one before us— *"the flood came, and took them all away."*

The destruction caused by the deluge was universal. It did not merely sweep away some who were out of the ark, but it swept them all away. There were, doubtless, distinctions in those days, as there are now, for never has there been one dead level of equality among the sons of Adam since men multiplied on the face of the earth. Many in that time were wealthy. They had accumulated stores of gold and silver. They were rich in merchandise, invention, or plunder. They were rich in the produce of the field. They owned broad acres of land. They had multiplied to themselves the conveniences and the luxuries of life, but the flood came and swept them all away. Not one rich man could escape with all his hoards, neither could he purchase life if he had given all his wealth, for the flood came and swept them all away. There were no rafts of costly cedar, or towers of expensive masonry which could out-top the devouring deluge: death laughed at miser and merchant, millionaire and monarch; all, all were swallowed up in the angry flood.

There were some in those days who were extremely poor. They worked hard to gain enough to keep body and soul together, and they were scarcely able to do that; they had to suffer every day—

*The oppressor's wrongs,
the proud man's contumely;*

but I do not find that as a reward for their sufferings they were spared. No; when the flood came it swept them all away. The pauper out of the ark perished as well as the prince. The poor and miserable peasant died, washed away from the filth of his mud hovel as monarchs were from their palaces. The beggar without a shoe to his foot died; the flood had no pity on his rags. He who swept the street crossing and stood waiting for a casual alms was taken away with the aristocrats who had pitied him. The flood came and swept them all away; the unrelenting billows meted out an equal fate to all who were outside the one ark of safety.

And so will it be at the last. As the great man will not purchase an escape by all that which he has stored up, so neither will the man be delivered because of his poverty. There was a rich man in hell, we read: poor men have been there, and are there now. As riches cannot save from hell, so neither can poverty raise to heaven. The grace and justice of God are independent of society and rank and state and condition. What matters it to the Lord how much or how little of yellow metal you have about you! He measures no man by his purse, but by his soul; and he whose soul is unpardoned is lost, be he rolling in plenty or pining in want. You must be born again; you must believe in Jesus; you must, in one word, get into the ark, or when the flood comes it will sweep you all away, be you rich as Dives or poor as Lazarus.

There were in those days *learned* men in the world—men who searched the stars at night; who had deciphered the constellations, who had pried into the secrets of matter; men who had ransacked science, and, so far as men had gone (and we do not know but what they went a very long way then), had pierced into the innermost recesses of knowledge; but when the flood came it swept them all away. There goes the philosopher; you can hear his dying gurgle. There, floating on the stream, is the head of an antediluvian Solomon. The flood has swept away masters of arts, doctors of law, and rabbis in divinity. No man was able to escape the deluge by all that he had ever learned. Knowledge is no life buoy, logic is no swimming belt, rhetoric no lifeboat. Down, down they go, and all their science with them, beneath the shoreless waves.

And as for *the illiterate*, who were, no doubt, numerous then as now, who could only count as many as the number of their fingers, who knew none of the niceties of learning or of eloquence, when the flood came it swept them all away. So that knowledge, except it be of one particular kind, namely, the heart knowledge of Christ Jesus, will not deliver us from the final destruction; and, on the other hand, although ignorance, if it be not willful, is some palliation for sin, yet is it never such an excuse for it as to suffer sin to go unpunished. There is a hell for those who knew their Master's will and did it not; and there is also a hell for those who would not know, but who lived and died willfully ignorant of the things of God. The flood came and swept them all away. You men who are orthodox in doctrine, you who can talk about theology, and claim to be masters in Israel, if you do not belong to Christ, the flood shall sweep you all away. And you who say, "What does it matter? Creeds, what are they but handles of old rubbish? We do not study our Bibles, and do not want to know the doctrines taught therein." I tell you, sirs, except you know Christ, and are found in him, your ignorance shall be no sufficient excuse for you, for when the flood of fire shall come, it shall sweep you all away.

I doubt not that among those who perished in Noah's flood, *there were many who were very zealous in the cause of religion;* perhaps some who had officiated as priests in the midst of their families, and possibly even at God's altar. They were not a godless race in those days, so far as the form and profession went; they had a religion; even those sons of Cain had a religion; and indeed, generally when men are worst at heart, they prate most about outward religion. We may suppose it was so in Noah's day. But when the flood came, these men being out of the ark, whether priests or not, did not escape; it swept them all away. And there were others, no doubt, who were *profane,* who lived in disregard of God, or who hectored out infidel expressions concerning him. But the flood made no distinction between the hypocritical priest and the direct blasphemer; when it came, it swept them all away. O you sons of Levi, you who wear the robes of priesthood and profess to be sent of God to teach others, with all your boasted magical powers, if you do not believe in Jesus as poor guilty sinners and look up to the cross alone for your salvation, when the flood comes, it will sweep you all away. You will drown, Sir Priest, despite your baptismal regeneration and your sacramental efficacy! You will sink with a lying absolution on your lips down to the nethermost hell!

And, O you who rail against religion and boast that you are no hypocrites, you doubtless think yourselves honest, but do not imagine that your impudent "honesty," as you choose to call it, will exonerate you at the last tremendous day, for in that day of wrath the fiery deluge shall sweep you also all away. Short work will God make with doubters then. They shall behold him and wonder and perish, for a short and sharp work will he make in the earth. Quick work will he make with the hypocrites in that day; for though they call, he will not answer them; and when they begin to cry to him, he will mock at their calamity and laugh when their fear comes. The flood shall sweep all at last—whether religious or profane—away, for they have not fled to the ark and so have rejected the one only shelter.

Let me solemnly remind you in this congregation tonight, that in that day of destruction *some of the oldest men that have lived perished*—older men than you, though your head be gray or bald; older women than you, though you have nourished and brought up children and dandled your grandchildren and your great-grandchildren upon your knee: they went down the stream with others, perishing as though they had never seen the light. And the young died too. That one dreadful destruction took away the little child in his beauty, and the young man in his strength, and the maiden in her bloom. The flood took them all away; and so with all of us who have attained to adult years and have arrived at knowledge so as to judge between good and evil; if we be found not in Christ, the flood shall take us all away. We know not at how young an age we may be responsible. Let the child never presume upon its youth. We have heard of fools of twenty pleading "infancy" in our courts of law, and of all pieces of roguery sanctioned by the law, I have thought that the plea of "infancy" from young men of nineteen and twenty years of age, who have purchased jewelry and I know not what, to spend upon their lusts—of all pieces of villany, I say, that seems to me to be the most intolerable. But there shall be no such plea of infancy for you boys and girls and young people, at the last great day. If you know right from wrong, and if you can understand the gospel of Jesus Christ, at your peril do you reject it, at your peril do you neglect it! No, neither shall the young nor the old escape except by coming to Christ. "Ye must be born again" is of universal application to you who are young and to you who are gray headed. No youth can excuse, no experience can exempt, but alike will the flood of divine wrath overwhelm every human soul unless we find refuge in the ark of the covenant of grace, even the work and person of Jesus, the bleeding Lamb of God.

This universality I shall have to illustrate in yet another way. I can suppose that when Noah built the ark—a most absurd thing to do upon all the principles of common reason apart from his faith in God—*there were a great many persons who heard of this and wondered.* It was a very huge ship—the greatest that ever had been built, a conception in navigation which altogether staggered the minds of men in his day. When Noah built this vessel and built it on the dry land, far removed from any river or sea, it must have been a very great wonder and have caused abundance of talk through all the neighboring nations. I should not wonder but what the tidings spread far and wide, and there were some who, as soon as they heard of it, said, "A madman! I wonder his friends do not confine him; what a lunatic he must be!" Having made that remark, they cracked a joke or two about it and fell into the habit of sneering at a thing so very absurd, so that it passed into a proverb, and when a man did a silly thing, they said, "Why, he is as foolish as old Noah!" Ribald jests were all that Noah could get from them; they despised, ridiculed, and contemned him utterly, but the flood came and took *them* all away, and there was an end to their jests, their sarcasms, their jeers.

The flood had silenced *them* most effectually. So will it be with any of you who have ridiculed the gospel of Christ; you will find in the great and terrible day of the Lord, that your laughter shall have no power over death and win you no reprieve from the agonies of hell. There will be no room for infidelity in that tremendous day. God will be all too real to you when he tears you in pieces, and there is none to deliver; and the judgment will be all too real when the thunderclaps shall wake the dead and the books shall be opened and read by the blaze of lightning, and the sentence shall be pronounced, "Depart, you cursed!" Beware, you despisers, and wonder, and perish. Beware, now, while yet there is a day of grace to light you to heaven, for remember it will not last forever. May eternal love save any of us from perishing in devouring fire as Noah's despisers did in the devouring flood.

There were other people, no doubt, who, when they heard about Noah, *criticized his building.* I can imagine some of the shipbuilders of the time look-ing on and telling him that the keel was not arranged quite rightly; and that ingenious plan of pitching the great ship within and without would be sure to be very closely criticized, for it seems to have been a great novelty, not an invention of man, but a revelation from God. Then there was the making of only one window—why, we who read about it now do not know what it means, and all the plans that have ever been drawn of Noah's ark do not seem to realize the description given of it. Why, said the wise shipwright, "that thing will never float on the top of the flood, if it should chance to come; and besides, it has been so long in building that it will be sure to get the dry rot." What wise things were said about it! If they had been able to print them in those days, how many critical treatises would have been published against "that old wooden box of Noah's," as they very likely would have called it! All these critics could have built it a great deal better, I have no doubt, but they did not build at all; and though they found fault, and could do it so much bet-ter than Noah did, yet, somehow or other, they were drowned, and he was saved.

So in this world now, we constantly find men who eat up the sins of God's people as they eat bread. "Oh! yes," they can say, "there is something in religion, no doubt, but then look at your imperfections and your faults!" And, brethren, they need not look long to find them out. They can soon find ten thousand points in which we might be a little improved, and sometimes I have no doubt that our critics are in some respects better than we are. Many a worldly man has a better temper than a genuine Christian. I am sorry to say it, but I have known unconverted people much more generous than some who are converted. They do excel in some qualities, but still, still, still, there is the solemn truth that the sharpest and most philosophical critic of other people, if he be out of Christ, will be swept away, while the men whom he criticized and condemned, if they be found humbly believing in Jesus, shall be saved through faith in him. It all hinges on this one matter, inside or outside the ark: inside the ark a thousand imperfections, but all saved; outside the ark a thousand excellencies, but all drowned without a single exception at last!

Now there may have been, on the other hand, among those who came to see father Noah and his big ship, *some who took his part.* I never knew a man so big a fool but what some sided with him. So, perhaps, there were some who said, "Well, after all, do not be too hard upon him, he is a respectable patriarch; he is a man who follows up his convictions: his convictions are very absurd, no doubt, but still it is a fine thing in these days to see a man really practically sincere; we do like to see the man so infatuated, but though we cannot help wishing that he was a sane man, yet still it is almost better to see a man insane and carry out his convictions, than to see him trifling as so many are childishly trifling with their principles." Many a gentleman who looked at the ark when he said that went home with wonderful ease of conscience, and thought, "Now I have said a very good thing; I have put a spoke in the wheel of some of those cavilers; I have stood up for the good old man, for a very good old man, I have no doubt he is, though very much deceived." Ah! but when the flood came, it swept all these people away as well. They were very kind in their remarks, and very patronizing in their air, but the flood swept them all away.

And do you not know such people now? Why, there are some of them here tonight. Listen to their gentlemanly talk, how generously they speak: "Well, yes; I like to see these Christian people so earnest; I daresay they do a great deal of good; you know, I like to hear a preacher speaking out so plainly; I like to see these people very zealous—in these days it is very refreshing to see people zealous about anything, for there is so much latitudinarianism and policy and so on, that we like to find people decided, even though we should think them a little too dogmatic and bigoted." O sirs, we thank you for your good opinion of us, but except you repent you shall likewise perish. Your excellent remarks will not save you, and your very lenient and gentlemanly and broad-church views of religion will not assist you. You may hold all those views which are so tolerant and so excellent, and we are glad you do hold them, and yet you may have no share in Christ's salvation. You are a sensible man for holding such charitable views, but, sensible as you are, except you come to Christ, you will have to perish, even as the most bigoted persecutors.

Besides these, there were some other people *who liked Noah better still;* they not only excused and defended him, but they sometimes grew very warm about it. They said, "Father Noah is right; we see his life, we mark his manners and conversation, and he is a better man than they are who ridicule and despise him; we are convinced by his preaching that his testimony is true, and we will help him and stand up for him; we do not like to hear the jeers and uncivil remarks that are made about him; they cut us to the quick." Then I suppose you are going into the ark, are you not? "Well, we do not know our-selves about that yet. Perhaps we may, by and by; we are thinking of it; we have taken the matter into very serious consideration, and we think it to be a very proper thing to do, a very right thing to do, but at the same time, it is hardly convenient yet; we will wait a little longer." "Why," says one, "I am not married yet." And another says, "There is a banquet to be held on such-and-such a day; I must go to that; you know men must eat and drink, and there-fore I am not going into the ark just yet." Well, now, these well-meaning, procrastinating people, who were postponing and putting off, what became of them? Did one of them escape? Alas! no; when the flood came, it took them all away. What, not save one of them, those who would be right if they had a little longer time? Not spare those who have good resolutions in their throats, who are almost persuaded to be Christians? No, not one of them; they all went down in the common wreck and perished in the universal destruction, for good resolutions save no man unless they are put into practice. Almost persuaded to be a Christian is like the man who was almost pardoned, but he was hanged; like the man who was almost rescued, but he was burned in the house. As old Henry Smith says, "A door that is almost shut is open; a man that is almost honest is a thief; a man that is almost saved is damned." Oh, take heed of that, you halters between two opinions, you awakened but not decided, you aroused but not converted! Noah's friends perished, his very dearest friends who were not in the ark. When the flood came, it swept them all away; and so must you, our sons and daughters, if you give not your hearts to the Lord.

So, to close this recapitulation, you have often been told that *the very workmen who worked for Noah,* and who were, no doubt, paid their wages, or they would not have worked, perished also. They helped to saw the wood, to lay the keel, to drive the bolts, to put in the oakum, to use the pitch, to strengthen the timbers, but after all that they had done, not one of them escaped. And so the chapel keeper, the pew opener, the elder, the deacon, the minister, the bishop, the archbishop, all those who have had a function in the church, who have had something to do with the good staunch vessel of Christ's gospel, except they, themselves, be in Christ by a living faith, they must perish as much as the despisers and the outcasts. Here, then, is the solemn truth: all out of Christ lost, all in Christ saved; all unbelievers perishing, all believers preserved in him. Here is a rule without an exception.

Very briefly we shall now have to speak upon a second subject.

2. It appears that when the flood came, it found them all eating and drinking, marrying, and giving in marriage, and, according to the text, *this also* was a rule without an exception.

Is it not a very solemn thing that it is so now, that without any exception the mass of mankind are still neglectful of their souls, still busy about their fleeting interests, and negligent of eternal realities? There are no exceptions to this rule among natural men. Gracious men care for these things, but all natural men are like these men in the days of Noah. While I was musing this afternoon, I felt surprised at it. I said to myself, "What, not one man in Noah's day that was anxious to be saved in the ark—not one?" Why, the population of the globe is supposed by some to have been greater at that time than it is now. Owing to the extreme length of years to which men then lived, the deaths were fewer, and the population increased more rapidly, and yet out of them all was there not one that sought after God naturally—not one? It was an extraordinary thing that there was not one who would believe in the reiterated prophecies of Noah and find a shelter in the ark. But is it not more strange still, only it is strangely true, that out of all the unregenerate, until they are quickened by divine grace, there is not one who cares to flee to Christ? "Ye will not come unto me that ye might have life" is a rule of universal application. Men will not come to Christ, but had rather perish in their sins than come and put their trust in him.

I suppose the reason lies in three things. First, there is men's *universal indifference* about their souls—a wanton carelessness about their noblest part, their truest selves. But that is a strange thing! A man is always earnest about his life—"Skin for skin; yea, all that a man hath will he give for his life." If a man thinks he is likely to perish by burning, what cries he will raise! What exertions he will make to get out of the room! If he is near to drowning, how he kicks and struggles! If he be sick, how quickly he sends for the doctor, and how anxious he is to get the best advice within his reach, so that his life may be preserved! And yet the preservation of his highest life seems to be to him a matter of no consequence at all! Every thinking man must feel that his true self is his spirit, his soul, that his body is not he himself, but simply a sort of garment that himself wears, a house in which himself lives; and yet men spend their time from morning till night in finding clothes and food for this outside house, but the tenant that dwells within is—poor creature!—quite forgotten. That is odd, is it not? Does it not seem to prove that man is degraded into something less than a reasonable creature by his sin, so that he acts like a beast?

When a man has to live but a little time in this world, he wishes to be happy in it. If a man only stops for an hour in an inn, what a noise he makes if the chimney smokes, if the tablecloth is not clean, if chops are not done to a turn; and while he knows that his better self must live forever in another world, he does not concern himself about that world, or whether he shall be happy in it or not! Strange! 'Tis strange; 'tis passing strange; 'tis wonderful.

It is a miracle of madness that men should be so indifferent to the interest of their souls, their immortal souls, that they should go to sleep, not knowing whether they will wake up with the never-dying worm or arise to enjoy with Jesus the surpassing splendors of eternity. Yet this indifference is universal. O brethren, you and I have need to pray that God would stir this dead sea, that he would speak with his quickening voice, and make men alive to these spiritual things, or else in the graves of their indifference they will rot forever.

The second reason for this indifference lay, no doubt, in universal unbelief. Is it not a strange thing that they did not one of them believe Noah? Noah was an honest man; some of them had known him for many years, yes, for hundreds of years they had known him, for they lived so long then. He spoke like an honest man. He preached with vehemence and power, but not one believed him, not one soul believed him so as to escape from the wrath to come, not one! Now that is odd, for as I have said before, no lie that was ever told was so incredible but what somebody or other was found to believe it, much more should some be found to receive the truth. Yet here was a truth that looked so probable, on account of the sin of man, and yet nobody was found to believe it, but they universally rejected it. Even so it is with the gospel of Christ. We come and tell our fellowmen that the Son of God was made flesh to redeem men, that whosoever trusts in him shall be saved. But they will not believe it, though we have proved it, hundreds of us, thousands of us, and we tell them as solemnly and as earnestly as we can, that we have tasted and handled of these things, that they are not cunningly devised fables, but are in very truth most precious and proven realities; and yet, without the grace of God, there is not a single one, high or low, rich or poor, that will so believe as to try for himself; but they shake their heads and go on their way, and universally live and die in unbelief, unless sovereign grace steps in. A strange thing, a marvelous thing! "Jesus marveled because of their unbelief," and well may we marvel because of the universality of this sin.

Then a third cause for this general indifference was, *that they were always and altogether given to worldliness.* The text seems to hint that they did not think of preparing for the coming flood because they were so busy in the base enjoyment of mere eating. Some of them were gluttons, and others who did not eat so much, yet ate right well when they did eat, and daintily. They were worshiping that god that Paul speaks of—the belly. Alas! good feeding ruins many, and men dig their way to hell with their teeth. Like brutes, they care only to be filled. Others were drunkards. Ah! how merry were they in their cups! How they judged a glass of wine and told its age to a year! They were bent upon swallowing hogsheads of dainty liquor. They were drowned, like Duke Clarence, in their butts [casks] of wine. No doubt they had, in their way, their lord mayors' feasts, and their aldermen's and companies' dinners, and I know not what besides, and they were all so occupied with these things, these crying necessities of the life of swine, that they did not and could not think of anything superior to that. They were married and given in marriage; this was a serious business, and must be attended to—how could they forsake their wedding feasts and their newly married brides? These things engrossed all their thoughts. And yet, friends, and yet, what was the use of eating and drinking, when they were to be drowned the next day? And what was the use of being married, when they were to be drowned on the morrow? If they had looked at these things in the light of faith, they would have despised them; but they only used the blear eye of sense, and thus they set great store upon these present things of mirth.

Yes, and so it is with the wicked man nowadays. He gets rich, but what is the use of being wealthy if you must be damned? Fool that he is, if he buys a gold coffin, how would that help him? Suppose he is laid out with a bag of gold in each hand, and a pile of it between his legs, how will that help him? Others seek to get learning, but what is the good of learning if you sink to perdition with it? Take up the learned man's skull, and what is the difference between that and the skull of the merest pauper that scarcely knew his letters? Brown unpalpable powder, they both crumble down into the same elements. To die in a respectable position, what is the use of it? What are a few more plumes on the hearse, or a longer line of mourning coaches? Will these ease the miseries of Tophet? Ah! friends, you have to die. Why not make ready for the inevitable? Oh! if men were wise, they would see that all earth's joys are just like the bubbles which our children blow with soap; they glitter and they shine, and then they are gone, and there is not even a wreck left behind. Oh, that they were wise to enter the ark, to look to Christ, so that when the floods arise they might be found safe in him.

Here, then, comes this general rule, never to be too much lamented, and which ought to make every Christian's heart break with heaviness, that universally and everywhere, in the very presence of the coming judgment, and between the very jaws of death and hell, the whole human race remains indifferent, unbelieving, worldly, and still will so remain until the flood of fire comes and sweeps them all away. Thus will they all sport until they perish, unless eternal love prevent.

3. The last consideration shall be but very briefly handled, but it is a very comforting one, namely, that *all who were in the ark were safe.*

Nobody fell out of that divinely appointed refuge; nobody was dragged out; nobody died in it; nobody was left to perish in it. All who went in came out unharmed. They were all preserved in it; they were all safely brought through the dread catastrophe. The ark preserved them all, and so will Jesus Christ preserve all in him. Whoever may come to him shall be secure. None of them shall perish, neither shall any pluck them out of his hand. Think what strange creatures they were that were preserved! Why, there went into that ark unclean animals two and two. May God bring some of you who have been like unclean animals unto Christ; great swine of sin, you have wandered furthest in iniquity and defiled yourselves—yet when the swine were in the ark they were safe, and so shall you be. You ravens, you black ravens of sin, if you fly to Christ he will not cast you out, but you shall be secure. If electing love shall pick you out, and effectual grace shall draw you to the door of that ark, it shall be shut upon you and you shall be saved. Within that ark there was the timid hare, but its timidity did not destroy it; there was the weak coney, but despite its weakness, in the ark it was all safe. There were to be found such slow-moving creatures as the snail; some darkness-loving creatures like the

bat, but they were all safe; and the mouse was as safe as the
was as safe as the greyhound, and the squirrel was as secur
and the timid hare was as safe as the courageous lion—n
what they were, but safe because of where they were, nam__,

Oh! what a medley the Lord's people are! What strange beings! Some ⸺
of them fathers, but not many; the great mass of them little children, who,
though they should have grown are still very carnal, and only babes in Christ
instead of full-grown men. Yet all safe; all alike in security, however much they
may differ; varying temperament, but unvarying security; differing in experience, but the same in oneness to Christ, and all in him. "Wherefore, being justified by faith, we have peace with God, through our Lord Jesus Christ"; and
so we have, whether we be great or small.

> To us the covenant stands secure,
> Tho' earth's old columns bow;
> The strong, the feeble, and the weak,
> Are one in Jesus now.

When the storm beat upon the ark, it might have destroyed the lion quite
as soon as the mouse, but it destroyed neither, because the sides of the ark
could bear the tempest; and when the floods came, the vessel could mount
higher and higher and nearer toward heaven, the deeper the waters were. So
with us: let storms and furious tempests come and our sins assail us, and our
sorrows too, yet we who are weakest are quite as secure as the strongest,
because we are in Christ, and Christ shall outlive the storm, and bear us
upward, nearer and nearer to the heaven of God.

May God grant us grace to be found of him in peace in the day of the
Lord's appearing, when the elements shall melt and the skies be rolled up like
a scroll. As I have already said, it all hangs upon that question, "Do you believe
in Christ?" If your heart trusts Christ, you are safe, come what may; but if
your heart rests not in him, you are lost, come what will. God save you, for
Jesus' sake. Amen.

> Come to the ark, come to the ark;
> To Jesus come away:
> The pestilence walks forth by night,
> The arrow flies by day.
>
> Come to the ark: the waters rise,
> The seas their billows rear

While darkness gathers o'er the skies,
Behold a refuge near.

Come to the ark, all, all that weep
Beneath the sense of sin!
Without, deep calleth unto deep
But all is peace within.

Come to the ark, ere yet the flood
Your lingering steps oppose!
Come, for the door which open stood
Is now about to close.

The Scales of Judgment

❦

Delivered on Sabbath morning, June 12, 1859, at the Music Hall, Royal Surrey Gardens. No. 257.

TEKEL; Thou art weighed in the balances, and art found wanting.
—DANIEL 5:27

There is a weighing time for kings and emperors, and all the monarchs of earth, albeit some of them have exalted themselves to a position in which they appear to be irresponsible to man. Though they escape the scales on earth, they must surely be tried at the bar of God. For nations there is a weighing time. National sins demand national punishments. The whole history of God's dealings with mankind proves that though a nation may go on in wickedness, it may multiply its oppressions; it may abound in bloodshed, tyranny, and war, but an hour of retribution draws nigh. When it shall have filled up its measure of iniquity, then shall the angel of vengeance execute its doom. There cannot be an eternal damnation for nations as nations; the destruction of men at last will be that of individuals, and at the bar of God each man must be tried for himself. The punishment, therefore, of nations, is national. The guilt they incur must receive its awful recompense in this present time state.

It was so with the great nation of the Chaldeans. They had been guilty of blood. The monuments which still remain, and which we have lately explored, prove them to have been a cruel and ferocious race. A people of a strange language they were, and stranger than their language were their deeds. God allowed that nation for a certain period to grow and thrive, till it became God's hammer, breaking in pieces many nations. It was the ax of the Almighty—his battle ax, and his weapon of war. By it he smote the loins of kings, yes, and slew mighty kings. But its time came at last. She sat alone as a queen, and said, "I shall see no sorrow," nevertheless, the Lord brought her low, and made her grind in the dust of captivity, and gave her riches to the spoiler, and her pomp to the destroyer.

Even so must it be with every nation of the earth that is guilty of oppression. Humbling itself before God, when his wrath is kindled but a little, it may for a while arrest its fate; but if it still continue in its bold unrighteousness, it shall certainly reap the harvest of its own sowing. So likewise shall it be with the nations that now abide on the face of the earth. There is no God in heaven if the iniquity of slavery go unpunished. There is no God existing in heaven above if the cry of the Negro do not bring down a red hail of blood upon the nation that still holds the black man in slavery. Nor is there a God anywhere if the nations of Europe that still oppress each other and are oppressed by tyrants do not find out to their dismay that he executes vengeance. The Lord God is the avenger of everyone that is oppressed, and the executor of everyone that oppresses. I see, this very moment, glancing at the page of the world's present history, a marvelous proof that God will take vengeance. Piedmont, the land which is at this time sodden with blood, is only at this hour suffering the vengeance that has long been hanging over it. The snows of its mountains were once red with the blood of martyrs. It is not yet forgotten how there the children of God were hunted like partridges on the mountains; and so has God directed it, that the nations that performed that frightful act upon his children shall there meet, rend, and devour each other in the slaughter, and both sides shall be almost equal, and nothing shall be seen but that God will punish those who lift their hands against his anointed.

There has never been a deed of persecution—there has never been a drop of martyr's blood shed yet, but shall be avenged, and every land guilty of it shall yet drink the cup of the wine of the wrath of God. And especially certain is there gathering an awful storm over the head of the empire of Rome—that spiritual despotism of the firstborn of hell. All the clouds of God's vengeance are gathering into one—the firmament is big with thunder, God's right arm is lifted up even now, and before long the nations of the earth shall eat her flesh and burn her with fire. They that have been made drunk with the wine of her fornication, shall soon also have to drink with her of the wine of the fierceness of his wrath; and they shall reel to and fro, their loins shall be loose, their knees shall smite together, when God fulfills the old handwriting on the rock of Patmos.

Our duty at this time is to take heed to ourselves as a nation that we purge ourselves of our great sins. Although God has given so much light, and kindly favored us with the dew of his Spirit, yet England is a hoary sinner. Favorably with mercy does God regard her, so much the rather then let each Christian try to shake off the sins of his nation from his own skirt, and let each one to the utmost of his ability labor and strive to purify this land of blood and oppression, and of everything evil that still clings to her. So may God preserve this land; and may its monarchy endure till he shall come, before whom both kings and princes shall lose their power right cheerfully even as the stars fade when the king of light—the sun—lifts up his golden head.

With this brief preface, I will leave nations and kings all to themselves, and consider the text principally as it has relation to each one of us; and may God grant that when we go out of this hall most of us may be able to say, "I thank God I have a good hope that when weighed in the scales at last I shall not be found wanting." Or, if that is too much to expect, may I yet trust some will go away convinced of sin, crying in their own spirits, "I am wanting now, but if God in his mercy meet with me, I shall not be wanting long."

I shall notice, first, that there are certain preliminary weighings which God would have us put ourselves to in this world, and which indeed he has set up as kind of tests whereby we may be able to discover what shall be the result of the last decisive weighing. After I have mentioned these, I shall then come to speak of the last tremendous weighing of the judgment day.

1. *Let us judge ourselves that we that we may not be judged.*

It is for us now to put ourselves through the various tests by which we may be able to discover whether we are, at this present time, short weight or not.

The first test I would suggest is that of *human opinion*. Now understand me. I do believe that the opinion of man is utterly valueless when that opinion is based upon false premises, and therefore draws wrong conclusions. I would not trust the world to judge God's servants, and it is a mercy to know that the world shall not have the judging of the church, but rather, the saints shall judge the world. There is a sense in which I would say with the apostle, "With me it is a very small thing that I should be judged of you, or of man's judgment: yea, I judge not myself." Human opinion is not to be put in competition with divine revelation. But I speak now of judging ourselves, and I do not think it safe, when weighing our own character, to prefer our own and exclude our neighbor's judgment. The esteem or contempt of honest men, which is instinctively shown without reference to party or prejudice, is not by any means to be despised. When a man knows that he is right, he may snap his fingers in the face of all men, but when a man's conscience tells him that he is wrong—if at the judgment bar of men he is found guilty, he must not despise it; he must rather look on the judgment of men as being the first intimation of what shall be the judgment of God.

Are you, my hearer, at this time in the estimation of all your fellow creatures condemned as one who should be avoided? Do you clearly perceive that the righteous shun you because your example would contaminate them? Have you discovered that your character is not held to be estimable among honest and respectable men? Let me assure you that you have good reason to be

r if you cannot stand the trial of an honest fellow creature—if the
/our country condemn you, if the very laws of society exclude you—
mperfect judgments of earth pronounce you too vile for its association,
ho٦. fearful must be your condemnation when you are put into the far more
rigid scale of God's justice, and terrible must be your fate when the perfect
community of the Firstborn in heaven shall rise as one man and demand that
you shall never behold their society? When a man is so bad that his fellow creatures themselves, imperfect though they be, are able to see in him, not the
mere seeds, but the very flower, the full bloom of iniquity, he should tremble.
If you cannot pass that test, if human opinion condemn, if your own conscience declare that opinion to be just, you have good need to tremble indeed,
for you are put into the balances and are found wanting.

I have thought it right to mention this balance. There may be some present to whom it may be pertinent, but at the same time, there are far better
tests for men, tests which are not so easily to be misunderstood. And I would
go through some of these. One of the scales into which I would have every
man put himself, at least once in his life—I say at least once, because, if not,
heaven is to him a place, the gates of which are shut forever—I would have
every man put himself into the scales of the *divine law*. There stands the law
of God. This law is a balance which will turn, even were there but a grain of
sand in it. It is true to a hair. It moves upon the diamond of God's eternal
immutable truth. I put but one weight into the scale; it is this: "Thou shalt love
the Lord thy God with all thy heart, with all thy mind, with all thy soul, and
with all thy strength," and I invite any man who thinks himself to be of the
right stamp, and flatters himself that he has no need of mercy, no need of
washing in the blood of Jesus Christ, no need of any atonement—I invite him
to put himself into the scales and see whether he be full weight, when there
be but so much as this one commandment in the other scale. O my friends, if
we did but try ourselves by the very first commandment of the law, we must
acknowledge that we are guilty. But when we drop in weight after weight, till
the whole sacred ten are there, there is not a man under the cope [covering]
of heaven who has one grain of wit left, but must confess that he is short of
the mark, that he falls below the standard which the law of God requires. Mrs.
Too-Good has often declared that she herself has done all her duty, and perhaps a little more; that she has been even more kind to the poor than there
was any occasion for; that she has gone to church more frequently than even
her religion requires; that she has been more attentive to the sacraments than
the best of her neighbors, and if *she* does not enter heaven, she does not know
who will. "If I have not a portion among the saints, who can possibly hope to

see God's face in light?" No, madam, but I am sorry for you; you are light as a feather when you go into the scales. In these wooden balances of your own ceremonies you may, perhaps, be found right enough, but in those eternal scales, with those tremendous weights—the Ten Commandments of the law—the declaration is suspended over your poor foolish head. "Thou art weighed in the balances, and art found wanting."

There may, perhaps, in congregations like this, be some extremely respectable body who has from his youth up, as he imagines, kept God's law; his country, family, or associates can bring no charge against him, and so he wraps himself up and considers that really he is the man, and that when he appears at the gate of heaven, he will be received as a rightful owner and proprietor of the reward of the righteous. Ah, my friend, if you would take the trouble just to sit down and weigh yourself in the scales of the law—if you would take but one command, the one in which you think yourself least guilty, the one that you imagine you have kept best, and really look at its intent, and spirit, and view it in all its length and breadth, in truth I know you would keep out of the scale and say, "Alas, when I hoped to have gone down with a sound of congratulation, I find myself hurled up, light as the dust of the balance, while the tremendous law of God comes sounding down and shakes the house." Let each man do this, and every one of us must retire from this place saying, "I am weighed in the balances, and I am found wanting."

And now the true believer comes forward, and he claimed to be weighed in another balance, for, says he, according to this balance, if I be what I profess to be, I am not found wanting, for I can bring with me the perfect righteousness of Jesus Christ, and that is full weight, even though the Ten Commandments of the law be weighed against it. I bring with me the full atonement, the perfect satisfaction of Jesus' blood, and the perfect righteousness of a divine being, the spotless righteousness of Jesus the Son of God. I can be weighed against the law, and yet sit securely, knowing that now and forever, I am equal to the law. It has nothing against me since Christ is mine. Its terrors have no power to frighten me, and as for its demands, they can exact nothing of me for they are fulfilled to the utmost in Christ.

Well, I propose now to take professors and put them into the scales and try them. Let each one of us put ourselves into the scale of *conscience*. Many make a profession of religion in this age. It is the time of shams. There were never so many liars in the world since the days of Adam, as there are now. The father of lies has been more prolific of children at this than at any other period. There is such an abundance of newspapers and of talkers and of readers: and consequently flying reports, wrong news, and evil tales, are far more numerous than ever. So, too, there is a great deal of vain show with religion. I sometimes fear we have not a grain more religion in England now than we had in the time of the Puritans. Then, though the stream in which it ran was narrow, it did run very deep indeed; now, the banks have been burst; a great extent of country is covered with religious profession; but I tremble lest we should find at last that the flood was not deep enough to float our souls to heaven.

Will each one now in this congregation put himself into the scale of *conscience*, sit down and ask, "Is my profession true? Do I feel that before God I am an heir of the promises? When I sit at my Savior's table, have I any right to be a guest? Can I truly say that when I profess to be converted, I only profess what I have actually proved? When I talk experimentally about the things of the kingdom of God, is that experience a borrowed tale, or have I felt what I say in my own breast? When I stand up to preach, do I preach that which I have really tasted and handled, or do I only repeat that which I have learned to utter with the lip, though it has never been fused in the crucible of my own heart?" Conscience is not very readily cheated. There are some men whose consciences are not a safe balance; they have by degrees become so hardened in sin that conscience refuses to work; but still I will hope that most of us may abide by the test of our own conscience, if we let it freely work. Dear friends, I would that you would often retire to your chambers alone; shut the door and shut out all the world, and then sit and review your past life; scan carefully your present character and your present position; and do, I beseech you, try to get an honest answer from your own conscience. Bring up everything that you can think of that might lead you to doubt. You need be under no difficulty here; for are there not enough sins committed by us every day to warrant our suspicions that we are not God's children? Well, let all these black accusers for death, let them all have their say. Do not cloak your sins. Read your diary through, let all your iniquities come up before you (this is the pith of confession); and then ask conscience whether you can truly say, "I have repented of all these. God is my witness, I hate these things with a perfect hatred. God also hears me witness that my trust is fixed alone in him who is the Savior of sinners, for salvation and justification. If I be not awfully deceived, I am a partaker of divine grace, having been regenerated and begotten again unto a lively hope." Oh, that conscience may help each of us to say, "I am not a mere painted image of life, but I trust I have the life of Jesus made manifest in my body." My profession is not the pompous pageantry with which dead souls are carried respectably to perdition; but it is the joy, the hope, the confidence of one who is being borne along in the chariot of mercy, to his Father's home above.

"Ah! how many people are really afraid to look their religion in the face! They know it to be so bad, they dare not examine it. They are like bankrupts that keep no books. They would be very glad for a fire to consume their books, if they ever kept any, for they know the balance is all on the wrong side. They are losing, breaking up, and they would not wish to keep an account of their losses or villainies. A man who is afraid to examine himself may rest assured that his ship is rotten, and that it will not be long before it founders in the sea, to his eternal shipwreck. Call up conscience; put yourself in the scale, and God help you, that the verdict may not be against you—that it may not be said of you, "You are weighed in the balances, and are found wanting."

I would have every man also weigh himself in the scales of *God's Word*—not merely in that part of it which we call legal, and which has respect to us in our fallen state; but let us weigh ourselves in the scale of the gospel. You will find it sometimes a holy exercise, to read some psalm of David, when his soul was most full of grace; and if you were to put questions as you read each verse, saying to yourself, "Can I say this? Have I felt as David felt? Have my bones ever been broken with sin as his were when he penned his penitential psalms? Has my soul ever been full of true confidence in the hour of difficulty, as his was when he sang of God's mercies in the cave of Adullam or the holds of Engedi? Can I take the cup of salvation and call upon the name of the Lord? Can I pay my vows now unto the Lord, in the courts of his house, in the presence of all his people?" I am afraid that the book of Psalms itself would be enough to convince some of you that your religion is but superficial, that it is but a vain show and not a vital reality. God help you often to try yourselves in that scale.

Then read over the life of Christ, and as you read, ask yourselves whether you are conformed to him, such as he describes a true disciple. Endeavor to see whether you have any of the meekness, any of the humility, any of the lovely spirit which he constantly inculcated and displayed. Try yourselves by the Sermon on the Mount—you will find it a good scale in which to weigh your spirits. Take then the epistles and see whether you can go with the apostle in what he said of his experience. Have you ever cried out like him: "O wretched man that I am! who shall deliver me from the body of this death?"? Have you ever felt like him, that "this is a faithful saying, and worthy of all acceptation, that Christ Jesus came into the world to save sinners"? Have you ever known his self-abasement? Could you say that you seemed to yourself the chief of sinners and always accounted yourself less than the least of all saints? And have you known anything of his devotion? Could you join with him and say, "For me to live is Christ, and to die is gain"? O brethren! The best of us—

if we put the Bible into the scales for the proof of our state, if we read God's Word as a test of our spiritual condition—the very best of us has cause to tremble. Before almighty God, on our bended knees, with our Bible before us, we have good reason to stop many a time and say, "Lord, I feel I have never yet been here, oh, bring me here! Give me true penitence, such as this I read of. Give me real faith. Oh, let me not have a counterfeit religion! Give me that which is the current coin of the realm of heaven—your own sterling grace, which shall pass in the great day, when the gates of heaven shall be opened, and, alas! the gates of hell wide open too." Try yourselves by God's Word, and I fear there are some who will love to rise from it, and say, "I am weighed in the balances and found wanting."

Yet again, God has been pleased to set another means of trial before us. When God puts us into the scales I am about to mention, namely, the scales of providence, it behooves us very carefully to watch ourselves and see whether or not we be found wanting. Some men are tried in the scales of adversity. Some of you, my dear friends, may have come here very sorrowful. Your business fails, your earthly prospects are growing dark; it is midnight with you in this world; you have sickness in the house; the wife of your bosom languishes before your weeping eyes; your children perhaps, by their ingratitude, have wounded your spirits. But you are a professor of religion; you know what God is doing with you now; he is testing and trying you. He knows you, and he would have you know that a summertime religion is not sufficient; he would have you see whether your faith can stand the test of trial and trouble. Remember Job; what a scale was that in which he was put! What weights of affliction were those cast in one after another, very mountains of sore trouble; and yet he could bear them all, and he came out of the scales proof against all the weight that even satanic strength could hurl into the scale.

And is it so with you? Can you now say, "The Lord gave, and the Lord hath taken away, blessed be the name of the Lord"? Can you submit to his will without murmuring? Or if you cannot master such a phase of religion as this, are you able still to feel that you cannot complain against God? Do you still say, "Though he slay me, yet will I trust in him"? O my friends, remember that if your religion will not stand the day of adversity, if it afford you no comfort in the time of storms, you would be better in that case without it than with it; for with it you are deceived, but without it you might discover your true condition and seek the Lord as a penitent sinner. If you are now broken in pieces by a little adversity, what will become of you in the day when all the tempests of God shall be let loose on your soul? If you have run with the footmen, and they have wearied you, what will you do in the swellings of Jordan? If you cannot endure the open grave, how can you endure the trump of the archangel and the terrific thunders of the last great day? If your burning house is too much for you, what will you do in a burning world? If thunder and lightning alarm you, what will you do when the world is in a blaze, and when all the thunders of God leave their hiding place and rush pealing through the world? If mere trial distress you and grieve you, oh, what will you do when all the hurricanes of divine vengeance shall sweep across the earth and shake its very pillars till they reel and reel again? Yes, friends, I would have you, as often as you are tried and troubled, see how you bear it—whether your faith then stands and whether you could see God's right hand, even when it is wrapped in clouds, whether you can discover the silver lining to the black clouds of tribulation. God help you to come out of the scales, for many are weighed in them and have been found wanting.

Another set of scales there is, too, of an opposite color. Those I have described are painted black; these are of golden hue. They are the scales of *prosperity*. Many a man has endured the chills of poverty who could not endure sunny weather. Some men's religion is very much like the palace of the queen of Russia, which had been built out of solid slabs of ice. It could stand the frost; the roughest breeze could not destroy it; the sharp touch of winter could not devour it; they but strengthened and made it more lasting. But summer melted it all away, and where once were the halls of revelry, nothing remained but the black rolling river. How many have been destroyed by prosperity? The fumes of popularity have turned the brains of many a man. The adulation of multitudes has laid thousands low. Popular applause has its foot in the sand, even when it has its head among the stars. Many have I known who in a cottage seemed to fear God but in a mansion have forgotten him. When their daily bread was earned with the sweat of their brow, then it was they served the Lord and went up to his house with gladness. But their seeming religion all departed when their flocks and herds increased, and their gold and silver was multiplied.

It is no easy thing to stand the trial of prosperity. You know the old fable; I will just put it in a Christian light. When the winds of affliction blow on a Christian's head, he just pulls around him the cloak of heavenly consolation and girds his religion about him all the tighter for the fury of the storm. But when the sun of prosperity shines on him, the traveler grows warm and full of delight and pleasure; he ungirds his cloak and lays it aside, so that what the storms of affliction never could accomplish, the soft hand and the witchery of prosperity has been able to perform. It has loosed the loins of many a mighty man. It has been the Delilah that has shorn the locks and taken away the strength of many a Samson. This rock has witnessed the most fatal wrecks.

> More the treacherous calm I dread,
> Than tempests rolling over head.

But shall we be able to say after passing through prosperity, "This is not my rest, this is not my God. Let him give me what he may, I will thank him for it, yet will I rejoice in the giver rather than the gift; I will say unto the Lord, you only are my rest"? It is well if you can come out of these scales enabled honestly to hope that you are not found wanting.

There are again the scales of *temptation*. Many and many a man seems for a time to run well; but it is temptation that tries the Christian. In your business you are now honest and upright, but suppose a speculation cross your path which involve but a very slight departure from the high standard of Christianity, and indeed would not involve any departure from the low standard which your fellow tradesmen follow. Do you think you would be able to say, "How can I do this great wickedness and sin against God?"? Could you say, "Should such a man as I do this? Shall I haste to be rich, for if I do, I shall not be innocent?"? How has it been with you? You have had your trial time. There has been an opportunity of making a little: have you taken it? Has God enabled you to endure when tempted, whether to unlawful gain or to lustful pleasure or to pride and vanity? Have you been enabled to stand proof against all these, and to say, "Get thee behind me, Satan, for thou savorest not the things which be of God, but those which be of man and of sin"? How have you stood the test of temptation?

If you have never been tempted, you know nothing about this. How can we tell the worthiness of the ship till she has been at sea in the storm? You cannot know what you are till you have been through the practical test of everyday life. How then has it been with you? Have you been weighed in the balance, and have you been enabled to say, "I know through grace I have been kept in the hour of temptation, and with the temptation the Lord has always sent a way of escape. And here I am glorying in his grace; I cannot rest in myself, but still I can say, 'I am truly his.' The work within me is not of man, neither by man: it is the work of the Spirit. I have found succor and support when my heart and my flesh have failed me"?

It is probable, my hearers, that most of you are professors of religion; let me ask you again very earnestly to test and try yourselves, whether your religion be real or not. If there be many false prophets in the world, and those prophets have followers, must there not be many false men who are fatally deceived? Do not suppose, I beseech you, because you are a deacon—or have been baptized, or are a member of the church, or are professors—you are therefore safe. The bleaching bones of the skeletons of self-deceived ones should warn you. On the rock of presumption, thousands have been split that once sailed merrily enough. Take care, O mariner! though your bark may be gaily trimmed and may be brightly painted, yet it is none the surer after all. Take heed, lest the rocks be seen beneath the keel, lest they pierce you through, and lest the waters of destruction overwhelm you. Oh! do not, I entreat you, say, "Why make this stir? I daresay I shall be all right at last." Do not let your eternal state be a matter of suspicion or doubt. Decide now, I beseech you, decide now in your conscience whether you are Christ's or not. Of all the most miserable men in the world, and the most hopeless, I think those are most to be pitied who are indifferent and careless about religion. There are some men whose feelings never run deeper than their skin; they either have no heart, or else it is so set round with fatness that you can never touch them. I like to see a man either desponding or rejoicing; either anxious about his eternal state or else confident about it. But you who never will ques tion yourselves —you are just like the bullock going to the slaughter or like the sheep that will enter the very slaughterhouse and lick the knife that is about to take its blood. I wish I could speak this morning somewhat more earnestly. Oh, that some sparks from the divine fire could now light up my soul, I think I could speak to you like some of the prophets of old, when they stood in the midst of a professing generation, to warn them. Oh, that the very voice of God would speak to each heart this morning! While God is thundering on high, may he thunder below in your souls! Be warned, my hearers, against self-deception. Be true to yourselves. If God be God, serve him, and do it truly; if the devil be God, serve him, and serve him honestly, and serve him faithfully. But do not pretend to be serving God while you are really indifferent and careless about it.

2. I must now close by endeavoring to speak of *the last great balance*; **and here would I speak very solemnly, and may the Spirit of God be with us.**

Time shall soon be over; eternity must soon begin; death is hurrying onward; the pale horse at his utmost speed is coming to every inhabitant of this earth. The arrow of death is fitted to the string, and soon shall it be sent home. Man's heart is the target. Then, after death, comes the judgment; the dread assize shall soon commence. The trump of the archangel shall awake the sleeping myriads, and, standing on their feet, they shall confront the God against whom they have sinned. I think I see the scales hanging in heaven, so massive that none but the hand of Deity can uphold them. Let me cast my eye upward and consider that hour when I must myself enter those scales and be weighed once for all.

Come, let me speak for each man present. Those scales yonder are exact; I may deceive my fellows here, but deceive God I cannot then. I may be weighed in the balances of earth, which shall give but a partial verdict, and so commit myself to a false idea that I am what I am not, that I am hopeful when I am hopeless. But *those* scales are true. There is no means whatever of flattering them into a false declaration; they will cry aloud and spare not. When I get there, the voice of flattery shall be changed into the voice of honesty. Here I may go daily on crying, "Peace, peace, when there is no peace"; but there the naked truth shall startle me, and not a single word of consolation shall be given me that is not true. Let me therefore ponder the fact, that those scales are exactly true and cannot be deceived. Let me remember also, that whether I will or not, into those scales I must go. God will not take me on my profession. I may bring my witnesses with me; I may bring my minister and the deacons of the church to give me a character, which might be thought all-sufficient among men, but God will tolerate no subterfuge. Into the scales he will put me, do what I may, whatever the opinion of others may be of me and whatever my own profession. And let me remember, too, that I must be altogether weighed in the scales. I cannot hope that God will weigh my head and pass over my heart—that because I have correct notions of doctrine, therefore he will forget that my heart is impure or my hands guilty of iniquity. My all must be cast into the scales. Come, let me stretch my imagination and picture myself about to be put into those scales. Shall I be able to walk boldly up and enter them, knowing whom I have believed, and being persuaded that the blood of Christ and his perfect righteousness shall bear me harmless through it all; or shall I be dragged with terror and dismay? Shall the angel come and say, "You must enter"? Shall I bend my knee and cry, "Oh, it is all right," or shall I seek to escape? Now, thrust into the scale, do I see myself waiting for one solemn moment. My feet have touched the bottom of the scales, and there stand those everlasting weights and now which way are they turned? Which way shall it be? Do I descend in the scale with joy and delight, being found through Jesus' righteousness to be full weight, and so accepted; or must I rise, light, frivolous, unsound in all my fancied hopes, and kick the beam? Oh, shall it be, that I must go where the rough hand of vengeance shall seize and drag me downward, into fell despair? Can you picture the moments of suspense? I can see a poor man standing on the drop with the rope round his neck, and oh, what an instant of apprehension must that be; what thoughts of horror must float through his soul! How must a world of misery be compressed into a second! But, O my hearers, there is a far more terrible moment still for you that are godless, Christless, careless: that have made a profession of religion, and yet have it not in your hearts. I see you in the scales, but what shall we say? The wailings of hell seem not sufficient to express your misery, in the scales without Christ! Not long before you shall be in the jaws of hell, without pity and without compassion.

O my dear hearers! if you could hope to get to heaven without being weighed—if God would believe what you say without testing you, I would not care about asking you this morning to ascertain the state of your own hearts. But if God will try you, try yourselves; if he will judge you, judge your own hearts. Don't say that because you profess to be religious therefore you are right—that because others imagine you to be safe that therefore you are so. Weigh yourselves; put your hearts into the balance. Do not be deceived. Pull the bandage from your eyes, that your blindness may be removed, and that you may pass a just opinion upon yourselves as to what you are. I would have you not only see yourselves as others see you, but I would have you see yourselves as God sees you; for that, after all, is your real state; his eye is not to be mistaken; he is the God of truth, and just and right is he.

How fearful a thing will it be, if any of us who are members of Christ's church shall be cast into hell at last. The higher we ascend, the greater will be our fall, like Icarus in the old parable, who flew aloft with waxen wings, till the sun did melt them and he fell. And some of you are flying like that: you are flying up with waxen wings. What if the terrible heat of the judgment day should melt them! I sometimes try to picture, how terrible the reverse to me if found to be rejected at last. Let what I shall say for myself suit for all. No, and must it be, if I live in this world and think I am a Christian and am not—must it be that I must go from the songs of the sanctuary to the cursings of the synagogue of Satan? Must I go from the cup of the Eucharist to the cup of devils? Must I go from the table of the Lord to the feast of fiends? Shall these lips that now proclaim the word of Jesus one day utter the wailings of perdition? Shall this tongue that has sung the praises of the Redeemer be moved with blasphemy? Shall it be that this body which has been the receptacle of so many a mercy—shall it become the very house and home of every misery that vengeance can invent? Shall these eyes that now look on God's people one day behold the frightful sights of spirits destroyed in that all-consuming fire? And must it be that the ears that have heard the hallelujahs of this morning shall one day hear the shrieks and groans and howls of the lost and damned spirits? It must be so if we be not Christ's. Oh, how frightful will it be! I think I see some grave professor at last condemned to hell. There are multitudes of sinners, lying in their irons and tossing on their beds of flame; lifting themselves upon their elbows for a moment, they seem to forget their tortures as they see the professor come in, and they cry, "Are you become like one of us? Is the preacher himself damned? What! is the deacon of the church below come to sit with drunkards and with swearers? Ah," they cry, "aha, aha, are you bound up in the same bundle with us after all?" Surely the mockery of hell must be itself a most fearful torture; professing sinners mocked by those who never professed religion. But mortal fire can never describe the miseries of a disappointed, blasted hope, when that hope is lost—it involves the loss of mercy, the loss of Christ, the loss of life—and it involves, moreover, the terrible destruction and the awful vengeance of almighty God.

Let us one and all go home this day, when yet God's sky is heavy, and let us bend ourselves at his altar and cry for mercy. Every man apart—husband apart from wife. Apart, let us seek our chambers of praying again and again, "Lord renew me; Lord forgive me; Lord accept me." And while, perhaps, the tempest which is now lowering over the sky, and before another tempest direr still, shall fall on us with its fearful terrors, may you find peace. May we not then find ourselves lost, lost forever, where hope can never come! It shall be my duty to search myself. I hope I shall be enabled to put myself into the scale; promise me, my hearers, that each of you will do the same. I was told one day this week by someone, that having preached for several Sabbaths lately upon the comforting doctrines of God's Word, he was afraid that some of you would begin to console yourselves with the idea that you were God's elect when perhaps you were not. Well, at least, such a thing shall not happen if I have done what I hoped to do this morning. God bless you, for Jesus' sake.

"I Would; but Ye Would Not"

Intended for reading on Lord's Day, October 7, 1894; delivered on Lord's Day evening, July 22, 1888, at the Metropolitan Tabernacle, Newington. No. 2381.

O Jerusalem, Jerusalem, thou that killest the prophets, and stonest them which are sent onto thee, how often would I have gathered thy children together, even as a hen gathereth her chickens under her wings, and ye would not!
—MATTHEW 23:37

This is not and could not be the language of a mere man. It would be utterly absurd for any man to say that he would have gathered the inhabitants of a city together, "even as a hen gathereth her chickens under her wings." Besides, the language implies that, for many centuries, by the sending of the prophets, and by many other warnings, God would often have gathered the children of Jerusalem together as a hen gathers her chickens under her wings. Now, Christ could not have said that throughout those ages, he would have gathered those people, if he had been only a man. If his life began at Bethlehem, this would be an absurd statement; but, as the Son of God, ever loving the sons of men, ever desirous of the good of Israel, he could say that, in sending the prophets, even though they were stoned and killed, he had again and again shown his desire to bless his people till he could truly say, "How often would I have gathered your children together!"

Some who have found difficulties in this lament have said that it was the language of Christ as man. I beg to put in a very decided negative to that; it is, and it must be, the utterance of the Son of man, the Son of God, the Christ in his complex person as human and divine. I am not going into any of the difficulties just now; but you could not fully understand this passage, from any point of view, unless you believed it to be the language of one who was both God and man.

This verse shows also that the ruin of men lies with themselves. Christ puts it very plainly, "I would; but ye would not." "How often would I have gathered thy children together, and ye would not!" That is a truth, about which, I hope, we have never had any question; we hold tenaciously that salvation is all of grace, but we also believe with equal firmness that the ruin of man is entirely the result of his own sin. It is the will of God that saves; it is the will of man that damns. Jerusalem stands and is preserved by the grace and favor of the most High; but Jerusalem is burned, and her stones are cast down, through the transgression and iniquity of men, which provoked the justice of God.

There are great deeps about these two points; but I have not been accustomed to lead you into any deeps, and I am not going to do so at this time. The practical part of theology is that which it is most important for us to understand. Any man may get himself into a terrible labyrinth who thinks continually of the sovereignty of God alone, and he may equally get into deeps that are likely to drown him if he meditates only on the free will of man. The best thing is to take what God reveals to you and to believe that. If God's Word leads me to the right, I go there; if it leads me to the left, I go there; if it makes me stand still, I stand still. If you so act, you will be safe; but if you try to be wise above that which is written, and to understand that which even angels do not comprehend, you will certainly befog yourself. I desire ever to bring before you practical rather than mysterious subjects, and our present theme is one that concerns us all. The great destroyer of man is the will of man. I do not believe that man's free will has ever saved a soul; but man's free will has been the ruin of multitudes. "Ye would not" is still the solemn accusation of Christ against guilty men. Did he not say, at another time, "Ye will not come unto me, that ye might have life"? The human will is desperately set against God, and is the great devourer and destroyer of thousands of good intentions and emotions which never come to anything permanent because the will is acting in opposition to that which is right and true.

That, I think, is the very marrow of the text, and I am going to handle it in this fashion.

1. First, consider from the very condescending emblem used by our Lord, *what God is to those who come to him.*

He gathers them, "as a hen gathereth her chickens under her wings." Let us dwell upon that thought for a few minutes. It is a very marvelous thing that God should condescend to be compared to a hen, that the Christ, the Son of the Highest, the Savior of men, should stoop to so homely a piece of imagery as to liken himself to a hen. There must be something very instructive in this metaphor, or our Lord would not have used it in such a connection.

Those of you who have been gathered unto Christ know, first, that *by this wonderful gatherer, you have been gathered into happy association.* The chickens, beneath the wings of the hen, look very happy all crowded together. What a sweet little family party they are! How they hide themselves away in great contentment and chirp their little note of joy! You, dear friends, who have never been converted, find very noisy fellowship, I am afraid, in this world; you do not get much companionship that helps you, blesses you, gives you rest of mind; but if you had been gathered to the Lord's Christ, you would have found that there are many sweetnesses in this life in being beneath the wings of the most High. He who comes to Christ finds father and mother and sister and brother; he finds many dear and kind friends who are themselves connected with Christ, and who therefore love those who are joined to him. Among the greatest happinesses of my life, certainly, I put down Christian fellowship; and I think that many who have come from the country to London, have, for a long time, missed much of this fellowship till, at last, they have fallen in with Christian people, and they have found themselves happy again. O lonely sinner, you who come in and out of this place, and say, "Nobody seems to care about me," if you will come to Christ, and join with the church which is gathered beneath his wings, you will soon find happy fellowship! I remember that, in the times of persecution, one of the saints said that he had lost his father and his mother by being driven away from his native country, but he said, "I have found a hundred fathers, and a hundred mothers, for into whatsoever Christian house I have gone, I have been looked upon with so much kindness by those who have received me as an exile from my native land, that everyone has seemed to be a father and a mother to me." If you come to Christ, I feel persuaded that he will introduce you to many people who will give you happy fellowship.

But that is merely the beginning. A hen is to her little chicks, next, a cover of safety. There is a hawk in the sky; the mother bird can see it, though the chickens cannot; she gives her peculiar cluck of warning, and quickly they come and hide beneath her wings. The hawk will not hurt them now; beneath her wings they are secure. This is what God is to those who come to him by Jesus Christ—*he is the giver of safety.* "He shall cover thee with his feathers, and under his wings shalt thou trust: his truth shall be thy shield and buckler." Even the attraction of your old sins, or the danger of future temptations—you shall be preserved from all these perils when you come to Christ, and thus hide away under him.

The figure our Lord used is full of meaning, for, in the next place, the hen is to her chicks *the source of comfort.* It is a cold night, and they would be frozen if they remained outside; but she calls them in, and when they are under her wings, they derive warmth from their mother's breast. It is wonderful, the care of a hen for her little ones; she will sit so carefully and keep her wings so widely spread, that they may all be housed. What a cabin, what a palace, it is for the young chicks to get there under the mother's wings! The snow may fall, or the rain may come pelting down, but the wings of the hen protect the chicks; and you, dear friend, if you come to Christ, shall not only have safety, but comfort. I speak what I have experienced. There is a deep, sweet comfort about hiding yourself away in God, for when troubles come, wave upon wave, blessed is the man who has a God to give him mercy upon mercy. When affliction comes, or bereavement comes, when loss of property comes, when sickness comes, in your own body, there is nothing wanted but your God. Ten thousand things, apart from him, cannot satisfy you, or give you comfort. There, let them all go; but if God be yours, and you hide away under his wings, you are as happy in him as the chickens are beneath the hen.

Then the hen is also to her chicks *the fountain of love*. She loves them; did you ever see a hen fight for her chickens? She is a timid enough creature at any other time; but there is no timidity when her chicks are in danger. What an affection she has for them; not for all chicks, for I have known her kill the chickens of another brood; but for her own what love she has! Her heart is all devoted to them. But, oh, if you want to know the true fountain of love, you must come to Christ! You will never have to say, "Nobody loves me; I am pining, with an aching heart, for a love that can fill and satisfy it." The love of Jesus fills to overflowing the heart of man and makes him well content under all circumstances. I would that God had gathered you all, my dear hearers. I know that he has gathered many of you, blessed be his name; but still there are some here, chicks without a hen, sinners without a Savior, men and women and children who have never been reconciled to God.

The hen is also to her chicks *the cherisher of growth*. They would not develop if they were not taken care of; in their weakness they need to be cherished, that they may come to the fullness of their perfection. And when the child of God lives near to Christ, and hides beneath his wings, how fast he grows! There is no advancing from grace to grace, from feeble faith to strong faith, and from little fervency to great fervency, except by getting near to God.

The emblem used by our Lord is a far more instructive figure than I have time to explain. When the Lord gathers sinners to himself, then it is that they find in him all that the chicks find in the hen, and infinitely more.

2. Now notice, secondly, *what God does to gather men*.

They are straying, and wandering about, but he gathers them. According to the text, Jesus says, "How often would I have gathered thy children together!" How did God gather those of us who have come to him?

He gathers us, first, *by making himself known to us.* When we come to understand who he is and what he is, and know something of his love and tenderness and greatness, then we come to him. Ignorance keeps us away from him; but to know God, and his Son, Jesus Christ, is eternal life. Hence I urge you diligently to study the Scriptures, and to be as often as you can hearing a faithful preacher of the gospel, that, knowing the Lord, you may by that knowledge be drawn toward him. These are the cords of love with which the Spirit of God draws men to Christ. He makes Christ known to us. He shows us Christ in the grandeur of his divine and human nature, Christ in the humiliation of his sufferings, Christ in the glory of his resurrection, Christ in the love of his heart, in the power of his arm, in the efficacy of his plea, in the virtue of his blood; and, as we learn these sacred lessons, we say, "That is the Christ for me, that is the God for me"; and thus we are gathered unto him.

But God gathers many to himself *by the call of his servants.* You see that, of old, he sent his prophets; now, he sends his ministers. If God does not send us to you, brethren, we shall never gather you; if we come to you in our own name, we shall come in vain; but if the Lord has sent us, then he will bless us, and our message will be made to you by means of gathering you to Christ. I would much rather cease to preach than be allowed to go on preaching but never to gather souls to God. I can truly say that I have no wish to say a pretty thing or turn a period or utter a nice figure of speech; I want to win your souls, to slay your sin, to do practical work for God, with each man, each woman, each child, who shall come into this tabernacle; and I ask the prayers of God's people that it may be so. It is thus that God gathers men to himself, by the message which he gives to them through his servants.

The Lord has also *many other ways of calling men to himself.* You saw, this morning, that Peter was called to repentance by the crowing of a cock; and the Lord can use a great many means of bringing sinners to himself! Omnipotence has servants everywhere; and God can use every kind of agent, even though it appears most unsuitable, to gather together his own chosen ones. He has called some of you; he has called some of you who have not yet come to him. The text says, "How often!" It does not tell us how often; but it puts it as a matter of wonder, "How often!," with a note of exclamation.

Let me ask you, how often has God called some of you? Conscience has whispered its message to the most of you. When you come to see men dying, if you talk seriously with them, they will sometimes tell you that they are unprepared, but that they have often had tremblings and suspicions; they have long suffered from unrest, and sometimes they have been "almost persuaded." I should not think that there is a person in this place who has not been sometimes made to shake and tremble at the thought of the world to come. How often has it been so with you? "How often," says God, "would I have gathered you?"!

The Lord sometimes speaks to us, not so much by conscience, as by providence. That death in the family, what a voice it was to us! When your mother died, when your poor father passed away, what a gathering time it seemed to be then! You soon forgot all about it; but you did feel it then. Ah, my dear woman, when your babe was taken from your bosom, and the little coffin left the house, you remember how you felt; and you, father, when your prattling boy sang the Sunday school hymn to you on his dying bed and well-nigh broke your heart, then was the Lord going forth in his providence to gather you. You were being gathered, but you would not come; according to our text, you "would not."

It has not always been by death that the Lord has spoken to you; for you have had other calls. When you have been brought low or have been out of a situation [employment], when, sometimes, a Christian friend has spoken to you, when you have read something in a tract or paper which has compelled you to pull up and made you stand aghast for a while, has not all that had a reference to this text, "How often, how often, how often would I have gathered thee?"? God knocks many times at some men's doors. I know that there is a call of his which is effectual; oh, that you might hear it! But there are many other calls which come to men, of whom Christ says, "Many are called, but few are chosen." How often has he called you? I wish you would try and reckon up how often the almighty God has come to you and spread out his warm wide wings, and yet this has been true, "I would have gathered you, but you would not."

One more way in which God gathers men is by continuing still to have patience with them, and sending the same message to them. I am always afraid that you, who hear me constantly, will get to feel, "We have heard him so long and so often that he cannot say anything fresh." Why, did I not use to shake you, when first you heard me, and compel you to shed many tears in the early days of your coming to this house? And now—well, you can hear it all without a tremor; you are like the blacksmith's dog, that goes to sleep while the sparks are flying from the anvil. Down in Southwark, at the place where they make the big boilers, a man has to get inside to hold the hammer while they are riveting. There is an awful noise—the first time that a man goes in he feels that he cannot stand it, and that he will die. He loses his hearing, it is such a terrible din. But they tell me that, after a while, some have been known even to go to sleep while the men have been hammering. So it is in hearing the gospel; men grow hardened, and that which was, at one time, a very powerful call, seems to be, at the last, no call at all. Yet still, here you are, and your hair is getting gray; here you are, you have long passed the prime of life; here you are, you were in a shipwreck once, or you had an accident, or you caught the fever, but you did not die, and here you are. God still speaks to you, not saying, "Go," but "Come, come." Christ has not yet said to you, "Depart, you cursed," but he still cries, "Come unto me, all ye that labor and are heavy laden, and I will give you rest." This is how God calls, and how he gathers men by the pertinacity of his infinite compassion, in still inviting them to come unto him that they may obtain eternal life.

3. Well, now, a third point, and a very important one is this, *what men need to make them come to God.*

According to the text, God does gather men; but what is wanted on their part? Our Savior said of those that rejected him, "Ye would not."

What is wanted is, first, *the real will to come to God.* You have heard a great deal, I daresay, about the wonderful faculty of free will. I have already told you my opinion of free will; but it also happens that that is the very thing that is wanted, a will toward that which is good. There is where the sinner fails; what he needs is a real will. "Oh yes!" men say, "We are willing, we are willing." But you are not willing. If we can get the real truth, you are not willing; there is no true willingness in your hearts, for a true willingness is *a practical willingness.* The man who is willing to come to Christ says, "I must away with my sins, I must away with my self-righteousness, and I must seek him who alone can save me."

Men talk about being willing to be saved, and dispute about free will; but when it comes to actual practice, they are not willing. They have no heart to repent; they will to keep on with their sin; they will to continue in their self-righteousness; but they do not will, with any practical resolve, to come to Christ. There is need of *an immediate will.* Every unconverted person here is willing to come to Christ before he dies; I never met with a person yet who was not; but are you willing to come to Christ now? That is the point. "Today, if you will hear his voice, harden not your hearts." But you answer, "Our hearts are not hardened, we only ask for a little more time." A little more time for what? A little more time in which to go on rebelling against God? A little more time in which to run the awful risk of eternal destruction? So, you see, it is a real will and an immediate will that is needed.

With some, it is *a settled will* that is wanted. Oh yes, they are ready! They feel as soon as the preacher begins to speak; they are impressed during the singing of the first hymn. There is a revival service, and after the meeting they begin telling you what they have felt. Look at those people on Wednesday. They have got over Monday and Tuesday with some little "rumblings of heart"; but what about Wednesday? They are as cold as a cucumber; every feeling that they had on Sunday is gone from them; they have no memory of it whatever. Their goodness is as the morning cloud, and as the early dew it passes away. How some people do deceive us with their good resolves, in which there is nothing at all, for there is no settled will!

With others, what is lacking is *a submissive will*. Yes, they are willing to be saved; but then they do not want to be saved by grace; they are not willing to give themselves up altogether to the Savior; they will not renounce their own righteousness and submit themselves to the righteousness of Christ. Well, that practically means that there is not any willingness at all, for unless you accept God's way of salvation, it is no use for you to talk about your will. Here is the great evil that is destroying you, and that will destroy you before long, and land you in hell: "You would not, you would not." Oh, that God's grace might come upon you, subduing and renewing your will, and making you willing in the day of his power!

4. My last point is a very solemn one. I shall not weary you with it. *What will become of men who are not gathered to Christ?*

What will become of men of whom it continues to be said, "You would not"?

The text suggests to us two ways of answering the question. What becomes of chicks that do not come to the shelter of the hen's wings? What becomes of chicks that are not gathered to the hen? Well, the hawk devours some, and the cold nips others; they miss the warmth and comfort that they might have had. That is something. If there were no hereafter, I should like to be a Christian. If I had to die like a dog, the joy I find in Christ would make me wish to be his follower. You are losers in this world if you love not God; you are losers of peace and comfort and strength and hope, even now; but what will be your loss hereafter, with no wing to cover you when the destroying angel is abroad, no feathers beneath which you may hide when the dread thunderbolts of justice shall be launched, one after another, from God's right hand? You have no shelter and consequently no safety.

> He that hath made his refuge God,
> Shall find a most secure abode.

But he who has not that refuge shall be among the great multitude who will call to the rocks and the mountains to fall upon them, to hide them from the face of him that sits upon the throne, and from the wrath of the Lamb. O sirs, I pray you, run not the awful risk of attempting to live without the shelter of God in Christ Jesus!

But the text suggests a second question, *What became of Jerusalem in the end?* "O Jerusalem, Jerusalem, how often would I have gathered thy children together, but you would not!" Well, what happened to Jerusalem, after all? I invite you, who are without God and without Christ, to read Josephus, with the hope that he may be of service to you. What became of the inhabitants of that guilty city of Jerusalem? Well, they crucified the Lord of glory, and they hunted out his disciples, and yet they said to themselves, "We live in the city of God, no harm can come to us; we have the temple within our walls, and God will guard his own holy place." But very soon they tried to throw off the Roman yoke, and there were different sets of zealots who determined to fight against the Romans, and they murmured and complained, and began to fight among themselves.

Before the Romans attacked Jerusalem, the inhabitants had begun to kill one another. The city was divided by the various factions, three parties took possession of different portions of the place, and they fought against one another, night and day. This is what happens to ungodly men; manhood breaks loose against itself, and when there are inward contentions, one part of man's soul fighting against another part, there is an internal war of the most horrible kind. What is the poor wretch to do who is at enmity with himself, one part of his nature saying, "Go," another part crying, "Go back," and yet a third part shouting, "Stop where you are"?

Are there not many of you who are just like battlefields trampled with the hoofs of horses, torn up with the ruts made by the cannon wheels, and stained with blood? Many a man's heart is just like that. "Rest?" says he. "That has gone from me long ago." Look at him in the morning after a drinking bout; look at him after he has been quarrelling with everybody; look at the man who has been unfaithful to his wife, or that other man who has been dishonest to his employer, or that other who is gambling away all that he has. Why, how does he sleep, poor wretch? He does not rest; he dreams, he starts, he is always in terror. I would not change places with him, no, not for five minutes. The depths of poverty, and an honest conscience, are immeasurably superior to the greatest luxury in the midst of sin. The man who is evidently without God begins to quarrel with himself.

By and by, one morning, they who looked over the battlements of Jerusalem cried, "The Romans are coming, in very deed they are marching up toward the city." Vespasian came with an army of sixty thousand men, and, after a while, Titus had thrown up mounds round about the city, so that no one could come in or go out of it. He had surrounded it so completely that they were all shut in. It was, as you remember, at the time of the Passover, when the people had come from every part of the land, a million and more of them; and he shut them all up in that little city. So a time comes, with guilty men, when they are shut up; this sometimes happens before they die; they are shut up; they cannot have any pleasure in sin as they used to have, and they have no hope. They seem cooped up altogether; they have not been gathered by God's love, but now, at last, they are gathered by an avenging conscience, they are shut up in God's justice.

I shall never forget being sent for, in my early days, to see a man who was dying. As I entered the room, he greeted me with an oath; I was only a youth, a pastor about seventeen and a half years of age, and he somewhat staggered me. He would not lie down on his bed; he defied God; he said he would not die. "Shall I pray for you?," I asked. I knelt down, and I had not uttered many sentences before he cursed me in such dreadful language that I started to my feet, and then again he cried and begged me to pray with him again, though it was not any good. He said, "It is no use. Your prayer will never be heard for me; I am damned already"; and the poor wretch spoke as though he really were so and were realizing it in his own soul. I tried to persuade him to lie down upon his bed. It was of no avail; he tramped up and down the room as fast as he could go; he knew that he should die, but he could not die while he could keep on walking, and so he kept on. Then again I must pray with him, and then would come another awful burst of blasphemy, because it was not possible that the prayer should be heard. It does not often happen that one sees a person quite as bad as that; but there is a condition of heart that is not so visible, but which is quite as sad, and which comes to men dying without Christ. They are shut up; the Roman soldiers are, as it were, marching all round the city, and there is no escape, and they begin to feel it, and so they die in despair. But then, when the Roman soldiers did come, the woes of Jerusalem did not end. There was a famine in the city, a famine so dreadful that what Moses said was fulfilled, and the tender and delicate woman ate the fruit of her own body. They came to search the houses, because they thought there was food there; and a woman brought out half of her own babe, and said, "Well, eat that, if you can," and throughout the city they fed upon one another; and oh, when there is no God in the heart, what a famine it makes in a man's soul! How he longs for a something which he cannot find, and that all the world cannot give him, even a mouthful to stay the ravenousness of his spirit's hunger!

And this doom will be worse still in the next world. You know that Jerusalem was utterly destroyed—not one stone was left upon another—and this is what is to happen to you if you refuse your Savior. You will be destroyed, you will be an eternal ruin, no temple of God, but an everlasting ruin. Destroyed—that is the punishment for you; destroyed from the presence of the Lord and the glory of his power, and so abiding forever, with no indwelling God, no hope, no comfort. How terrible will be your doom unless you repent!

> *Ye sinners, seek his grace*
> *Whose wrath ye cannot bear;*
> *Fly to the shelter of his cross,*
> *And find salvation there.*

I pray you, do so, for the Lord Jesus Christ's sake! Amen.

Index to Key Scriptures